THE METHODOLOGY OF MAURICE HAURIOU

VIBS

Volume 218

Robert Ginsberg
Founding Editor

Leonidas Donskis
Executive Editor

Associate Editors

a volume in
Studies in Jurisprudence
SJ
Vincent L. Luizzi, Editor

THE METHODOLOGY OF MAURICE HAURIOU

Legal, Sociological, Philosophical

Christopher Berry Gray

Rodopi

Amsterdam - New York, NY 2010

Cover photo: Toulouse (author: chantrybee, Flickr.com)

Cover Design: Studio Pollmann

The paper on which this book is printed meets the requirements of "ISO 9706:1994, Information and documentation - Paper for documents - Requirements for permanence".

ISBN: 978-90-420-3007-7
E-Book ISBN: 978-90-420-3008-4

Printed in the Netherlands

Studies in Jurisprudence
(SJ)

Vincent L. Luizzi
Editor

Other Titles in SJ

Randall E. Osborne and Paul Kriese, ***Global Community: Global Security.*** 2008. VIBS 198

Formerly

Natural Law Studies
(NLS)

Other Titles in NLS

Kenneth Bryson, ***Persons and Immortality***, 1999. VIBS 77

Roger T. Simonds, ***Rational Individualisms***, 1995. VIBS 20

Virginia Black
Editor Emerita

This work is dedicated to my wife Kathleen Gray.

CONTENTS

EDITORIAL FOREWORD

Studies in Jurisprudence publishes works in all areas of philosophy of law and maintains a special interest in the relationship between values and morality and the laws of nations and peoples. *The Methodology of Maurice Hauriou: Legal Sociological, Philosophical* by Christopher Berry Gray offers a cogent study of Hauriou's institutionalism within that context.

French jurist Maurice Hauriou (1856–1929) is best known for his institutionalism, which is both a theory and a method. According to institutionalism, the social reality is populated by institutions, one of which is law. It holds that the proper way to study and understand society and social development is to attend to these institutions.

However much Hauriou was revered as a sociologist and philosopher in his day and remains influential in Latin America and Europe, he is largely unknown in the English-speaking world. Gray work seeks to rectify that omission with a comprehensive study of the man, his works, thought, and place within the context of the theory of law and social theory.

The work includes an account of the life and times of Hauriou; but, in the main, concentrates on his three methodologies. Throughout, the theory and methodology are firmly grounded within the context of the historical fabric against which Hauriou formed them.

Grey's concluding chapter, "The Philosophical Status of Hauriou's Methodology," is especially useful for locating Hauriou's work within the discipline of current philosophy and theory of law, and for clarifying its significance for our studies in jurisprudence.

Vincent Luizzi, Professor of Philosophy
Texas State University
Studies in Jurisprudence Special Series Editor

PREFACE

Maurice Hauriou (1856–1929) stands at the head of twentieth-century philosophical considerations upon social studies in law. His contribution to current Latin American concerns, as well as to European Community projects, is profound. English-speaking insulation from his work is a loss whose remedy begins with study of Hauriou's interfacing methodology in social science, law, and philosophy.

Writers in the late twentieth century have recognized the relevance of Hauriou's work to legal and social changes in France during its Third Republic (1870–1940) and to political change in its Fifth Republic (from 1958). During this renaissance, commentators must avoid misapprehensions concerning Hauriou, stated largely in terms of his methodology, suffered during its overly parliamentary Fourth Republic (1945–1958).

Since Hauriou stands in the grand tradition of continental social philosophy, the methodological appreciation of his work is even more appropriate to philosophical study.

Some aspects of Hauriou's work, particularly his theory of the institution, have been addressed by others. In this study, I will present an introduction to his career and influence, and then detail his explicit methodology of law, sociology, and philosophy. My purpose is to clarify the basis for other research based on Hauriou's work and to evaluate the adequacy of his ways of knowing in social philosophy.

Portions of some chapters have been published previously. I gratefully acknowledge copyright permissions that have been granted from the publishers of these works: "The Criterion of What Is a Classic for Maurice Hauriou," *Vexillum* 23 (1984), pp. 3–6; and "Prolegomena to Methodology in Philosophy of Law and Social Philosophy," *Methodology and Science* 17 (1984), pp. 178–180. In addition, I wish to acknowledge that this volume expands and further develops some of the ideas that have been published previously as: "Critique of Legal Philosophy from Rousseau to Kelsen," 14 (1983) 401–417; "A Forgotten Link in Legal Sociology: Maurice Hauriou on his Predecessors," 15 (1984) 256–267; "The Nature and Methodology of Law for Maurice Hauriou," 25 (1995) 335–365; and "Theory and Philosophy of Law in Maurice Hauriou's Institutionalism," 37 (2006) 193–214, which were all published in *Rechtstheorie*; and "Theory and Practice in the Sociology and Jurisprudence of Maurice Hauriou," *Perspectives* 15 (1981) 50–60.

To conform with Rodopi/VIBS format, works previously published in a footnote or endnote format have been converted to the author-date system of documentation. Translations throughout the manuscript are done by the author unless otherwise noted. The original quotations are included with the translations for the convenience of the readers.

Thanks are due to Elizabeth D. Boepple for her intensive editorial assistance; to my proofreaders, Kathleen Gray and Pierre Daigneault; to Vincent Luizzi for supporting this work at VIBS; to Concordia University for its financial support by the Faculty of Arts and Science and the Vice-Provost's Research office.

One

MAURICE HAURIOU (1856–1929)

1. Career

Jean Claude Eugène Maurice Hauriou was born 17 August 1856, in Ladiville, which is in the Charente region of France. He earned baccalaureates in science and arts at Angoulême. He took the law degree from the University of Bordeaux: license, 1876; doctorate, 1879; and aggregation, the final research degree, in 1883 (Mestre, 1929, pp. 269–279; Sfez, 1966, pp. 66–75).

Taking charge of courses in the history of law at Toulouse, Hauriou continued study in a wide variety of fields. He also credited highly his vigorous daily discussions at Café Capitole, which he aptly called the bracing education of the café [*le fort éducation du café*], with his colleagues, the philosophers, Frédéric Rauh, Jean Jaurès, Georges Dumesnil, and Viktor Delbos. In 1888, Hauriou was appointed to the chair of administrative law at Toulouse, a position he first considered a personal tragedy due to the chaotic state of the subject. In the following year, he began to publish a series of commentaries on the decisions of the administrative courts. Two years later, he published the first of the twelve editions of his *Précis de droit administratif* (*Treatise of Administrative Law*). He became Dean of the Faculty of Law at Toulouse in 1906.

Hauriou's *Principes de droit public* (*Principles of Public Law*) appeared in 1910, and his *Précis de droit constitutionnel* (*Treatise of Constitutional Law*) in 1923, each followed by a second edition. The latter work accompanied his appointment to the chair of constitutional law in 1920 at the same university. During this time, he developed a close personal relationship to the philosopher, Jacques Chevalier.

In 1926, because of ill health Hauriou retired from the program of student legal workshops or "laboratories" he had developed at Toulouse. He continued his writing and teaching from home until he suffered a brief worsening of his illness; he died on 12 March 1929, survived by his wife and his son André, a professor of law at the University of Paris.

2. Development

Not all would agree with Marcel Waline that Hauriou was "as important in the history of ideas as [Karl] Marx" (1929, p. 57), or with Roland Maspétiol that he was "the very first major jurist to see the need of sociology in law" (1968, p. 265), but few could deny him the factual role of being "the leading legal philosopher of France in the early twentieth century" (Timasheff, 1946, p. 493), as courts and scholars interpret him more correctly today.

A standard issue in Hauriou criticism concerns the periods of development of his career subsequent to the earliest concentration on the history of law. With his appointment to the chair of administrative law, Hauriou begins a series of books and articles on the use of sociology in law. All agree that the stimulus to end Hauriou's phase of writing on the use of sociology in law was the stillbirth of his major work in social science, *La science sociale traditionnelle* (*Tradition in Social Science*) of 1896. That Hauriou was well aware of the conspiracy of silence by the power brokers of orthodox monistic positivism toward his book is clear from his *"Les idées de M. Duguit"* ("The Doctrine of Duguit") and *Précis de droit constitutionnel* (1911a, p. 38n2; 1929c, pp. xxii–xxiii).

Hauriou having passed successfully to more plainly legal writing, his sixth edition of the *Précis de droit administratif* is taken by nearly all commentators as the key point when his thought achieved coherence around the notions of order, equilibrium, and institution. In his *"A propos des droits réels administratifs"* ("On Administrative Real Rights"), Hauriou expresses the coherence in the project carried out by his *Précis de droit administratif* (1914b, p. 336; 1906a; 1907a; 1910).

Most will find a shift in Hauriou's positions shortly before World War I, between the two editions of his *Principes de droit public* in 1910 and 1916, with a movement toward a more centralized, hierarchized, and state-oriented conception. Maspétiol feels representatively that from the first edition of the *Droit public*, "the most personal and reflective work of Hauriou" [*"l'ouvrage le plus personnel et le plus médité de Hauriou"*], and its second edition, a totally new and narrowed work has transpired (1968, pp. 255, 258). The difference is that some philosophers, such as Roland Maspétiol, and the early Georges Gurvitch, believe this illustrates a loss of Hauriou's achieved talents, while others, such as Joseph Thomas Delos and the later Gurvitch, take it to be consistent with where Hauriou's development would naturally have led him. Hauriou himself however, finds the two nearly identical with the difference being that the theoretical logic of the second is tightened up over the loose materials of the first, as this chapter will illustrate later (cf. 1918b, p. 813; 1916e, p. vi).

3. Influences on Hauriou's Doctrine

The three rather lengthy studies of Hauriou that focus on his secondary materials need some justification for their presence in this discussion of Hauriou's methodology. It is perhaps as true today as in 1941 that "the thought of Maurice Hauriou has not yet been the object of a study deep enough to place it adequately in any determinate philosophical current" (Lissarrague, 1941, p. 197) and as true for all the other dimensions of Hauriou as for his philosophy. But this has been no hindrance upon facile slotting of Hauriou into a determinate category, as shown in this chapter. But that categorization has succeeded in making distasteful by association any memory of his contributions.

My first study in the rest of this section focuses on Hauriou and on his sources, and is not an attempt to reduce him to them. The second, discussed in the section of this chapter titled, "Effects of Hauriou's Theoretical Work: Institutionalism," is a study of the various directions Hauriou was led by different national aims, and is not intended to substitute for direct knowledge of Hauriou. The third, in the second chapter, more closely presents a factual account of Hauriou's legal, sociological, and philosophical methodology and is a résumé of the extraordinary significance given by authors critical of Hauriou because of his methodology, either to laud him for it or to damn him for it.

A. Historical Influences

Dominance by Legislatures. The major formative influence on Hauriou and on his France was the French Revolution. Its effect in his eyes was to leave France shaken and unsure. In 1896, he wrote, "We have still not recovered our balance after the violent revolutionary upset of 1789" (1896, p. 192) [*"Nous n'avons pas retrouvé notre équilibre depuis la violente refonte révolutionnaire de 1789"*]. The mediocrity of the results condemned its violence; anything founded on force must be maintained by force. True, the egalitarianism—the Revolution's essential idea—increased social life; but the net result was to leave the individual naked and unprotected before the state. There remained no buffer of associations between individuals and state more proximate to individuals than the state to soften the harsh direct governance.

The guilds of the old regime [*ancien régime*] were suppressed, leaving workers unprotected for a century until the rise of unions in the late nineteenth century. There was no place left for institutions that were not state-initiated. The Revolution allowed only for the direct assembly of the people; it destroyed all the corporative social organizations and it substituted the unique mystic demos, or the people as a whole (ibid., pp. 75, 372; 1907a, p. 6n11; 1916c, p. 639).

The source of these difficulties was the Revolution's exclusive stress on reason. Cartesianism, scientific success, the metaphysical concept of legal justice, the growth of political economy all manifested this. Reason, as oppressive planning, could progress indefinitely. Reason made all people equal; this was the driving force of the Revolution, and it is, for Hauriou, false to substitute liberty as the Revolution's energy. Reason was individualist, leaving no trust in what experience in society reveals—tradition and custom—as a source of truth. The individualist economic theory that the Revolution spurred raised individualism to the order of a dogma (1896, pp. 73, 81, 103; 1916c, p. 776).

The individualism of the Revolution was not essentially subjective in its tenets, for Hauriou; it became so by serving as a pretext for its promoters to attack all institutions and all law, becoming subjective by trying to throw down an existing order and substitute another totally discontinuous with the pre-Revolutionary order. This substitution was the revolt of principles of matter over that of spirit. The lasting effect of the Revolution on the French mind was to leave it disorganized and confused even about itself: exclusively practical while incorrigibly theoretical. Hauriou harmonizes both tendencies in speaking of "the tradition of French idealism balanced by age-old Gallic good sense" [*"la tradition de l'idéalisme français corrigé par le vieux bon sens gaulois"*].

The practical turn of mind he loves leads the French to ignore presumably theoretical controversies without ever thinking that there may be practical consequences to them; thus, he says the moral personality of institutions to the French is a mere fiction founded solely on positive law. On the other hand, the passion for a politics of pure ideas [*la passion de la politique d'idées pures*] destroys the solidity of party politics for the French, as compared with the British system of basing politics upon friendship and interest in addition to ideas.

This mania for generalized formulations [*manie de la formule générale*] sometimes guarantees Revolutionary equality, by treating citizens alike. More often, however, it restrains liberties by unnecessarily submerging individual differences. To remedy both traits of laziness, of neglecting either practicality or reasonability, what is needed is exact analysis, but analysis of real situations. Of particular relevance here are Hauriou's notes on the Mogambury Case (1894b) and the Sourisse Case (1926) (1894b, p. 316; 1899d, pp. 143, 156; 1902b, p. 346; 1926a, p. 546; 1929c, pp. 38, 62).

The French Revolution effected social and intellectual disorganization, "and all these confusions have lain heavy on our public law for a hundred years now" (Hauriou, 1912d, p. 8) [*"Toutes ces confusions pèsent sur notre droit public depuis cent ans"*]. The counter of total individualism was strong interventionism by the state, for in a nation without internal structure there could be only one sole agent. Interventionism, in Hauriou's opinion, was the legislative crisis threatening the regime of the state as that regime had been known since the renaissance.

The capital dogma of French law held that the general will of the sovereign nation is formulated directly in suffrage and embodied in law. Legislation was the activity that expressed political sovereignty with the executive branch of government a mere functionary of it. This was the stifling found in the *Code civil* in France, whose practical application since the Revolution required rigorous deduction from its principles for any application (ibid., p. 130; 1896, pp. 213, 349; 1907a, p. 2).

Industrial Revolution and Administrative Law. The revolutionary coming to power of the bourgeoisie was the second formative influence on Hauriou's French world. The extension of state intervention required by the excessive individualism of bourgeois growth in industrial activity increased the state bureaucracy and led it deep into economic business. As a result, employees of the state treated the state as a private employer and the state often acted as a private industrialist; eventually there threatened to be no longer a political government but only another grouping with an economic interest. "The political government will end up by being absorbed for having wished to overextend its activity" (Hauriou, 1896, pp. 392–393; cf. p. 32) [*"Pour avoir voulu trop étendre son action le gouvernement politique sera resorbé"*].

A recognizably new form of control gradually evolved as "bourgeois justice, as the workers call it, is recognized as being unable to control the conflicts between capital and labor" (ibid.) [*"La justice bourgeoise, comme on dit dans le monde ouvrier, s'est reconnue incapable de regler les conflits entre le capital et le travail"*]. The control by judicial administration was new because the administrative change involved a different separation of powers between the branch of government exercising control over civil and criminal offenses in terms of deductions from the *Code civil* and the branch judging the new industrial growth unforeseen by the *Code*. These novel growths required regulation for the good of the state and citizens regardless of lacunae in the legislative foundations. The administrative agencies, which regulated industrial society, had to do with these social bodies for which the *Code*'s reduction of society to state as the general will did not provide.

Conflicts of these regulating agencies with the regulated bodies fell outside the purview of regular courts and eventually required a due process other than the decisive pronouncement by the same minister who was involved in the conflict. This due process proceeded from government concession and not from the popular will, as legislation according to the Code was defined to do in Revolutionary dogma. The administrative law bypassed medieval reliance upon the sheer weight of custom and the Revolutionary reliance upon individual invention and reason. This intermediary posture is the characteristic of what Hauriou called the half-middle age [*demi-moyen âge*], the most desirable social situation, when custom is found to manifest social values, but only by conscious and administrative custom.

The seat of administrative law was the transformed organ of the Directorate known as the *Conseil d'État* (Council of State) (Hauriou, 1893d, pp. 5–6; 1896, p. 339; *L'introduction à l'étude du droit administratif français*, n.d., p. ii). Under the old regime, the *Conseil d'État* had been part of the confusion between judicial and administrative powers, performing civil and administrative functions, just as the local councils [*parlements*] made police decisions in addition to citing ministers of the government before them. The Constitution of Revolutionary year VIII, 1800, created the body of administrative law by giving the *Conseil d'État* control over ministers' appeals against decisions. Directed little by statute, this body developed a thoroughly case-based law, formed by jurisprudence. For the first several decades, its decisions were ignored and unknown as precedents; the end of the imperial wars led to a period when these precedents became known.

The outcome of the revolution in 1830 was to focus upon the broad administrative functions for anything involving the public funds; this is a theory called the "state-debtor." One outcome of the Revolution of 1848 was a tribunal for contentious matters [*Tribunal des Conflits*] to take from the *Conseil d'État* some of its excess functions. Suppressed in the coup d'état of 1851, the Tribunal did not reappear to differentiate civil and administrative areas for the *Conseil* until 1872. By that time, the *Conseil*'s power to annul ministerial acts through an action for exceeding jurisdiction [*recours pour excès de pouvoir*] had been widely expanded.

The organizing activity of commentators had convinced lawyers to see the administrative personality as the center of administrative law. They saw administrative acts as the manifestation of will of the administrative person. As a result, nearly the first case that the reinstituted *Tribunal* decided (TC 8 February 1873 [Blanco]), refused the simple discrimination of administrative from civil law in terms of the public bursary. Jurists had to develop new rules distinct from rules in the Civil Code for administrative cases.

This history of the administrative law's institutions set the scene for Hauriou's research and discoveries, and led his research toward the distinction of public and private personalities of the administrative body to obviate the danger of state dominance. In this study of influences on Hauriou's work, we need not trace his alignment of the administrative courts with the act of management [*gestion*] exercised in ordinary litigation [*recours contentieux ordinaire*] and based upon the social relation of *collaboration* as opposed to *cohabitation*. This latter relation would put the state into a self-confirming legality [*situation d'état étant en soi légale*].

This alignment, however, was authoritatively affirmed in the *Conseil d'État* case, Terrier, 6 February 1903 (Hauriou, 1903c), making administrative law a matter of the public services, an alignment which endured until World War I when, due to an increasing number of public contracts for private services, the criterion of public service was assimilated to that of public power [*puissance publique*] (Hauriou, 1899a, Broderick, 1967, pp. 51–53). Administrative agencies took on the role of autonomous authorities.

World War I and the Centralized State. The situation in which Hauriou began his work was defined by the legal institutions of two Revolutions, French and Industrial, the *Code Civil*, whose judicial interpretation purported to be strictly deductive, and the *Conseil d'État*, which operated with the more practical method by trial and error. These four stimuli just mentioned were intensified by World War I, with the result that Hauriou's corresponding alterations in his theory described in this book appeared to betray his earlier revolutionary liberalism, to some admirers of liberalism.

Hauriou believed, however, that the war only hastened a fated confrontation of equity with unforeseeability [*imprévision*] that would force parties to modify contracts. The enemy's occupation of coalfields, the difficulty of transportation by sea while under attack, the rise in the use and price of carbons, which were the raw materials for natural gas—all resulting from the length of the war—were all factors which tended to overthrow an economy based upon contracts. The monopolies conceded by towns to gas companies and the service guaranteed by those companies were severely compromised. Nonetheless, to ensure continued delivery of gas, a crucial public service, the government had to take extraordinary measures. Hauriou commented on the Maritime Message Company Case (1917a, pp. 621, 623) and the Nice Gas Authority Case (1920, p. 635).

Before the war, Hauriou had thought that one law applied during war and another during peace. During war, the government could suspend rights constitutionally guaranteed during peacetime. But during World War I, Hauriou came to believe that the ordinary contracts of life are done for peacetime; in order not to surrender the aims of the nation to the goal of winning the war, special guarantees, without compromising national goals for the long run, must continue during wartime as well.

During a short war, it may be possible to suspend guarantees; the economic life of the nation may be subordinated to the military interlude. But for a long war, military objectives must be aligned with the economic needs of the nation. Hauriou's notes on the Winkell Case (1909b p. 172), the Bordeaux Gas Authority Case (1916b, pp. 60–603), and the Vions and Son Case (1916d, pp. 41, 46) reflected his thoughts in this regard. The remedy to this dilemma of wartime needs and enduring guarantees is for a judge to suspend the contracted delivery of goods and services destroyed by circumstances.

However, contrary to this being a kind of superstructure that does not touch a contract but only assures the delivery of the service [*situation extra-contractuelle*], Hauriou insists that the contractual framework remains dominant. A judge may suspend the deliveries of contracts, but immediately substitutes other deliveries; the length and terms of the original contract remain in force, these terms constitute the normal economic life of the nation. "These benefits are as contractual as the others; you cannot rescind the contract" (1920, p. 646) [*"Ce sont des bénéfices contractuels comme les autres: vous ne pouvez pas scinder le contrat"*] (Gaz de Nice case, 1919; Postal Vehicles Case, 1923a).

Although Hauriou believed that from 1900 "[until World War I], the whole State organization has been political, not economic" (1900a, pp. 416–417) [*"Jusqu'à present, toute l'organisation de l'état a été politique, non point économique"*], by the 1920s, the state would be mired in the economic life of the nation (Gignac Canal Case, 1900). Hauriou was not pleased with this; he believed it would be the end of the political state and a loss of the distinctive form of human life that it makes possible. But he also believed this transition was inevitable. This development had begun even before the war. In the pre-war years, Hauriou thought of decentralization of government from a unified central authority, by granting legal authority to organizations intermediate between state and citizen, as an unqualified progress from the legal and the political points of view (1892a, p. 59).

Hauriou came to see in mid-career that "we must realize that real decentralization is complicated and expensive" (*Introduction à l'étude du droit administratif français*, n.d., pp. viii–ix) [*"il faut bien savoir que la décentralisation veritable, c'est de la complication et des debours"*]. In a France at the start of the twentieth century, little true decentralization yet existed and the French would want no more. Centralization allows easier direction of life and major projects. All that the war adds to the appeal of centralization is citizens' recognition that a yet further strengthened central government is the sole guarantee of civic life against the massive military complex built for the war purpose that I described in this section. For the whole sweep of these social influences on Hauriou, see his *Précis de droit constitutionnel* (1923d, p. 148n1).

B. Sociological Influences

Even more than the socio-political data of Hauriou's professional environment, we should examine his literary influences from his point of view. There may be other likenesses to other scholars that we can find, but they remain only likenesses until he claims them as influences or sources. In this work, I have ranked the importance of Hauriou's sources by its quantity (the number of times it appears in his writing), its quality (how deeply Hauriou penetrates it) and duration (the length of time it appears) over the course of his career.

Sociology was the area of science in which Hauriou was most active; but he also studied thermodynamics, anthropology, physiology, and psychology. His writings evince respect for the scientific impulse and its relevance to law and sociology. Still, for him, social science remains the grand metaphor of existence:

> If I do not think it useful to employ these analogies [from sciences other than social science], this is because it is superfluous to support the greater with the lesser. It is in social matter that the phenomenon of the organization of balances is most apparent and that its true *raison d'être* best reveals itself. It is psychology and biology, which will have to make use of the elements drawn from social matter. (1909a, p. 19) [*Si je ne crois pas utile d'user de ces analogies, c'est qu'il est superflue de renforcer le plus par le moins. C'est en matière sociale que le phénomène de l'organisation des équilibres est le plus apparent et que sa véritable raison d'être se révèle le mieux. Ce sont la psychologie et la biologie qui auront à invoquer les éléments tirés de la matière sociale.*]

It is not intoxication with science [*ivresse de la science*]—the optimism that prefers knowledge of being to being itself—that is Hauriou's scientific impetus. For this, he criticizes Ernest Renan, Cesare Lombroso, and Theodor Ribot. Hauriou does not refer to any works by the modern penologist, but does mention Renan's *Qu'est-ce qu'une nation?* (*What is a Nation?*) (1882). Despite Hauriou's agreement with Marx that "materialism makes the world go" and Marx's theory of surplus value, he conflates Marx with the others in the criticism that this intoxication is sheer ineffectual fantasy. Ineffectual is the operative term, for all their projects lead to socialism. But on the one hand, collectivizing only in part is futile; on the other, we have no evidence that total collectivization is bearable, not even that we have evolved to that tolerance. These doctrines defeat themselves in time [*laissons agir le temps*] (Hauriou, 1894c, p. 294; 1894d, p. 391; 1896, pp. 127, 162, 189, 288, 290–292; 1899d, p. 133).

The sense of Hauriou's scientific influence is given by his commitment to Auguste Comte, upon whom he reflected later in his life: "I was a positivist to the second power, in the style of Comte rather than that of [Herbert] Spencer" (1916c, p. xxiii) [*"J'étais positiviste à la seconde puissance, à la façon d'Auguste Comte plutôt qu'à la façon de* (*Herbert*) *Spencer"*], meaning that there was no excision of religious and moral data on theoretical grounds. Hauriou agrees with Comte in great part that the political life unifies social life; and that the "dead" (a culture's predisposition to certain ideas) rule a society more than the living. Hauriou also mostly agrees that one invention entails another one, and that stages of history—religious, metaphysical and positive—succeed one another.

Hauriou believed Comte's error was the theory of simple succession in the three stages, whereas Hauriou believed that we should, instead, recognize a rotation among these three stages from the third back to the first. The succession view requires that each previous one be subordinated in value to its successor, while the rotation view allows each to have more or less valuable effects. Comte lost the pragmatic perspective by exempting his positive age from his principle that in social science something false can have great practical value, the only point of view for social science (Hauriou, 1894c, p. 306; 1896, pp. 16, 44, 75, 181, 209, 255, 241, 261, 277, 297, 361; *Introduction à l'étude du droit administratif français*, n.d., p. xxiii; 1912d, p. 16; 1923d, pp. 13, 41; 1929c, p.16).

So far is Hauriou from disowning Spencer, however, that later in his career he holds Spencer up to contemporary sociologists as a model of the theory on the origin and succession of society. Spencer is an individualist, but he abetted the collectivists; he discovered that complication in structure is a sign of social progress, but neglected to study other signs, to study the reverse movement away from differences of social practice toward their likeness, and to make differentiation a question of multiple social roles, not of fragmented social being.

Many have criticized Spencer for his reduction of morality to science and his exclusion of irreducible morality. To Hauriou, this was an overextension of Hauriou's laws of conservation of energy and of parsimony (1909a, p. 25; 1923d, p. 44; 1894c, p. 294; 1896, pp. 7, 37, 44, 316; 1899d, pp. 2,9,117,163). Hauriou appears to have been familiar with Spencer chiefly through a secondary source, Howard Collins' *Résumé de la philosophie de Herbert Spencer* (*Summary of the Philosophy of Herbert Spencer*) (1891). He also mentions, however, Spencer's *"Loi et cause du progrès"* ("Law and the Cause of Progress") (1857).

Hauriou borrows the ideas that a sense of togetherness is needed even for non-human animal groups (Alfred Victor Espinas), and that among earliest humankind, only groups, not persons, were present (Henry Sumner Maine). But it is Numa Denis Fustel de Coulanges who shows a profound knowledge of ancient periods [*une si profonde connaissance des temps antique*]. Hauriou limits the central thesis, that religion affected ancient society more than any other factor, by giving the role of religion not as creation but as redemption. He extends Fustel de Coulanges' thesis from the ancient city to the whole Western culture, which he calls "sedentary" to distinguish its permanence from nomadic civilizations. Hauriou refers to Espinas's *Des sociétés animales; étude de psychologie comparée* (*Animal Societies: Studies in Comparative Psychology*) (1877). He may also have known Espinas's translation of Spencer's *Principles of Psychology* into French as *Principes de psychologie* (1874–1875). Hauriou names Fustel de Coulanges's *La cité antique* (*The Ancient City*) (1866), and cites works of Maine: *L'ancien droit* (*Ancient Law*, 1861) and *"Le propriété du manoir"* ("Manorial Property") (see Hauriou, 1898, p. 10; 1894c, pp. 301, 315; 1896, pp. 137, 118, 203, 224; 1909a, p. 36; 1927d, p. 61).

Related to these ideas on the origin of society, Hauriou occasionally refers to Gaston Richard on the origin of law today as at its beginnings. Law arises from voluntary submission by the parties of their disputes to arbitration and voluntary acceptance of the results; for Hauriou this continues to characterize law. Hauriou takes the observational morality, empirically based on observation of social practice that Richard suggests, to be a morality differing from spiritualist morality in that its origin is social rather than the uprightness of the individual, though both moralities have the individual as their end (Hauriou, 1894c, p. 301; 1896, p. 118; 1909a, p. 36). Hauriou cites Richard's *"Essai sur l'origine de l'idée du droit"* ("Essay on the Origin of the Idea of Law") (1892, pp. 290–296).

Hauriou finds Gustave Le Bon roughly reminiscent of Fustel de Coulanges, since Le Bon learns from studying crowds that their beliefs are religious in that they imply abandonment of will. Preferable to Le Bon's submerging of individuality is Frédéric LePlay's view that individuals and their values are the strength of society; but Hauriou considers LePlay's attempt to restore the belief system of Christian Middle Age for this sake an outmoded and impossible overreaction. However, Hauriou never mentions writings by LePlay, the thoroughness of whose engineering mind in his massive case histories of French family life must have been forbidding. The multiplication of social circles in contemporary society is a greater guarantee of individual liberty because of their limiting of each other's scope (Georg Simmel). Walter Bagehot realized that the nature of society is to alternate between periods of different types of society. Hauriou admits this notion, with a change only in the names of those types, or stages as was discussed above several pages ago.

More to the point of characterizing societies in France, Hauriou believes the great merit of Hippolyte Taine was to discriminate, according to his too little known criterion of the classical, a society from a state whose blurring was detrimental, as shown previously in the first section of this chapter; he recognized the disaster of having no external check upon the French legislative state, which could originate no spontaneous social growth within it (Hauriou, 1895a, p. 538; 1896, pp. 65, 181, 346, 388, 392–393; 1899d, p. 18; 1907a, p. 6; 1909a, p. 16; 1911a, p. 18; 1923d, p. 14; 1929c, p. 162).

Hauriou refers to Simmel's *Aufsätze 1887 bis 1890: Über soziale Differenzierung: Die Probleme der Geschichtsphilosophie* (1892) (*Writings 1887 to 1890: On Social Differentiation: The Problem of the Philosophy of History*) (1989); Taine's *Les origines de la France contemporaine* (*The Origins of Contemporary France*) (1876); Le Bon's *Psychologie des foules* (*Psychology of Crowds*) (1895), and *L'évolution de la matière* (*The Evolution of Matter*) (1905); Bagehot's *Lois scientifiques du développement des nations dans leurs rapports avec les principes de la sélection naturelle et de l'hérédité* (*Scientific Laws of the Development of Nations in their Relation to Principles of Natural Selection and Heredity*) (1882). While the social theorists just mentioned do have an implicit methodology in their work, Hauriou is more concerned with theorists who give their attention directly to social scientific methodology.

The method of science is of some concern to Hauriou. On this he scatters a handful of references through his work on Henri Poincaré, Jules Lachelier, and especially Émile Boutroux. Other than Poincaré's work in physics that he cited in *Leçons sur le mouvement social* (1899d), Hauriou names as sources only Boutroux's two works, *De la contingence des lois de la nature* (*On the Contingency of the Laws of Nature*) (1874) and *De l'idée de loi naturelle dans la science et la philosophie contemporaine* (On the Idea of Laws of Nature in Science and in Contemporary Philosophy) (1895). Hauriou always used them in the same way: insistence upon the merely relative determinism of scientific—statistical—laws. This leaves Hauriou opportunity to restore freedom and hence morality into social science.

Marcel Bernès also insists upon the liberty implied in social science; but Hauriou's chief indebtedness to Bernès is that he was the first to show that the object of sociology is a practical synthesis of social facts instead of their scientific or theoretical complexity. Since society, the object of social science is a modification of reality, the way of studying this it is to observe the modifications it undergoes instead of its explanation or how it relates to the rest of the universe. This study of its changes is the theory of progress Hauriou insists upon in sociology; only this makes sociology suitable for directing practice (1896, pp. 3, 24; *Introduction à l'étude du droit administratif français*, n.d., p. xiii; 1899d, pp. 3, 130). He makes reference to Bernès' *Sociologie et morale: deux années d'enseignement sociologique* (*Sociology and Morality: Two Years of Sociological Teaching*) (1894), and *"Sur la méthode de la sociologie"* ("On the Method of Sociology") (1895, pp. 233–257, 372–399). Hauriou is also impressed by Albert Fouillée's striking formulation [*formule saissisante*] for the possibility of including the study of ideas in observational social science. Even if not objective enough to be observed as mental concepts, ideas become ideas as forces [*idées-forces*] when they move a party or a people as a current of ideas (1896, p. 19; 1899d, pp. vi, 3, 90, 129; 1912b, p. 9). Hauriou makes reference to Fouillée's *La science sociale contemporaine* (*Contemporary Social Science*) (1880).

Hauriou adopts theoretical formulations from physiology and psychology to supplement the descriptions of society from social science. Hauriou takes from Armand Sabatier the claim that specialization eventually exhausts both organisms and societies, and causes them to degenerate away from their well-developed condition.

Contrary to the view of Émile Durkheim on specialization to be discussed shortly, Hauriou adopts Georges Chavreau's view that the organism develops and continues its life by producing heat and power. Hauriou notes that the social organism does so, too. He also uses Albert Dastre's theory that, in nature, physical and social life lack sufficient regulation on their expenditure of energy. From this physical and social principle, Hauriou inferred the psychological and social principle of Henri Mazel, who espoused the thesis that justice and good are principles of cohesion and preservation, since the better and more just a mental or a social synthesis is, the more coherent it is. He verified and applied this theory later in his career when he learned of the Belgian psychologist, George Dwelschauvers' theory of mental synthesis [*synthèse mentale*]: the center of synthesis for impressions is the individuality of the perceiver.

Each synthesis is different, a function of the individual and not of natural laws. In human beings, individuality relates to freedom; mental impressions reach equilibrium around the individual as a center; human individuality is associated with freedom; similarly, in the social order, the balance of political powers also fosters freedom. Adopting the insights in Dwelschauver and Fouillée's theories made it possible for Hauriou to recognize that Claude Bernard's directive idea [*idée directrice*] served as the axis for development not only in biological systems but in social groups as well.

Hauriou makes reference to Mazel's *Synergie sociale* (*Social Synergy*) (1896); Albert Dastre's *La vie et la mort* (*Living and Dying*) (1903); Sabatier's *Essai sur la vie et la mort* (*Essay on Life and Death*) (1892); Chavreau's *Le travail physiologique* (*Physiological Effort*) (1888) and *Le travail musculaire* (*Muscular Effort*) (1891); and Dwelschauvers' *La synthèse mentale* (*Mental Synthesis*) (1908). Although he does not explicitly cite Bernard's classic of experimental medicine, the content of his notes indicates that he evidently knows of it directly (Hauriou, 1894c, pp. 304, 321; 1896, p. 331;

1899d, pp. 39, 166; 1909a, pp. 65, 82; 1911a, p. 36; 1923d, p. 51; 1933c, pp. 30–31; 1933e, p. 109).

Finally, by far more influential on Hauriou's work than any other influence from the human sciences were the classical theories of Durkheim and Gabriel Tarde. In several works Hauriou makes reference to these works of Durkheim: *De la division du travail social: étude sur l'organisation des sociétés supérieures* (*The Division of Labor in Society: Study on the Organization of Developed Societies*) (1893); and *"Règles de la méthode de la science sociale"* ("The Rules of Sociological Method") (1894) (1894c, pp. 299, 312–320; 1896, pp. 18, 32, 37, 57, 60–61, 123, 158; 1899d, pp. 48, 84; 1911a, pp. 32, 34, 38; 1923d, p. 46; 1933c, p. 28). He also refers often to nearly all of Tarde's works: *La Criminalité comparée* (*Comparative Criminality*) (1886); *"Les deux sens de la valeur"* ("The Two Meanings of Value") (1888); *Les lois de l'imitation: étude sociologique* (*The Laws of Imitation: Sociological Study*) (1890); *Philosophie pénale* (*Penal Philosophy*) (1891); *Études pénales et sociales* (*Studies on Penalty and Society*) (1892); *Transformations du droit* (*Transformations in the Law*) (1893); *La logique sociale* (*Social Logic*) (1895); and *Les lois sociales: esquisse d'une sociologie* (*The Laws of Society: An Essay in Sociology*) (1898) (1893c, p. 7; 1894c, pp. 299, 301–302, 312; 1894d, p. 394; 1896, pp. ii, 14, 68–69, 143, 158, 261, 279–280, 346; 1899d, pp. 35–38; 58, 86, 100; 1902b, pp. 357–358).

Respecting both, on the whole Hauriou refuted Durkheim and accepted Tarde, but neither completely. These were the poles that Hauriou worked between and to which he referred heavily through the whole stretch of his long career. In his earliest commentary on Durkheim, he disputed the view that the advance of society is dependent on the division and specialization of labor and that likenesses among members' social practices decrease as specialization increases.

This view of Durkheim's for Hauriou is nominalism; it reduces human beings to isolated atoms. The species of human individuals is suppressed following Durkheim's view; individual persons are left isolated, when their functions are specialized and lose contact with each other. Later on in the twentieth century, Hauriou's attack on Durkheim focuses on Durkheim's view of society as restraint and thus as the source of morality, Hauriou holds that freedom reacts to constraint and that society reveals morality rather than creating it. Society is a protection more than a restraint on the individuality of human beings according to Hauriou.

Only late in his career does Hauriou begin to tax Durkheim with the critique customary among scholars that the collective consciousness absorbs individual consciousnesses. Hauriou refers to "that unfortunate sociology" [*la triste sociologie*] of Durkheim. Hauriou rejects the group mind because Durkheim's theory represents the popular mass as unconscious and unreflective, whereas any constraining force would have to be active, and therefore reflective and conscious—personified.

Hauriou's relation to Tarde early in his career is clearly that of an obedient disciple. He pays attention from the start to Tarde's theory of imitation: what can appear to be a sheep-like following within society, once it is interpreted as a following of genius, thereby surpasses dumb repetition. In Hauriou's *"La crise de la science sociale"* ("The Crisis in Social Science") (1894c), a study wholly devoted to showing the superiority of Tarde over Durkheim, he finds the positivist nature of Tarde's work attractive; Tarde can explain criminal responsibility not by appealing to the hypothesis of freewill but by the social self-identity of the criminal, from which the criminal is alienated by his crime. The criminal has not imitated society's moral ideal. Our individual reality is reached only by the intermediary of the likenesses manifested in social reality, a realist position Hauriou favors.

By the time Hauriou wrote *La science sociale traditionnelle*, which he dedicated to Tarde, "whose works have aroused this one" (1896, p. vii) [*"dont les œuvres ont suscité ce livre"*], he credits Tarde as being the first to class imitation among the significant social data and the first to occupy himself with the psychology and the crimes of crowds. But he has broken with Tarde on other issues, finding the positivism of his master more restrictive than he had seen at first.

Hauriou insists that imitation is not an ultimate datum, that human beings imitate only because they have the idea that imitation benefits society. Though language is a social creation as Tarde describes it, Hauriou finds it not as such a material phenomenon identified with ideas. He finds Tarde even going as far as Durkheim by making morality a conformity to social likeness rather than an individual event. Finally, Hauriou does not accept Tarde's reduction of unconscious to conscious, as the mechanical residue of habitual conscious acts. There is something irreducible to unconsciousness, something important for ideas.

This ambivalence continues into subsequent works. Still believing Tarde's theory of imitation to be the consummate work of contemporary French sociology [*l'œuvre capitale de la sociologie française contemporaine*], Hauriou goes beyond what he views as Tarde's mere numerical repetition to the more formal idea of repetition according to an image or a concept. It is not mere organic adaptation to needs, but representative adaptation to ideas. Hauriou believes Tarde should have reached this point, because he, too, considered the mass of common ideas to be the categoreal deposit of societies [*fonds catégorique des sociétés*], an essential element of societies; but he did not go far enough out of his positivism, because he never admitted any form of representative knowledge, and because he never accepted will as an incontestably original and irreducible factor in society.

Tarde gradually falls into unimportance in Hauriou's thinking; Hauriou made reference to Tarde every now and then only as an example of a positivist who could avoid reducing human activity to an effect caused by its environment. No longer seen as the master, Hauriou did view Tarde as the "precursor of dualism," the dualism of matter and spirit Hauriou felt himself to develop much more fully, as we shall see in the chapter on his sociological methodology. Durkheim remained as an opponent longer than Tarde as an ally, because Hauriou's constant opponent in legal theory debate, Léon Duguit, followed Durkheim as his philosophical and scientific mentor.

C. Legal Influences

Hauriou viewed seventeenth- and eighteenth-century German metaphysicians, in their role as social thinkers, as a formative influence upon the state of jurisprudence to which his legal theory responded. The only textual reference Hauriou makes to any of these thinkers important to law is found in *La science sociale traditionnelle*, which is a secondary reference to his colleague, Jaurès' 1891 thesis, *"De primis socialismi germanici lineamentis apud Lutherum: Kant, Fichte, Hegel"* ("First Outlines of German Socialism in Luther: Kant, Fichte, Hegel"). The German jurists' balance between subjectivism and objectivism could not persist as will be shown next. Subjectivism prevailed in France and Germany, although in different forms. The contemporary legal thinkers with whom Hauriou was preoccupied and in terms of whom he developed his views can be related to this phenomenon of concern with subjectivism.

In Hauriou's estimation, Hugo Grotius and the school of the law of nations [*école de droit des gens*], in which Hauriou counted Samuel Pufendorf, Gottfried Wilhelm Leibniz, Christian Wolff, Emmerich de Vattel, while secularizing medieval natural law by reducing its dependency upon deity, nevertheless maintained its universality, which it had depended upon deity to provide. Hauriou understood Leibniz's whole project of law to be that of completing law with sociology.

Law came even closer to belonging to only one territory or another with the assertion of Immanuel Kant and Charles Bernard Renouvier that the state is rational and so we should consider it as freely accepted by all. This philosophy of law was separated from metaphysics and made empirical sociology by Antonio Rosmini. The philosophical subjectivism of Georg Wilhelm Friedrich Hegel—subjective thought becomes the essential form of being—was the final blow to objective jurisprudence, in Hauriou's estimation. Instead of interpreting René Descartes' cogito [*"je pense . . ."*] to mean objectively, "there is thought in me; thought is a form of being," it comes to mean, "I am thought; conscious thought is the form of being." The result is that Jean-Jacques Rousseau makes human beings the source of their own morality, as Friedrich Carl von Savigny makes nations the source for theirs (Hauriou, 1884, p. 7; 1896, p. 395; 1899e, p. 133; 1899f, p. 463; 1933c, pp. 15, 16, 28).

French Subjectivism. "O Jean-Jacques, you who wanted to liberate man from man!" (1912b; 1896, p. 30) [*"O Jean-Jacques, toi qui voulais affranchir l'homme de l'homme!"*] Hauriou writes in appreciation of Rousseau's project of liberation and in sorrow at objectivism's loss of Rousseau's subjective values. His quotes from the Marquis Nicolas de Condorcet and Anne Robert Turgot, and his references to Jean Domat and Abbé Sieyes show his schooling in Rousseau's social contract theory. Hauriou believes that social contract theory is right insofar as it means that for a state to be an interest that individuals will take risks to protect, it must be rational and stem from the consent of the governed. In this conciliarist sense of canon law, Hauriou takes canon law to be the origin of social contract theory. He agrees social conditions exist prior to the existence of a political state, a social condition in which individuals have the liberty to render justice for themselves. Without what Hauriou calls "these great truths" it would be incomprehensible how Rousseau's ideas attained such wide and deep effects by entering into the political foundations of all Western states. His judgment is that Rousseau's error was not that he was too individualistic, but that he was not individualistic enough (1896, pp. 11, 46–47; 73–77, 99; 1923d, pp. 184–185n1).

Rousseau's intention in separating law governing individuals from customary institutions was to theorize the possibility for people to return to the freedom of a primitive state of nature. What Rousseau, in Hauriou's view, did not understand was that the primitive state is not free but fated; people are the slaves of natural laws, of instinct, of species. Society, instead, frees individuals, because, by exercising reason, the collectivity pools efforts to obtain necessities by taking the provision of necessities upon the collectivity as its task. But being the first to make this distinction and to conceive of general will as the unique foundation for law, Rousseau is responsible for a cult of the law exclusive of social fact among Hauriou's contemporaries by belief in its omnipotence. Society becomes a force constraining man, and human beings are made only for society.

This cult of law is the Durkheimian derivative from Rousseau. The general will and the legislative will are assimilated to each other by Rousseau; and this is, for Hauriou, an error, which vitiated Rousseau's whole thinking, and vitiated all French public law thenceforward. Equating the general will with the electoral or legislative will, and inevitably a majoritarian will of particular persons, makes decisions that are essentially contested among the several parties and deprives the social order of potential for unanimity (1894c, p. 314; 1895a, p. 549; 1896, p. 13; 1907a, p. 18; 1912d, pp. 26–29).

Hauriou believed morality cannot be rooted in human beings, as Rousseau wished, or in society either, for neither man nor society is completely good. But because of Rousseau's aversion to superior force, due to the excesses of the *ancien régime*, this was his only recourse. He confused the material force of coercion and the spiritual power of legitimated direction. This in turn fails to distinguish societies founded on force, from those founded legitimately. But Hauriou sees society based not on force or violence, but on power which becomes socially acceptable because of the consent of the governed. Power is, then, as natural as liberty, and so are the institutions built upon it. The institutions are not the whole of society; they never substitute for primitive, individual, natural liberty (1923d, p. 4; 1933c, p. 28; 1933e, p. 89).

It is in the sense of the Baron de Montesquieu's desire to propagate power that Hauriou understands Rousseau's fellow revolutionary and his celebrated doctrine of separation of powers. Hauriou devoted increasing attention to the concept of separation of powers as his career progressed: a thought "brilliant on some points, but lacking explicit developments and legal precision" (1929c, p. 353) [*"fulgurante sur certains points, mais manquante de développements explicites et de précision juridique"*].

Hauriou early explicates what he takes to be Montesquieu's implicit doctrine on balances, interpreting him to mean that the state is legally constituted only when it is instituted by freely consenting citizens, and that it is instituted only when powers are separated. Montesquieu becomes a source of Hariou's identification of social order with balances of powers; Montesquieu was a source for balances only to the extent that he laicized order by claiming order remains a characteristic of nature instead of a manifestation of some divine will. Montesquieu mobilized order by showing that the balance of powers cannot be inert since history moves them. Hauriou believes he has improved Montesquieu's guarantee of power moderated by its separation from power by adding that separation of powers also creates routine.

Routine allows mutual expectations to be relied upon, and thereby security. Security in reliance permits persons to increase their liberty by acting in ways that they might not have dared, before. Difficulties lie not in separation in Hauriou's thought, but in the rigidity given separation of powers to be achieved by followers. To Hauriou, separation means simply that powers must proceed together [*aller au concert*], thus increasing the power; rigidity in the divisions of powers or in the number of powers only cripples power (1907a, p. 12; 1909a, p. 12; 1929c, pp. 355, 358).

German Objectivism. Perhaps an even greater influence on Hauriou than Rousseau's subjectivism of the social contract, and definitely one of which he was more conscious, was German objectivism. From the same metaphysical parentage as the French theories, the growth of German objectivism was freer in what Hauriou called Germany, the country of theories [*Allemagne pays des théories*], because there social science was purely speculative, without active consequences, and without any use of tradition.

Objectivism means here that law arises from social fact rather than from individual wills, wills that in France were identified with the will of the legislative assembly. But the German theories that Hauriou studies—some critically, some approvingly—do include strong emphasis on will of another form—state will—identified with social fact. Identifying state with social fact is the Willensmacht theory of right, running from Savigny through Carl Friedrich von Gerber, Paul Laband, Georg Jellinek, and Theodor Mommsen, to Ernst Troeltsch; the will of the state is dominant over other social bodies and individuals. Endorsing only the dominance theory [*Herrschafttheorie*] in Hauriou's description of the Willensmacht theory of right, Rudolf von Jhering, followed by Johann Kaspar Bluntschli, Otto Mayer, and Lorenz von Stein, saw no need to introduce the concept of will into the theory of right and substituted for it the notion of interest [*Zweckvermoegung*].

In a third German variety of state will, Otto Friedrich von Gierke postulated a theory of will [*Willenstheorie*], which was unique to him at that time, which identified the will directly with the organs or officers of the state, not the state itself. Comparison to the bodily organism leads to naming this an organic or corporative theory. Of all these theories, Hauriou is perhaps least impressed with von Gierke's, yet it is from him that Hauriou receives the most significant concept for his own theory, the theory of unification [*Vereinbarung*] as the key to legitimation (1896, pp. ix–x; 1898, p. 125; 1899a, p. 64; 1906a, pp. 156–158; 1907a, pp. 3, 30, 131; 1909a, pp. 4, 75; 1933e, p. 91).

Hauriou constantly refers to Savigny with professional appreciation for his historical acumen [*aperçu historique*] on Roman law. He also approves of Savigny's analysis of law into its individualist tendencies. From 1910, Hauriou realizes that what Savigny had done was to make the power of decision and the force of will the only basis of rights; the consciousness of each people, not universal reason, is the first principle of a people's law. The danger is that Savigny's doctrine tends to lead people to ignore the functions that people expect the state to carry out; Savigny himself retained the distinction of right and force (Hauriou, 1899f, p. 463; 1909a, p. 75; 1933c, p. 16).

However, when speaking more generally, Hauriou is willing to ignore these distinctions among theories he makes elsewhere, and to group their adherents all into a category of Bismarkian jurists he characterized as legal brigands because of their objective identification of law with unlegitimated fact. The legal nationalism [*nationalisme juridique*] of Savigny prepared for this identification by breaking with the universality of natural law in Grotius' school, casting natural law as a variable of the particular national legal system.

Eventually, these two movements of Savigny and nineteenth-century German objectivists culminated in the "legal collectivism" of Troeltsch, theorist of the German superstate, which he considered the new transcendent realm of God, superior to nation and individual, and wherein liberty meant obedience to the state (Hauriou, 1933c, pp. 15–18). Hauriou broke his usual restraint to call these German theorists and their French followers, during the war years, "more a fashionable snobbery than a profound conviction" [*"beaucoup une mode et un snobisme plutôt qu'une conviction profonde"*], and to say of them:

> Basically, we are just tired out with "new schools" and "realist schools," with "new philosophies" and "objective theories," with which people have been abusing our ears for thirty years; a reaction is under way, which ever so gently is bringing us back to the old subjective themes. (1919b, pp. 691–692) [*Au fonds, nous sommes fatigués des "écoles nouvelles" et des "écoles réalistes," et des "philosophies nouvelles" et*

des "théories objectives," dont on nous avait rebattu les oreilles depuis un trentaine d'années; une réaction se produit, que nous ramène tout doucement aux vieux thèmes subjectifs.]

It was "the venerable Gerber" who consciously equated the rule of law with the subjective will of the state. State was "the subject of the rights of domination over free men" thus equating public law and private law. Hauriou holds that only in private law is the legal person a subject of rights, the central principle of law. He refers to Gerber's (1865) *Grundzüge eines Systems des deutschen Staatrechts* (1909a, pp. 4–6; 1933e, p. 91). Following Gerber's lead, Jellinek developed a theory of state of affairs [*Zustand*], analogous to Hauriou's theory of statutory right [*droit statutaire*]. In Jellinek's state of affairs, the state has the sole recognized right to authorize conduct and the sole individual right against the state is that of being recognized as a member of the state: its citizen. The citizen has the right to be on the electoral rolls, but the right to vote is delegated to him by the state. This is essentially the state as Hegel postulated it, believes Hauriou.

Quoting Hegel, "the life and death of the state are matters of history. It alone judges them, not the rules of a jurist" (Hauriou, 1909a, p. 5) [*"La naissance, la vie et la mort des États ne relève que de l'histoire. A elle seule, il appartient à les juger, et ses lois ne sont certainement pas celles du juriste"*], Hauriou wonders whether this would mean that every time a law exists, a state exists. He concludes this is impossible, for no one would consider ancient political groupings with their laws to be states in any modern sense. Nonetheless, he thinks Jellinek is well worth studying once we have at hand the guiding thread [*fils conducteur*], Christian revelation of the rights of individual persons against any body. Hauriou cites Jellinek's *Allgemeine Staatslehre*, *System der subjektiven oeffentlichen Recht* (*General Theory of State: System of Subjective Public Law*) and *Staatenverebindungen* (*Relations between States*), but their lack of dating and the lateness of the references suggests that these were secondary sources mentioned in Jellinek's (1904) *L'état moderne et son droit* (*The Modern State and its Law*) (1906a, p. 138; 1914b, p. 335; 1923d, pp. 11, 88).

Laband continues to develop Jellinek's theory, but believes that to call the weak power of citizens against the state a "right" is incorrect. The most a functionary of the state can do is see that proper form is followed. The functionary cannot judge the state's deeds; the only limitation of the person-state is self-limitation [*autolimitation*]—limitation of the state's acts only by itself. Hauriou wishes to adopt the concept of self-limitation, but does not find it necessary to postulate any legal personality of the state for this purpose; he makes state rather an organization of fact, which limits and institutes itself impersonally in one phase of its history, citing Laband's (1895) *Der Staatsrecht der deutschen Reiches*, translated into the French (1900) as *Le droit public de l'empire allemande* (1906a, p. 138; 1911a, p. 8; 1907a, p. 17).

Hauriou calls von Jhering, the prominent Hanoverian jurist [*l'illustre jurisconsulte hanovrien*], the greatest of the *Herrschaft* theorists. Von Jhering empties the "will" of the Savigny school of all risk and responsibility. Power of decision is the crucial factor. Law always has a practical end; it is the way to satisfy a need. Rights are justified by their practical ends; state supremacy is built upon law; and force is the state's essential quality. "Law is the politics of force" [*"Le droit est la politique de la force"*], says Hauriou about von Jhering's theory. In this regard, he cites von Jhering's *Geist der roemischen Rechts* (*The Spirit of Roman Law*) (1883) and *Der Zweck im Recht* (*Purpose in Law*) (1877–1883). But only Hauriou's citation of the translation, Jhering's *Les Indo-Européens avant l'histoire*, bears the reference date, 1895 (1933c, p. 16; *Introduction à l'étude du droit administratif français*, n.d., p. xv).

Herrschaft theory with which Hauriou deals was diametrically opposed to that developed by Max von Seydel, though it bore the same name of *Herrschaft*. Hauriou never mentions von Seydel's theory, which recognized the need for an indominable *Herrschaft* in the German federation (cf. Neumann, 1934, p. 13; Emerson, 1928, pp. 73–96; Waline, 1949). Instead, von Seydel insisted it remain in the original component states, even citing John C. Calhoun for his "states rights" doctrine. He denied legal personality to the state, endowing *Herrschaft* upon the ruler as a personal attribute, instead.

Hauriou agrees with von Jhering's objective insistence on interest and power, not just on will; but he disagrees with what he considers von Jhering's "overly fiscal" theory of state, because it assimilates state to private law and therein loses the political phenomenon to legalism, which is the same error in principle as Savigny (1898, p. 133; 1907a, pp. 7, 31; 1909a, p. 75; 1911a, p. 31; 1933c, p. 16).

Von Gierke, while asserting, with the *Herrschaft* School, the real moral personality of groups, moves in a different direction from it by founding this personality directly upon the objective collectivity without the intermediary of will. The administrators' will is that of the collective because it is produced within the collectivity, not as its representative but as its organ, deprived of liberty because of dependence upon the legal organism.

State is not free, but is organically determined, having no right that can be set against the collectivity; it can be opposed by individuals' rights. Yet as a collective legal personality, and using its organs' wills, the state does have rights that in turn, are opposable to those of the members. It is because of this inference, that von Gierke infers a personality from a collectivity, that Hauriou holds that this construal of the concepts is unjustified. Individuation of the group must occur between social collectivity and state personality. Von Gierke's concept of personality is built upon a plurality of individuals, not a single individual. In this regard, Hauriou refers to von Gierke's huge works, *Johannes Althusius und die Entwickelung der Naturrechtlichen Staatstheorien* (*Johannes Althusius and the Beginnings of the Natural Law Theory of*

State) (1880) and *Die Genossenschaftstheorie und die deutsche Rechtsprechung* (*Theory of Knowledge and German Pronouncement of Law*) (1887) (1898, p. 129, cf. pp. 125–126n2, 129nl, 137–138nl; 1899d, p. 157; 1907a, pp. 3, 30, 34).

Although disagreeing with von Gierke's foundation of collectivity upon plurality, what is valuable for Hauriou is the means by which this plurality performs a single act. Von Gierke was the first to show how the act called unification [*Vereinbarung*] differs from any act of individual life, and consists of the unilateral will of the group-to-be that persists thereafter. When a collection of individuals takes on a body and affirms itself to be a group, this does not constitute a contract, for it has only one party. Von Gierke runs into an inconsistency in his theoretical formulation when he describes a future corporation, however, since he states such an entity requires some procedure determined by an institution that already exists.

Von Gierke called this type of *Vereinbarung* a fusion [*Verschmelzungen*], but one of wills because their object is the same. This is the more proper meaning of *Vereinbarung*; but Hauriou finds it possible to trace the history of another type, which is more useful, the collective act [*Gesammtakt*], as Gierke calls it, the fusion of wills by external common act, moving together in parallel [*la marche parallèle*] as Hauriou calls it. Hauriou admits, however, that he has borrowed the citations of von Gierke and other German authors from French sources, particularly Geoffre de Lapradelle's *Des fondations* (*Foundations*) (1895), and borrowed interpretations from Raymond Saleilles and Léon Michoud. In addition to this evidence and that in previous mentions of Hauriou's acquaintance with the German school only through translation, he also cites Bluntschli only by his *Le droit public général* (*General Public Law*) (1881) and *La politique* (*Politics*) (1883), and Mommsen only by his *Droit romain public* (*Roman Public Law*) (1894).

La marche parallèle dispenses with the need for a pre-existing institution to determine the procedure for personal fusion; this happens because the act to be performed—the adherence of individual wills to an acceptable common existence—is not an immediate and common act, but an acceptance of a state of affairs, a fact, which can only be accepted or rejected, and this over a period of successive history. The corporate entity carries the procedure for adhering to it within itself, not in a different preexisting fusion. This procedure becomes Hauriou's procedural act or operation for combination (1906a, pp. 155–158) [*acte ou opération complexe à procédure*].

Contemporary French Legal Theory. Hauriou was not a professional Germanist; his interest in the foregoing theorists was conditioned by their influence on French jurisprudence. Hauriou often relates Saleilles's work to von Gierke's position, and subjects the work to the same criticisms. On the positive side, however, Hauriou is heartened to see that Saleilles takes the notions of moral and legal personality seriously, moving away from the traditional French dismissal of them as mere fictions. Although Hauriou refers to

Saleilles less over time, as late as 1912, he still endorses Saleilles's work relating personality and property. With him, Hauriou holds that the basis of institutions is property, interiorized as common in a universality of consciousnesses, worked out individualistically by law, and thereby organized into a subjective personality. Hauriou refers to Saleilles's *Étude sur la théorie générale des obligations dans la seconde rédaction du projet du code civil pour l'Empire d'Allemagne* (*Study of the General Theory of Obligations in the Second Redaction of the Civil Code of the German Empire*) (1895), *Étude sur l'histoire des sociétés en commandité* (*Study of the History of Limited Partnerships*) (1895), and *Leçons de la personnalité morale* (*Lessons on Moral Personality*) (1910) (1898, pp. 120–130; 1902b, pp. 155, 162; 1912d, p. 148).

An heir of the *Herrschaft* School, particularly of von Jhering, is Michoud, who begins earlier and continues later in Hauriou's attention than Saleilles, having a complete brochure devoted to him. Michoud holds that interests are the spontaneous facts; will and its expression as subjective personality is artificial and legally organized.

Hauriou believes Michoud is only partly correct; he holds that interest justifies individuality but not personality. If Michoud's authorities are only creations, they are organs and have no rights against the institution they represent. Apparently Hauriou found a shift in Michoud's later position, for in 1925, Hauriou is able to agree that the organs of government carry the idea of the state equally as much as the citizens; Michoud could not earlier have said this. Hauriou cites Michoud's *"Étude sur la responsibilité de l'état à raison des fautes de ses agents"* ("Study on the Responsibility of the State for Wrongdoing by its Agents") (1895), *La théorie de la personnalité morale et son application au droit français* (*The Theory of Moral Personality; Its Application in French Law*) (1906), and *"La personnalité et les droit subjectifs de l'état dans la doctrine français contemporaine"* ("The Personality and Subjective Rights of the State in Contemporary French Legal Theory") (1911) (1898, pp. 125, 132, 134; 1906a, pp. 138, 171; 1907a, pp. xi, xiii–ix, 29, 31, 35, 37; 1917b; 1933e, p. 102; *Introduction à l'étude du droit administratif français*, n.d., p. 20).

The dominant legal impact on Hauriou, as generally on French law of the period, came from Duguit. Starting from shortly after his first work, Hauriou wrote constantly in disagreement with Duguit, devoting three full articles to him and half of another (1902b, pp. 346–366; 1911a, pp. 1–40; 1912b, pp. 3–10; 1933a, pp. 72–86). Within Hauriou's ostensibly total opposition to Duguit's positions, we find ambivalence as evinced by his characterization of Duguit variously as anarchical and authoritarian. "We fear he has not recognized his tour de force in being a socialist and an anarchist at the same time" (1911a, p. 40) [*"Nous craignons bien qu'il n'ait réalisé le tour de force d'être à la fois socialiste et anarchiste"*].

Duguit's theory of social solidarity "that I will call English or American" (1914b, p. 337) [*"que je qualifierai d'anglaise ou d'Americaine"*], was also derived from the school of von Jhering and from von Gierke's corporativism (ibid., p. 336; 1907a, pp. xi, xvi; 1911a, p. 32; 1933a, p. 84; 1933e, p. 93). More immediately it used the sociology of Durkheim, Duguit's colleague at the University of Bordeaux. Hauriou recognized Duguit's career of writing, as lengthy and rich as his (Duguit, 1901; 1903; 1907; 1911; 1912, vol. 11, pp. 125, 126, secs. 40, 42). His position can be succinctly stated: the given fact is social solidarity—the interdependence of individuals; the consequent duty is a tacit and categorical imperative, to will that solidarity; the resultant rule of conduct and of law is an act for solidarity (1907a, p. 18n2). When the suppositions and corollaries are explicated, his stand on it is clearer.

Duguit's need, in violent reaction to the almighty *Willenstheorie* state, was to suppress power as a source of law, to submit the state to law. Duguit had to build law without the state and without its power. From his philosophy of phenomenalism (only phenomena are real), determinism (everything real is determined), and monism (everything determined is reducible to a single series of kinds of entities), Duguit must start as well without metaphysics (entities are real and undetermined). Hauriou believed Duguit must begin with the positive fact of the nation, a fact which, as positive, takes this social fact as a prolongation of the physical. Duguit appeared, to Hauriou, to be justified by the condition of his contemporary law that existed at his time, which appeared to have passed from a metaphysical to a positive phase with stress upon the objective social community, upon the fulfillment of social functions as the justification for this community, and upon the lessened importance of voluntary contract as a source of social relations.

From this point of view, subjective law, individual rights, moral personality, sovereignty, authority, all are extra flourishes that only serve to confuse law. With no moral personality, logically no individualized, sovereign nation could exist, and therefore, no executive power or function could exist. Because power is non-legal, Duguit sees that a citizen must refuse all obligation to obey governmental legislation or orders until such orders have been discussed before a judge. This is the respect in which Hauriou considers Duguit's theory "American," in that Hauriou feels the United States judiciary to be sovereign over legislature and executive, crippling their functions (1929c, p. 25). Governments have no right to command; the only authority is the ideal rule of social fact.

The only authoritative law, then, is the law that applies to civil servants, what Duguit calls "constructive law," the law needed to organize the services of the state. Positive law, the law for the citizens, is not authority but is fact; called "normative law," it is the existing social fact. Citizens act not *because of* law (causal), but for *the sake of* law (final); the fact of their solidarity is their conceived and willed interdependence, equivalent to law (Hauriou, 1902b, pp. 346–366; 1911a pp. 4–5; 1912b, pp. 4–5; 1912d, p. 74; 1914b, p. 336; 1933a, p. 84).

Hauriou disclaims what he believes is not just an anarchical but a metaphysical conception of human action. Human acts are not all and totally conscious. Human acts are not just voluntary; they are also caused by events. Solidarity is not only a formal end of the will and a fully foreseen contract, but also has content conditioned by circumstances and inclined toward its own ends irrespective of the willed ends. Therefore, conflict can arise between conditioned practical ends and willed social ends. Individuals may do something to achieve solidarity, but they must bring what they do into line with the value of *why* they do it. Actions have no guarantee of becoming so aligned without the action upon them by agents; the social is not identical with the moral or with the legal. Duguit appears to Hauriou to have fallen prey to the revolutionary optimism that progress can be indefinite and that reason is ubiquitous.

The result of denying subjective power to create law is that there is no guarantee for liberty, and no way for law to make swift adjustments to social reality. Law will tend toward the immobility of custom, since the only way for new norms to arise is by the long drawn-out process of alteration in social customs. This is another way in which Hauriou finds Duguit "American," as distinct from French law's *"prœtorian"* nature. The only way to mobilize law is for two systems of law to coexist, one based on political sovereignty and the other on the rule of legislation. Duguit's monistic determinism would never accept this sort of dualism. The first system establishes material peace, the other makes peace secure in legislation. Duguit's doctrine provides a presumption in favor of the former's validity; citizens must obey it because it is needed.

But this is a presumption which can also be corrected; this correction is the function of the second system, the rule of legislation, which follows behind. Hauriou believed that Duguit erred in identifying the political phase with the economic phase. Hauriou holds that the political sovereignty is valid, not because it conforms to legislated statutes already passed, for then there would be no need for the authority. Political sovereignty is presumed to conform instead to the subjective sentiment of law. The discipline that permits acceptance of authority while not providing a guarantee for it is the discipline of organization and procedure, not the whimsical discipline of internal will. The authoritative will is autonomous; but only insofar as disciplined and the discipline is procedural. Authority is presumed conformed to law until it is proven contradictory to the very rule of law; but this rule is itself another form of law.

Hauriou claims that the objectivity Duguit seeks is already given in existing French law; rights are produced by subjective acts, to be sure, but the acts themselves are objectively possible according to a rule of procedure. In primitive cultures, acts are clearly objective not subjective. Duguit confuses subjective with objective because, with the civilizing influence of law, it becomes less clear whether subjective acts or objective rules engender rights.

This confused situation can be penetrated, but to dare try it, one has to be a tough worker.

Duguit is fighting the excessive theoretical impetus of *Herrschaft*; but his theory does not escape legal conceptualism. Its failure illustrated for Hauriou that the only worthwhile attitude is a purely practical one. Duguit's is a selective realism, which excludes all candidates for reality but collective ones. A complete realism would accept the effects of autonomous wills and the currents of ideas even if the wills and the ideas are not themselves observed. Unwilling to accept power or the factual superiority of an elite, Duguit cut off the sources of power and left society powerless. In trying to avoid placing the rule of law *over* society and its institutions, Duguit placed law on par with society, when he should truly have placed law beneath society (Hauriou, 1902b, pp. 350, 355–356, 360, 364, 366; 1907a, p. 7; 1911a p. 10; 1912b, pp. 9, 14–31; 1923c, p. 341; 1933e, p. 125).

Akin to Jellinek's version of *Herrschaft* theory, but entering Hauriou's awareness only very late in his life, was the formal objectivism or legal positivism of Hans Kelsen and its French counterpart in Raymond Carré de Malberg's wide and worthwhile work [*considérable et précieuse œuvre*]. Hauriou cites Kelsen's *Hauptprobleme der staatsrechtlehre entwickelt aus der lehre vom rechtssatze* (*Major Problems of Public Law Doctrine: Derived from the Doctrine in Legal Opinions*) (1911) and *Allgemeine Staatslehre* (*General Theory of the State*) (1926), but, not surprisingly, most of all his *"Aperçu d'une théorie générale de l'état"* ("Overview of a General Theory of State") (1926, pp. 561—646). He also cites Carré de Malberg's *Contribution à la théorie générale de l'état* (*Contribution to the General Theory of State*) (1920–1922).

Kelsen makes the same objectivist error as Duguit in his most rigorous and elegant [*très hardi et très elegant*] system in Hauriou's estimation: he identifies the social organization and law, the state and law, coercion and validity. Beyond these as a source for them both are transcendental norms. Instead of deriving law from state as *Herrschaft* theory did, or identifying norms with social fact as Duguit did, it derives both from something more metaphysically remote. Kelsen's system lies open to the same result as Duguit's brand of objectivism in that this system makes law static, since Kelsen knows law must be stable and he identifies the stable with the immobile. Hauriou allowed stability to be found in movement, leaving relative immobility to customary social facts by distinguishing from them the active order of political power, and then adding further stability in the dynamic balance of one against the other (1933a; cf. 1929c, pp. 1–14, 97–103).

The system of the absolute legitimacy of the law of the state [*système de la légitimité absolue du droit de l'état*] of Carré de Malberg can be summarized succinctly: state is the sole creative power of law, properly so called; the foundation of state—constitution—is also that of law; law is not the foundation of the state. The first constitution is merely an historical fact, to which law attaches itself only later. Subsequent constitutions can be legitimate only by virtue of the rules of previous constitutions, successively back to the first; so no revolutionary constitution can be legitimate, being only a series of historical and not legal facts (Hauriou, 1923d, pp. 284–285).

Hauriou criticizes Carré de Malberg for having overly theoretical attitudes. No one form of law—state law—excludes any law but it. To think that what enacts state law is not political power but the moral personality of the state, superior to individuals, is erroneous. The root difficulty of the theory of absolute legitimacy is the abandonment of a theory of power—a refusal to admit that the will of one may be superior to the will of another. This view ignores the rights of superiority that characterized the will of the chief in every primitive legal society. It canonizes the cultural stage, ignoring that while persons protected by the state surrender their right to achieve justice for themselves, that right devolves to them when they are not so protected. Although Duguit looks for a legal foundation to the state while Carré de Malberg refuses any, both subordinate power to the rule of law, Carré de Malberg by going so far as to subordinate even the constituting power to the constitution. The difficulty with this and like systems is that they are so judicial that they can leave no place for power or for liberty, a narrowness that comes from conceiving jurisprudence as a pure science, rather than as the science of an art (ibid., pp. 178, 285–287; 1929c, p. ix).

If the largest group of French jurists upon whom Hauriou hones his thought is heir of the German school, still his is thoroughly native and represents the updating of Rousseau's thinking on national power. Paul Esmein, "the most classical of our authors" (*"le plus classique de nos auteurs"*), wrote a multi-edition work in constitutional law (1896), to which Hauriou refers for legal information and support for more than a decade before taking up the deeper questions it roused. Its explicit "theory of function" lay latent in many other French jurists.

Hauriou recapitulates the theory in this way: the state is the personification of the nation; the nation has legal functions, not created by state but serving the nation; the ensemble of these functions is the organized nation-individuality; the nation-individual is the state as an objective legal institution. The final proposition sums up the other functions: if each social function is a legal institution, then their ensemble also is one (1907a, p. xiv).

All this is similar to Hauriou's ideas. His only complaint lies once again with the source of power, which Esmein, with Duguit, Kelsen, Carré de Malberg, and the *Herrschaft* School, tries to legitimate in terms of something other than the people. Hauriou is not at odds with Esmein's claim that the representative government's personnel act autonomously and arbitrarily. He agrees with Esmein's claim that the representative source of their power is the nation. What he objects to is the failure to recognize that the personnel actually constitute the nation, and that consequently they give themselves the power.

Hauriou asserts that power is not delegated by the general will of the nation as a legal institution. If the government's personnel were delegated by other than themselves, they would not be autonomous. If they were delegated by the nation to serve the nation, this would mean that the nation they succeed in organizing is already organized. The only sense in which they are delegated, if this is truly a sense of the word, is delegated by themselves.

Unlike the theory of function, the nation occurs as a spontaneous fact. People affirm themselves as electors. Enough people doing so constitutes a majority affirmation. Legislation can confirm this affirmation, but it starts as a fact based on individual rights or the political rights of the people. Esmein views political rights as social functions delegated by the legal institution—the state. Hauriou views political rights to be among individual rights, since they are founded on equality. To think otherwise is to see only dead facts instead of active, passionate beliefs, as the objects of faith in the political life. Esmein accepted the confused effects of the French Revolution, illogically combining an organic with a representative doctrine into the general will of the nation, equating this combination with the legislative will (ibid., 1912d, pp. 99–105; 1923d, pp. 40, 100; 1916c, p. 620).

D. Philosophical Influences

The study of Hauriou's influences in the categories of scientific and legal theory thus far could equally well have considered them as philosophical influences. Hauriou's tendencies, however, as shall appear in the chapter on methodology, were to mean by philosophy something more limited, a realist epistemology and the consequences derived from it. This can be described in terms of method much more adequately, but we are not at the end of this study. The loose use of the term philosophy to cover the broader theoretical realm was just the contrary of what Hauriou wished; for, limiting himself explicitly to a positive study of society, he wished to bring the sociological, psychological and legal theorizing into a realm usable for his purposes by considering them as observational and positive. There is mention of an experimental metaphysics [*métaphysique expérimentale*] in regard to Hauriou; but this is not the first sense in which Hauriou speaks of philosophy. The influences that could be called philosophical, then, have to be such as Hauriou looks at within the scope he himself chooses to consider philosophical; this realm is chiefly the order of classical objective idealism or realism, verging toward contemporary life-philosophy.

Thomism. Often accused of latterly embracing a rigid Aristotelean Thomism, Hauriou is very light on both philosophers in all stages of his work, with one marked exception. His use of Aristotle is chiefly to refer to the *Politics* for the commonplaces used by all political writers, even the most non-Aristotelean: Society is in some sense a living thing; to live is to act; law is reason freed from passion; democracy is the rotation of commanding and obeying; money is a tool for avoiding constant re-measurement of kind (1896, pp. 18, 335; 1912d, pp. 14, 63, 131; 1916c, pp. 78, 367, 628; 1923d, 139).

Hauriou employs Thomas Aquinas even more lightly, being taken at almost every occurrence rather as a representative of the medieval point of view (a point of view outdated for Hauriou) than as an independent thinker. He now lumps Aquinas with Boethius on the concept of person, now with Suarez on natural law (1898, pp. 5, 9; 1899d, p. 147; 1912b, p. 8; 1933c, pp. 21, 30). He never makes explicit the radical modification he makes here in Aquinas for his own purposes, despite the verbal quotation: person is a system of rational mental representations; person as a concept has the function of conciliating contradictions; the relation of creature to God is real, and as a real relation it should be open to observational research along with other realities of the milieu.

While Hauriou quotes Aquinas' *Summa Theologica* on these questions, most of the knowledge he has of Aquinas on social questions such as revolution and popular rights seems to be derivative from his reading of von Gierke on the social theory of the Middle Ages. Not even a secondary acquaintance, it comes fourth-hand from Jean de Pange's (1914) translation of Frederick Maitland's (1900) English translation of von Gierke's (1868) *Political Theories of the Middle Ages*. Hauriou prefers to refer to this work in 1923, although fifteen years earlier, he had made the same point from Aquinas' *De Regimine Principum* directly (1923d, pp. 119, 172; cf. 1909a, p. 56). While he registers pleasant surprise at how non-authoritarian Aquinas is in dividing sovereignty between prince and people, he does not take the opinion as a serious social theory, instead reducing it to a strategy in the medieval fight between papacy and empire (1923d. p. 172).

The striking exception to this disinterest is the total and unqualified commitment to Aquinas in an introductory essay to his second edition of the *Droit public* (1916c, pp. xxiii–xxiv). Aquinas is his metaphysics, Aquinas is his "better inspiration and needed guide" [*"meilleure inspiration et martingale nécessaire"*], Aquinas is the reason he is "Comtean positivist become a Catholic positivist" [*"un positiviste comtiste devenu positiviste catholique"*]. Hauriou restates his social doctrine of moral personality as a corporative organization endowed with objective individuality to which can be added a subjective existence; he calls this the transposition of Aquinas' doctrine that the body of the human individual is organized first, containing the soul in potency, and passes its life bringing soul to act and realization. Hauriou also reads this back into the first edition of *Principes de droit public* of 1910. This is incomprehensible in the light of its isolation; the solution found preferable is that the essay in question is written as a response to François Geny's attack on the first edition.

In answer to Geny's accusation that Hauriou identifies the rational and the factual in the manner of Hegelian metaphysics, Hauriou admits a metaphysics, which as immediately as possible precedes the late medieval beginning of the movement toward totalitarianism, that from Grotius through Savigny to Troeltsch. This is the metaphysics of Aquinas.

Platonism. Hauriou is not reluctant to claim philosophical allegiances; on the contrary, the rest of this study of influences will look at the way he placed himself among the Platonists. But the most forthright statements he has to make about Aristotelean-Thomistic philosophy, with the exception of the above, concern its doctrine of the soul as the form of the body. This doctrine he finds to be a much inferior solution to the nature of humans and their evolution than is the Platonic doctrine of human soul as a motor superadded to an already mental body. In the Platonic view, the soul has influence; but the doctrine leaves intact the evolutionary origins of psyche in the body. The Platonic doctrine is like the Eucharist: for the transcendent human soul cannot be inserted into an evolved psychic life that is only relative and animal except by a partial transubstantiation of that psychic life. This is the only way to explain how beneath sense appearances of the body there can be an intelligible existence. Most importantly, Hauriou claims this to be true not only of the personal human existence but also of the political-social human existence, the institution (1896, pp. 169n11, 359–360, 360n).

Other places Hauriou makes references directly to Plato are not as significant. Other than some short remarks against Platonic communism, Hauriou sees that Plato gives hints of the connection between economic and political power; he is one of the first to decentralize doctrine, giving it to all and not just initiates. More illustrative, Plato is searching out, as do all utopias, the "human type" (ibid., p. 97; cf. pp. 36, 96, 103, 248; 1895a, p. 541). Overall, however, Hauriou does not refer to Plato frequently and most of the occasions on which he does refer to Plato fall into the earliest part of his career.

Other than these mentions, Hauriou's Platonism is manifest rather in his reliance upon the realist theory of ideas as a restorative of moral issues into a rational context, countering Kant. Hauriou looks to the intuition of Blaise Pascal as the more adequate way of encountering the ideas that support this project, and calls to his service his lycée teacher, Delbos and his colleague Fréderic Rauh for substantiation of his thesis by their research (Delbos, 1893; Rauh, 1890; 1892). Maurice Blondel, Dumesnil, Henri Bergson, and Chevalier figure with Pascal in this project, but I will consider the latter three more closely below.

Pascal's awareness that man is placed between good and evil is the very picture of human and social life developing in the midst of contradictions. For Hauriou, Pascal is the very first to find this perspective. In addition, Pascal's *Pensées* (1670) is the unique way out: together with the contradictions mentioned above, a cosmic and religious mediator appears. Pascal's profound view, for Hauriou, is that of a narrowly Cartesian thinker becoming a Christian thinker, combining the ideas of perfection of reason with individual perfection, so that the human race grows in just the way individual human beings do. Their power in society is an intellectual one, that of a thinking reed [*ro-*

seau pensant]. The power in question, though, is intuition, the reason of the heart. Truth is substantial for all true things, namely, the person of the mediator. That doctrine may appear false to the abstracted scholar in that it dissipates into utopias, but can be quite true for the person of action who works with his whole being (Hauriou, 1896, pp. 46, 105, 122, 46; 1894c, p. 297; 1899d, p. 51; 1933c, p. 30; 1912d, p. 117; 1893c, pp. 7–8; 1927f, p. vii).

We can see the Bergsonism that Salvador Lissarrague and Gurvitch sometimes alleged of Hauriou, but in a less heady dose than alleged. Shortly after Bergson's publication of *L'évolution créatrice* in 1907, and again in 1929, Hauriou spent lengthy footnotes on the relationship (1909a, pp. 17–19; 1929c, p. 7). Recognizing an analogy between his and Bergson's views but several times denying that he himself was doing philosophy, Hauriou insisted that their work was independent from each other, and that he had published his thought fifteen years earlier in his books on social science. He called it simply a coincidence [*une simple rencontre*].

Both Hauriou and Bergson find a vital drive continually creating reality anew, thereby creating the duration in reality by the life force's irreversible movement. To grasp this life force, intuition, and instinct are better than formal intelligent reasoning. What Bergson had called vital impetus [*élan vital*] Hauriou had, since 1896, called "social tradition" or "social revelation." Where Bergson and Hauriou differed was in a precision Hauriou made in the idea of continual creation—in the role of time in social life.

Continual creation corresponds well to the irreversibility of time, but less well to its stability or durability; yet the duration is of more interest to the statesman since from it social benefits accrue. It would not follow from creation anew unless the rhythm of the vital force were slowed to a uniform movement by meeting and reaching a balance with resistances. These resistances are the enduring species in nature, and in society they are the institutions created just for that purpose. Without them, the vital force "would ignite as suddenly as bursts of fireworks that burn out in an instant" (Hauriou, 1909a, pp. 17–19) [*"eût jailli avec la soudaineté des bouquets de feu d'artifice qui sont flambé en un moment"*].

Pierre-Joseph Proudhon (1846) is, for Hauriou, the visionary of contradiction. He refers to Proudhon's *Système des contradictions économiques* (*System of Economic Contradictions*) (1846), seeing that no social fact of any duration can develop apart from contradiction. His was a classical optimism to hope ever definitively to exorcise contradiction (1896, pp. 95, 106, 109, 234, 361; 1899a, p. 15; 1911a pp. 11–12). His more basic influence on Hauriou's Platonism appeared only in Hauriou's later books (1933c, p. 29; 1929c, p. 65). Proudhon began his thinking from historical revelation by concretizing spiritual force into historical events, in contrast to Marx's historical materialism and to the abstract principles of French idealism. Proudhon opposes this historical revelation of ideas to evolutionism; a great idea contains virtualities, which will continue to unfold in historical events, rather than succumb to changes in intellectual fashion. To clarify this aspect of Proudhon, I modify the usual method here of strict attention to Hauriou texts by inserting this excerpt from Proudhon's letter to Edmund in 1852: "Ideas, be well assured of it, are action; and one acts sufficiently when he scatters into the intellectual atmosphere the germs of future society"; this, in contrast to "mere revolutionary agitation," which Proudhon refused to deem "action" (Lubac, 1948).

Of immense importance to Hauriou's development, on a par with his debt to Tarde in social science and to Duguit in legal theory, is his relationship to the philosopher, Dumesnil, from his university years onward. He dedicated his *La science sociale traditionnelle* to Tarde, and to the work of Dumesnil "one of the most profound philosophical works of our time" (1896, p. vii) [*"l'une des œuvres philosophiques les plus profondes de ce temps"*], although Dumesnil is hardly known today. Hauriou refers to Dumesnil's *Du role des concepts dans la vie intellectuelle et morale* (*The Role of Concepts in Intellectual and Moral Life*) (1892) and *"Le spiritualisme"* (1904, pp. 453–563). Dumesnil's rotation helped Hauriou to develop his notion of the alternation between periods of renaissance and medievalism, between periods of objective, absolute faith and those of subjective, relative criticism. Hauriou's first introduction of the eventually crucial notion of institution occurred in a section of his 1896 *La science sociale traditionnelle* entitled *"Progrès comme le forme du salut"* ("Progress as the Form of Salvation"), a conception he borrowed in its entirety from Dumesnil.

The key concept Hauriou adopted from Dumesnil's thought was the reintroduction of moral questions into social science. Dumesnil's contribution was to furnish a theory of concepts and of conceptualism, which postulated that as opposed to a stream of consciousness—to the perceptual life described with scientific intoxication [*ivresse de science*]—concepts introduce disruptions in consciousness and discontinuity in the mechanism of bodily movement. Discontinuity allowed a reintroduction of liberty as a first step back toward a culture that respects human inspiration. Hauriou also recognizes the contribution of Emile Boutroux and William James to this restoration of spirited society (1894c, p. 297; 1895a, p. 538; 1896, pp. vii, 187, 253, 360; 1899d, pp. 7, 43, 44; 1911a p. 17).

Forty years after the publication of Hauriou's *La science sociale traditionnelle*, he said in retrospect that Dumesnil was the first to begin the work of founding the new phenomenal objectivity of ideas upon a substantial spiritual reality. Ideas could be real only on the condition that, according to Platonic doctrine, they are the ideas of God. Dumesnil showed that the penetration of principles and of beings by one another is of the order of liberty and grace—the supernatural order; yet he realized that this interpenetration was essential not only for religious life, but equally so in personal and social living (1933e, p. 128; 1923d, p. 721; 1923c, p. 342).

Late in Hauriou's career appeared a philosophical successor to, and on par with, Dumesnil's work. The personal friendship Hauriou struck up with philosopher, Jacques Chevalier of Grenoble, much better known today than Dumesnil, ran in the same idealist tradition as that of the older philosopher, Dumesnil. Chevalier, too, believed that the ideas, which people observed were real, not merely phenomenal, could be so only if they were the ideas of God. The libertarian discontinuity of concepts in Dumesnil was balanced by the personal continuity of ideas in Chevalier; this strongly influenced Hauriou's ever more forward analysis of the subjective continuity of corporate personality in terms of ideas. What Hauriou tried to derive from Chevalier was the metaphysical construction lying behind the physics of vitalism, which is social institution. These refer to Chevalier's (1923) *L'idéalisme français au dix-septième siècle* (*French Idealism in the Seventeenth Century*) and to his (1927a) *"Le continu et le discontinu"* ("The Continuous and the Discontinuous") (1923c, p. 343; 1923d, p. 721; 1933e, pp. 116, 128). Chevalier also writes on Hauriou, in his *"Le concept et l'idée"* ("Concept and Idea") (1929, pp. 113–136).

Though Chevalier's work influenced Hauriou's thinking, it might have had a greater impact had Hauriou discovered it earlier. In Chevalier's essay, Hauriou finds John Henry Newman holding a notion of development, which, in keeping with his thinking and that of Proudhon, claimed ideas' potentialities to unfold only in the course of history (Chevalier, 1927b; cf. Hauriou, 1929c, p. 65). From this Platonic context, it would have been likely that Hauriou, interested in the reality of ideas and conversant with German literature of the period, was aware of Edmund Husserl's work, yet we find no such reference or familiarity in published Hauriou literature. He does, however, express vigorous approval of it in a personal letter to Gurvitch, written in the year of his death, 1929:

> Phenomenology, there is the philosophy needed to let the social sciences found themselves on the method of observation, for it founds the objectivity of ideas right in the interior of the human consciousness. It is twenty years that I have been affirming this objectivity of ideas and following it out. (Gurvitch, 1932, p. 123n2; reprinted in Sfez, 1966, p. 505n41) [*La phenomenologie, voilà la philosophie qu'il fallait pour permettre aux sciences sociales de se fonder sur la méthode d'observation, car elle fonde l'objectivité des idées jusqu'à l'intérieur de la conscience humaine. Il y a vingt ans que j'affirme cette objectivité des idées et que je marche en conséquences.*]

4. Effects of Hauriou's Theoretical Work: Institutionalism

The effect of Maurice Hauriou's work on jurisprudential theory is much the same as the subsequent history of his theory of institution—the great devotion of my life [*la grande affaire de ma vie*] as he called it. We can trace this history by nationalities, because several of the directions of institutional theory are tied up with the political developments in different countries.

In France, André Hauriou has called himself "a disciple of my father" (1966a, p. 23n1) [*"un disciple de mon père"*], editing much of Hauriou's material posthumously (1929a; 1929c; 1933e; 1930b; *L'introduction à l'étude du droit administratif français*, n.d.). A minor development was the positivist theory of Waline; remnants of Waline's positivism are found in the work of René Clemens, André Desqueyrat, and Joseph Thomas Delos, who wished to extend the theory of institution from a partial legal theory to cover the whole scope of law by letting institution absorb even contracts (Clemens, 1935; Desqueyrat, 1935; 1939, pp. 65–115; Delos, 1929; 1931, pp. 97–153; 1950). Because the institution was an adequate sociological model, and because for them, the legal world merged with the social world, they believed such an extension on an empirical basis was possible. But the dominant French development, coming through Delos, and above all in the work of Georges Renard, was to cast Hauriou as a Thomist social philosopher.

From his earliest writings, Renard interpreted Hauriou as modernizing the principles of the Thomistic social theory. Hauriou considers the work that became Renard's 1931 work *La théorie de l'institution: essai de l'ontologie juridique* (*The Theory of Institution: Essay in Legal Ontology*) in a favorable but relatively non-committal way in *"L'ordre social, la justice, et le droit"* (Renard, 1922; 1924–1928; 1930; 1931; 1933; 1939). Delos added the dimension of the papal social encyclicals in his series of communications at the *Semaines sociales de France* (LeHavre, 1926; Paris, 1928; Marseilles, 1938; Lille, 1932; France, 1932; Alger, 1933; Nice, 1934; Angers, 1935; Versailles, 1936; Clermont, 1937; Strasbourg, 1946; Lyon, 1948; Pau, 1953). Through this dominant interpretation, reading Hauriou in any other way in France soon became quite difficult.

The most influential of all Hauriou's French commentators, Gurvitch, adopted the Thomist interpretation of Hauriou's work. However, contrary to the sentiments of Renard, Georges Gurvitch meant this not as praise, but as criticism. A "late Hauriou" emerged with Gurvitch, on much the same basis as he did for Renard, namely, the self-interpretation by Hauriou (discussed above) in the introduction to the second edition of his *Principes de droit public*. Thomistic conceptualism, personalism, and teleology are the critical agents in this transformation of Hauriou into Thomist. The "early Hauriou" had founded community upon the idea, the indeterminate and virtual idea of Plato; as a result, he could appreciate the legal validity of the unorganized social order. But scholastic teleology deforms the spontaneity, subjecting it to an end and making it hierarchical. When idea ceases to be an objective mind [*nous*] and becomes something interpenetrating consciousnesses [*comme une "interpénétration" de consciences*], then it is no longer equivalent to a fact. It becomes a hierarchical manipulation by the established government of authority. In Hauriou's development, the privacy of Thomistic substantialized persons triumphs over the transpersonal openness of Bergson and Proudhon. In the late Hauriou, social bodies have ceased to be agents, resigning their dynamism to the administrators of the person-state (Gurvitch, 1931a, p. 163; 1931b, pp. 658, 668, 678, 696, 697). Gurvitch attributes this transition to Renard's Thomistic influence on Hauriou and attributes to these heterogeneous theses the marked lack of effect institutionalism yielded on legal and political theory.

Fifteen years later, Gurvitch returned to his criticism (1947, p. 115). No longer interpreting Hauriou's alleged statism as an alien Thomist thesis, he now found it to be an intrinsic result of Hauriou holding only one basis for the institution, namely, communion in the idea. This, in turn, allowed only one form of institution, which monolithically had to culminate in the state.

Hauriou fell into even worse luck, if possible, among the German legal theorists. Rudolf Smend and especially Carl Schmitt, arch-apologists for what came to be National Socialism, took up Hauriou's theory as quite useful to justify the concrete law they were seeking to legitimate. As a result, Hauriou came to be known as the grandfather of the Nazi Reich (Smend, 1928; Schmitt, 1934). "Concretized legal thought or words have a sliding value, which becomes determinate through a context of some order" (Viehweg, 1937, p. 88) [*"Der (konkretisierte) juristische Begriff (oder das Juristische Wort) hat seinen verschiebbaren Stellenwert, der durch eine Ordnungs vorstellung bestimmt wird"*].

This Schmittian interpretation of Hauriou meant that the concrete "context" comprised the wishes of the present regime, freed now of any restriction by unalterable principle. Despite the attempt of Viktor Leontoweitsch to reorient the German version of Hauriou more textually toward classical teaching on the relation of subjective and objective elements in law (1936–1937, p. 234, quoted in Friedrich, 1963, p. 63), Erich Schwinge and Leopold Zimmerl still found it possible to criticize not the use of Hauriou but only the effectiveness of his technically jural use for Nazi ends (see Theodor Viehweg's interpretation and citation in Schwinge and Zimmerl, 1937). Viehweg's criticism of Nazi legislation amended and completed Leontowitsch's recovery again to dissociate Hauriou from Schmitt's use of him (1937). But his influence was not yet strong enough to overcome these other writers' belief in a Schmitt-Hauriou heritage.

As late as 1965, Wolfgang Friedmann, in the fourth edition of a work begun in the post-Nazi reaction, can still say that Hauriou's directive idea [*idée directive*] can be used to reinforce the collective over against the individual, and that this is close to the fascist mystique submerging individuals into service to something higher than themselves, subordinating one class to another. His grudging admission that Hauriou may not himself have been a fascist is not too gracious because "the political result is a Latin, Catholic, depersonalized version of the German, atheist, personal autocratic state theory" (Friedmann, 1965, p. 193) [*"Le résultat politique est finalement un pendant latin, catholique, dépersonnalisé de l'État autoritaire germanique, irreligieux et personnalisé de la théorie allemande"*].

Arnold Gehlen's view of Hauriou for political anthropology approximates closer to Vieweg, however (Gehlen, 1958, pp. 414, 425, 436). The thesis of Hansjürgen Friedrich realizes that either exclusively legal or exclusively sociological interpretations of Hauriou's work play into the hands of those who would force law into a peculiar national mold and direction, rendering Hauriou's useless for any non-French usage except in sociology (1963). This view, however, is countered by the even more recent claim of Roman Schnur that Hauriou's demise is just ending, that his theory of the strengthened executive was out of season in the Third and Fourth French Republics, coming into its own environment only in the Fifth Republic (1965, pp. 21–22; cf. Marty and Brimo, 1969, pp. 255–270).

An unlikely defender from Papist, Nazi, and socialist labels of Hauriou is Hermann Dooyeweerd, leader and theoretician of the Dutch Calvinist Party, since none of these labels make Hauriou useful to the party. But the inherently moralistic science of society built on natural law of divine origin brings him to bear on their needs. Dooyeweerd separates Hauriou from any taint of Thomist social philosophy, but refuses him unqualified acceptance because the humanist dialectic (the scientific ideal of objectivity versus the ideal of personal freedom) and the Christian dialectic (nature versus grace) do not merge as Hauriou was thought to claim, but rather denature each other (1940, p. 336; 1941, p. 61).

About the Schellekens thesis of 1945, which reaffirmed a Dutch Renard-like Hauriou (Schellekens, 1945), Dooyeweerd held that despite the attempt to make Hauriou's system a legal one, the original sociological character of it remained (1948, p. 2). Tjalling Ulbo Sixma van Heemstra's thesis in 1954 agrees with this sociological estimate of the institution, but holds that such a view is inadequate as it denatures state and nation (1954, pp. 109–110). Addressing the topic again in 1957, Dooyeweerd adds that Hauriou's ideas do not ensure a good community if implemented. By unfaithfulness to Platonic morphological ideas and dallying with Aristotelian substantial form, Hauriou must accept both "good" and "bad" ideas (Dooyeweerd, 1957, p. 579).

All this becomes clearer in a more recent addition to Dutch Calvinist institutional interest: J. D. Dengerink intends to do for the later Hauriou what Dooyeweerd did for the early Hauriou. It is the Calvinist motivation that restrained total usage of Hauriou: no ultimate dialectics can exist because there is *perfect* redemption from sin back to the unique will of God; there can be no autonomy of will against God.

So Hauriou's relatively autonomous ideas [*idées*] must be brought into strict dependence on their Creator, or the need to introduce a scholastic supernature will be admitted, instead of the Calvinist sole human nature in submission to divine sole agency (Dengerink, 1965, pp. 360–362).

The influence of Hauriou's institutionalism on Spanish thought is quite strong and comes to Spain chiefly through the work of Carlos Ruiz del Castillo (Hauriou, 1927f; 2003; Ruiz del Castillo, 1929). Ruiz del Castillo is one of Hauriou's more literal interpreters, who stresses the personality of the state in his view of corporative democracy.

Roberto Saboia de Medeiros repeated nearly verbatim a Gurvitch-like critique of Hauriou's Thomism (1938, pp. 103–159). Lissarrague, as mentioned earlier, refutes the Thomism but accuses Hauriou of statism nonetheless (1941, pp. 197–219). The interest in Hauriou's theory continued, however (Lustosa, 1938, pp. 5–14; Gimenez, 1945), spilling over into the South American legal world chiefly in the form of Gurvitch's institutionalism (Gascón y Marin, 1945, pp. 173–181; Hübner Gallo, 1951; Recaséns-Siches, 1948; cf. Lacambra, 1968, pp. 241–254).

Institutionalism in Italy chiefly takes the form of the positivism of Santi Romano. Hauriou believes that their work is only parallel: "A noteworthy parallel effect was made in Italy to organize the theory of institution. I refer to Romano's *L'ordinamento giuridico* (*Legal Order*), 1917, and Cino Vitta's *Gli atti collegiali* (*Collective Acts*), 1920" (1923d, p. 75) [*"Un effort parallel le très remarquable est fait en Italie pour organiser la théorie de l'institution. Je citerai Santi Romano, L'ordinamento giuridico, 1917, et Cino Vitta, Gli atti collegiali, 1920"*].

In Julius Stone's analysis of Romano, Hauriou's *idées* are no longer the Platonic ideas, but the concrete content of consciousnesses. In Stone's estimation, Romano considers this necessary to broaden the bases of community, in response to the Gurvitch critique, and to allow the explanation of criminal organizations in answer, for example, to Dooyeweerd. The series of works appearing in the years from Romano to the mid-twentieth century (Vitta, 1929; Monaco, 1932; Goretti, 1933; Poulopol, 1936; Forti, 1939; Mazzantini, 1946; Barbera, 1949; Bobbio, 1936) allow Alexander Passerin d'Entreves to ignore all but this Romano institutionalism not only in Italy but on the continent generally. Romano's is "the version which has most widely influenced contemporary legal and political thought" (1967, p. 127).

Hauriou's increasing use in Italy, as well, is to provide pointers for European Union and not only for national law and politics. While unattributed studies appreciate this same feature. Hauriou mentions *"Teoria normative-Istituzionismo-Teoria relazionale"* ("Normative Theory-Institutionalism-Relational Theory," n.a., n.d.) and L. Lucchetti's *"Istuzione sulla formazione dei Budgets"* ("Institution in the Drafting of Budgets," n.d.) as realizing the three Revolutionary ideals, as did Cesare Goretti's *Il liberalismo giuridico de Maurice Hauriou* (*The Juridical Liberalism of Maurice Hauriou*). In the spirit of Romano, it was left to the Catholic paper *Circoli Dossetti* (Rome) to load Hauriou with plaudits such as "most original of French publicists," "a daring spirit," and "lucid and sincere terms of candor and genius" (n.a. *"Funzioni e ordinamento dello stato modern"* ("Sorting Functions of the Modern State") 12 November 1951).

Hauriou stimulated comparative law at his university and over the continent, devoting large sections of his final works to English and American judiciary law. He borrowed ever more freely from American jurists (such as Maine, Woodrow Wilson, C. Dicey, S. F. Goodnow, James Bryce, Harold Laski, James W. Garner). Hauriou brought his concern for "social revelation," as bursting the rigidity of the Napoleonic Code into contact with the common law. In view of this effort, he found the Anglo-American response to be disappointing.

The first studies in English are simply non-committed; they become frankly poor in their interpretation in the World Wars I and II years, and begin to improve again during the 1960s. Frederick Hallis's study in 1930 is in the Continental tradition just discussed, appreciative but dismissing Hauriou as too busy about historical analysis to be the creator of a legal synthesis.

Moorhouse T. X. Millar is interested in the Thomism and finally frees Hauriou from Thomism, but only by alleging that Hauriou embraces a stoic naturalism or voluntarism: he attributes to Hauriou the view that each human being has total control over its destiny.

Ivor Jennings' study (1933) is masterful, also characterizing Hauriou outside Thomism, while faulting Hauriou's lack of crowd study as a basis for his social theory, and for introducing values as Jennings thought a scientist should not do (Hallis, 1930; Millar, 1932, p. 596; Jennings, 1933, p. 84).

Roscoe Pound passes "Continental institutionalism" off as a "recrudescence of absolutism" (1939, pp. 6–7), since the only justification for its law is divine authority. Morris R. Cohen notices favorably Hauriou's distinction of contract from institution in his *Law and the Social Order* (1933, pp. 108–109). Nikolai Timasheff and Thomas Morris Haynes use the Gurvitch critique. Haynes repeated the overall demand for a greater variety in the "work ideas" of society; the ideas should include not only those around which institutions are formed, but the full range of human endeavors. Timasheff misinterprets his sources by adopting the criticism of the later Hauriou's conceptualism as too hierarchical but attaching it to his Platonic ideas, quite the opposite of Gurvitch's intentions (Timasheff, 1946, pp. 498, 510; Haynes, 1949).

Of late, the Australian Julius Stone (1946; 1966) has reviewed Romano's work on Hauriou favorably; he believes Romano has no hidden criterion for institution. Stone relieves institutionalism from the suspicion of hiding a crypto-natural law within Platonic ideas.

The American, Joseph Albert Broderick, has been concerned with refocusing attention back on the Hauriou texts and placing them into contemporary legal practice instead of attempting to make Hauriou representative of any particular tradition (1963a; b, pp. 277–284; 1964, pp. 95–125; 1965, pp.

281–308; 1967, 1968a, pp. 271–280; 1968b, pp. 459–478; 1968c, pp. 144–160; 1970).

5. Late Twentieth-Century Effects

Appreciation of Hauriou's works in the last third of the twentieth century was the residue of more critical engagement during its first half. While hardly a glimmer persisted of his fellow institutionalists Renard and Delos, Hauriou entered into the pantheon of public law curricula and reference texts.

While some older interpretative texts are singly repeated (de Laubadère, 1980), Yann Tanguay puts the question of institution with contemporary relevance (1991). Hauriou's is a treasury of varied meanings of institution, not only his. He places his work in context for psychiatrists, educators, and sociologists, not only jurists, and for jurists of private law, not only public law. Tanguay takes the institutional elements of goal, power, and communion to show two current relevancies of the doctrine, due to its reliance on the founding idea: it supplies the pragmatic dimension, of institutionalism. First, founding idea (neither conceived end nor already actualized function) gives dynamism to the action needed to bring the idea to realization; second, founding idea gives stability to a permanent process of refounding, due to the idea's need to be constantly refounded by new participants.

Bjarne Melkevik (1989) takes the same three elements of institution to explain Yevgeny Pasukanis' surprising validation of Hauriou, in 1924, from Hauriou's 1910 first edition of *Principes de droit public*. Pasukanis' Marxist affiliation would not have suggested that this support was likely. But he presents Hauriou as the theorist whose insistence on the institution's elements, here called its interest, decision, and function, best unveils the bourgeois law's representation of individuals' personhood under the legal personality of the state.

Olivier Beaud also finds Hauriou ideologically affiliated, but this time with Thomism (1989). Following the lead of Albert Brimo (1969), Beaud says Hauriou is an "ardent natural lawyer," defending Aristotelean-Thomist principles versus legal positivism. The Thomism appears in Hauriou's rehabilitating a plurality of sources of law, including case law and convention, in addition to legislative practice. His only critical characterization in an otherwise positive assessment, that Hauriou is "brilliant but confused" for not being Thomistic enough, may be explained by Hauriou's not being Thomist at all, despite his approval of Thomism in the second edition of the *Droit public* in 1916, as earlier in this chapter. Another of Beaud's sources is worth pursuing (Dufour, 1983).

Eric Millard seeks to situate the influence of Hauriou into a school of Hauriou's own but devotes most of his efforts to puzzling out the methodology of that attribution (2005). He names only Lucien Sfez, Jean Rivero, and Georges Vedel as defenders, and Charles Eisenmann as principal critic of such a school. More helpfully, he identifies two key concepts of such a school: that public power is dominant over public service; and that auto-executory decision characterizes administrative decisions. Millard takes Hauriou's defenders to have confined him by insisting that executory decision making is not a unilateral act, while an auto-executory one is. Hauriou was willing, however, to reconcile those two and to conciliate public power with public service. According to Marie-Luce Pavia (2001), professional risk and administration as public service are Hauriou's chief contributions, despite Hauriou's explicit rejection of Duguit's claim to that effect.

In an earlier more substantial work, Millard (1995) already remarks that Hauriou's own work can help reduce resistance by his supporters by conciliating institution to public service. Primarily, though, Millard's study is a long reappreciation of Hauriou's theory of institution as a valuable tool for analysis of social reality, a method of institutional analysis [*l'instituant*], without committing to Hauriou's theory of institution as involving the identity of social entities [*l'instituée*]. The first opens new avenues for developing research programs by proposing an authentically juridical appreciation for the social dimension of state and law. Nonetheless, generalizing Hauriou's methodology to all sorts of institutions left Hauriou unable to resolve the basic inconsistency that Millard sees between state as the transcendent legal entity and state as another social entity competing for its own interests.

Millard blames "Catholic idealism" for giving the dominance to the idea of task over the other two elements of institution—its organized power and its manifestations of communion—and for the resulting incoherence in handling the state as institution. The supposed incoherence is that state is an institution like others, but is transcendent to others; a materialist dialectic then must be forced upon idea for state to mediate the conflict between competing institutions, unless its raw power is called upon to do this work. Millard forgets that the idea of state not as entity [*état*] but as the rational social fabric [*tissu étatique*] recognizes its role as rationally resetting the excesses of economic and political social fabrics. That role is limited, however, by state's lacking any power of social initiative that the other fabrics generate.

Bernard Roman (2001) tells the *Assemblée nationale* that on Hauriou's view, the president of the republic is not responsible before the high court except for treason. For Stéphane Leclerc (2002), Hauriou's institutional feature of full participation is what most informs his ideas on planning European Union. Christian Lequesne and Andy Smith (2002) find Hauriou's idea of task and not the feature of full communion of primary usefulness for this project. The duration of institution on the other hand, is what most impresses Gérard Mondiaire and Sylvie Durousseau (1999) and Alain Barrere (1971) for providing security to the European Union's process of centralization despite the tension among the Union's contradictory interests.

Duration as allowed by Hauriou's stress upon ideas is what permits F. Daviet to answer "yes" to his question (2000), "Is the public service still capable of innovating?" The most valuable feature of institutional theory is found to lie in its emphasis upon procedure, for Laurent Duclos (2001) and Alexandre Siné (2000). The way that this value of procedure achieves effect is shown by François Perroux (1980). In reflecting upon the student conflicts at Paris, ongoing since 1968, Perroux observes that the university as an institution as defined by Hauriou is neither subordinated to society nor to state, but elaborates its own law.

Bruno Silhol (2002), as well as Duclos and Olivier Mériaux (1997), apply Hauriou's work to labor law, as does the Dutch thesis by Filip Dorssemont (2001). Claude Olivesi (1997) finds Hauriou's work in constitutional law most useful for exploring the tension between direct democracy and representative government. Resolving that tension by requiring the "sacrifice" of direct democracy to representative order is enough for the International Young Catholic Workers (IYCW) to claim a Catholic affiliation for institutional theory; they see "sacrifice" as necessary for law to achieve social "salvation." Adopting Olivesi's strategy permits Luc Heuschling (1999) to identify institutionalism as a naturalism. Joseph Pini (1997) believes this strategy is better understood as Hauriou's equilibrium between authority and contract.

Melina Kurdjian-Fath (1997) gives greater contemporaneity to Hauriou's legal doctrine by locating it among the constitutional issues of the Fifth Republic. Virginie Meyrier (2002) and Laurence Melle Bonadei (1998) focus upon Hauriou's institution by asking whether theatre is a public service. Yann Landot (2002) applies institutional theory as a tool for evaluating French developments in litigation, while V. Philippe Cossalter (1999) includes Hauriou's appreciation of the cases in administrative jurisprudence on which Hauriou published commentaries. François Fourni (2005) locates Hauriou's decentralization where it belongs in law, instead of applied to more extended matters.

Fared Lekeal (1989) writes that first Renard, then Hauriou, influenced the doctrine of Paul Boncour, his favored source in Lekeal's thesis. The institution's features of autonomy, cooperation, subsidiarity and participation also influenced André Marc's *Ordre nouveau*, Maurice Barres' *Action française* and Emmanuel Mounier's *Esprit* movement, also says Lekeal, right down to Jacques Maritain and his use of Aristotle and Aquinas in the manner of Delos, says Lekeal. Again, Hauriou should not be assimilated uncritically into some Catholic wave. Remi Cheno (2008) intends the more scientific home than speculation upon religious outcomes from Hauriou's theory, as does Ludger Mueller (2000) in the German context.

Hauriou's stature among great French publicists is shown in *"Éloge du doyen Georges Vedel"* ("In Praise of Dean Georges Vedel") (Maus, 2002). In it, Didier Maus goes some distance to correct the wild claim by Dominique Gros (2002) that Maurice Hauriou did not object to Vichy's disqualification of Jews. Gros' reason for his claim is that André Hauriou's 1943 complete revision of the 5th edition of his *Précis élémentaire administratif* did not make this objection. Recall that the father died in 1929!

Wolfgang Schild (1974) fully details Hauriou's institutionalist theory. He concludes that Hauriou succeeds in humanizing the two extremes of positivism and naturalism. Humanizing is the work of idea, which yields less detail on its criteria for application.

Günther Teubner's mentions of Hauriou dismiss his ideas because they freeze normative interlegality into static and separate systems (Teubner and Korth, 2008). Teubner is also dismayed that Hauriou's talk of collective agents misses the agency of "talk incorporated," as his own replacement for agents that discourse theory's orthodoxy prefers (2006).

Some German works do focus directly on Hauriou (Bleich, 1998), but more frequently, his idea of task is used to facilitate others' doctrine (Amm, 1999; Melville, 2001). Equally compelling is his institutional theory's closely related attachment to law being not primarily a set of norms or values, but a communion in action. Teubner (1996) opines that by fostering a worldwide corporativist law-merchant, Hauriou's theory still fails to accomplish what Teubner's own mediating discourse theory of law does for the European Union.

While Hauriou has become nearly invisible in both Iberian countries, one exception is Lino Rodriguez-Arias Bustamente's extended study on institutionalism, which compares French institutionalism (Hauriou's) to Italian (for example, Romano), and prefers French institutionalism as leading to the state's balancing individual rights with law, as opposed to totalitarianism (1972).

On the other hand, an explosion of reference occurs today in Spanish- and Portuguese-speaking countries of Latin America. The translations of Hauriou made prior to 1970 are supplemented by more recent ones that fuel the explosion of interest (Hauriou, 1927f; 2003; Lopes Meirelles, 1977).

Meso- and South American thinkers write Hauriou's doctrine into addresses before professional conferences and legislatures, in journal articles, and books. Hauriou's development of administrative morality as the public order of personified institutions is the contribution that impresses legislators (Gomes, 1996; Escarrá, 1999; Flores, 2001; Canhim, 1994), and professionals (Trejo, 1999; Giacomuzzi, 2001; Cafarro, 2000; Quintão, 1998; Salomoni, 2001; Rossi, 2001). This thrust provides intelligibility to reforms of municipal law (Aguilar Sahagún, 2001; Zuccerino, 2000; Reyes, 2000; Manchego, 2000). It influences issues of human rights (Capizio, 2000), of penal law (Bento, 1994) and contractual relations. The directive force of institutional idea (Reale, 1994) explains the division of powers, although with primacy of executive power and law's ability to go beyond texts in order to achieve finalities (Escobar, 1980).

The sociological reality of institutional personality is what allows the uses of Hauriou's doctrine by these Latin authors for their administrative and constitutional law (Ruiz, 1999; Machado, 2000). The socio-legal method of institutionalist theory for treating legal reality is what lets Hauriou characterize institution (Rioldan, 1980).

Stress upon Hauriou's contribution to administrative morality characterizes numerous Latin studies (Miranda, 1999; Farías, 1996; Borges, 2000; Pinheiro, 1999; Vélez, 2001).These authors who refer to Hauriou's work use the references to establish firm doctrinal positions before the authors provide their own arguments.

In the Anglo-American world, even Hauriou's use as such a cliché is usually absent except when professionals try to grasp the civilian rationales of either European Union or Organization of American States in public law (Olsen, 2000; Lee, 1998). David Bates (2004) appreciates Hauriou's institutionalism for attempting to develop the legal relation between foundational communities and the organizing powers that preserve them, but less by a metaphysical approach than by deriving an example from the legal order of the Catholic Church (2006). This "Catholic imagery" for expressing his new republican concept comes down to state's embodiment of directive idea just as any other institutions do (2005), a claim that does not appear to be "Catholic" at all.

In English language literature, David E. Apter (2001) details the fall during the 1950s, and rise during the 1990s, of institutionalism, including Hauriou's. Jean Leca (Roux, 2004) places Hauriou prominently among the founders of political science in France, as does Eric Jabbari (2006). Gordon (2000) finds Hauriou to have been less than well served by his adoption into Eric Voegelin's (2000) works.

One surprising focus on the institutionalism of Hauriou's student Joseph T. Delos (1944) occurs in Hannah Arendt's reviews of Delos' book as "brilliant" (1946; 1951). His book traces totalitarianism to nationalism, not to state, as Arendt traced imperialism to nationalism. Instead of destroying individual rights, state protects them. Hauriou had claimed since 1896 that state is the "redemptive" social fabric.

No authors claim kinship of Hauriou to the Anglo-Scandinavian theory called institutionalism (MacCormick and Weinberger, 1986); Massimo La-Torre does compare them, to the detriment of Hauriou, because La Torre prefers the analytical methodology to a realist one (1999).

Beyond the commonplace use, H. Stuart Jones highlights Hauriou's contribution to the question whether public service unions should be subject to a regime of labor law different from private law (1988). His *The French State in Question* (1992) sets this question within the context of more recent French law.

Other jurisdictions have found new uses for Hauriou's theories in Hungary (Vilmos, 1993), Turkey (Gözler, 1998; Gözler, 1999; Bocaç, 2004), Japan (Saito, 1993; Imaseki, 1982) and Africa (Nguini, 1998). The website run by Stefan Gigacz (http://www.hauriou.net) has become a location that assimilates Hauriou into the Sillonist social movement of Marc Sagnier.

6. Conclusion about Influences On and By Hauriou

In this chapter, I intended my introductory survey of the influences by and upon Maurice Hauriou to show that his methodology is a core issue to which his work and others' use and commentary upon it keep returning. Hauriou adopts some of his sources because they allow the results of social science to influence the practice of law. He resists other sources because they refuse that influence. Or else they go too far by assimilating the methods of law and social science to each other, so that both disciplines suffer. Throughout his study of their mutual influence, he applies philosophical terminology to these methods in his sources, and in his own work, terms such as "subjectivist" and "objectivist," "positivist" and "realist," "pragmatic" and "idealist." This adds the third dimension, that of philosophy, to his and his sources' methods in law and social studies.

Hauriou is usually perceived in terms of the relationship he drew among law, politics, and sociology, says Simone Goyard-Fabre (1998). The authors who deal with Hauriou are focused upon issues of his methodology. Some have supported his accomplishments for bringing into mutual reinforcement the methods of social science and law. Others have reduced their reliance upon him, out of concern that the distinctive features of one of these two disciplines are confused with the other, by reason of faulty philosophical foundation. During the first forty years after the closure of his work, and in the more recent forty years, his commentators' concerns about Hauriou parallel his own concerns about his own sources.

Because of local issues in the several national settings where Hauriou's doctrine was received, this chapter has easily collected his sources and his respondents according to national traditions of reception. For completeness, I have pointed out even the less studious citations of Hauriou's contribution to the several areas of law. Nonetheless, the more substantial studies in the main national settings center on issues that return attention to his methodology.

To treat these issues of methodology, I have organized the remaining chapters to clarify first the legal, then the sociological, and finally the philosophical methodologies that Hauriou developed, by devoting one chapter to each. Two chapters considering methodology at large, and then Hauriou's own general treatment of methodology, precede the central chapters on these three methodologies. The chapters on law and on social science are completed by a chapter which integrates the two, and by another chapter which applies them to Hauriou's dominant focus, the institution. The final chapter completes the chapter on Hauriou's philosophical methodology by my philosophical appraisal of its claims.

Two

METHODOLOGY

1. Importance of Methodology

The issue of methodology is important for the sake of more than scholarly tidiness. The interest of a study may well be its conclusions, but the conclusions do not speak for themselves. They are not simply present, they are reached. The way of arriving at them is part of what they mean, as well as the source of their justification in part. The conclusions of a sociological study, for example, must be evaluated in terms of the expectations and canons of sociology, the way the sociologists do things. But while this allows for an intra-communicative body of knowledge, it does not allow for the creativity and innovation needed to keep a body of knowledge open by expanding its limits or exhausting them.

What makes expanding the limits of tradition possible is that our hypothetical sociologists are working not only in terms of what others are doing but also in terms of what they believe others ought to be doing—what they believe sociology should be or become. So also do students of law and philosophy endeavor to expand the limits of their fields, despite protestations by some traditional, possessive philosophers who may protest that philosophy should remain confined within its limits. This is not because philosophy as a science is different from others; no science is "just another" science; the model of each science should be unique. The difference arises because philosophy deals with human issues and no human tools stand unmade, neutral, or objective. Human beings are not alienated from their tools, for those are also products, human purposes incarnate.

The logic, models, and the metaphors authors use are not independent of their results, or to judgments that we make upon those results. Our sociologist using legal models will get legal, albeit hybrid, results. What the sociologist would consider true in a legal sense have neither truth nor falsity in sociological terms. The judgments do not have the same meaning when they are arrived at differently.

It is true by definition that the object of a discipline is not known until the research is exhausted; but the intention to describe it suffices to postulate an object. The intention to describe the object may be frustrated; for instance, carrying out the description may prove that the object in question is untenable as conceived, or that we did not correctly anticipate its reality. But the methodology does not have to wait upon the end of an investigation. The projects investigators conduct may have an implicit methodology that conflicts with the explicit one, but which may truly be called theirs because they cannot dissociate themselves from the projects they initiate; they describe what in fact we do, and what we intend to do in practice. Hauriou may not distinguish his implicit from explicit methodology, but that construction can well be made.

The difference between explicit and implicit methodology is quite significant in the case of Maurice Hauriou. For example, the institutionalism that he and others felt to be his chief contribution demands that we judge whether institutions exist. But it is not possible to make this judgment or others of the type unless we know just the kind of thing we are to affirm or deny. We may affirm that Hauriou's institution exists sociologically while denying it any legal reality, or vice versa; or we may admit an institution is a real legal community but refuse to admit that it has any metaphysical stature comparable to the legal one.

The object of the study in this volume is not to determine the truth-value of the theory of institution, not to decide what the category of methodology is to which its construction belongs. The institution is not under scrutiny here, although we surely must consider it as the context in which Hauriou's writing evinces his methodology and toward which the methodology is directed. Judgment here is properly directed toward analysis of the way institution is presented, both implicitly and explicitly. Hauriou took fifty years to work out his theory of institution; much preparation of a humbler sort is owed to him before making the judgments that the critics of his methodology surveyed in Chapter One have made precipitously. The attempt to carry out this effort by no means requires the prerequisite of a rigid distinction between disciplinary methods in Hauriou. Theoretically, the way is even left open for us to find the interpreted Hauriou saying that all three—philosophy, sociology, law—are one and the same, or that any two are. That outcome is unlikely, however.

From the present methodological study, I expect to elucidate the relationships between philosophy, social science, and law. These three strands are too patently in evidence in Hauriou; my expectation finds sufficient rationale in that evidence. But it is striking to find that this issue, that of methodology, is just the one on which all authors criticize Hauriou. When reduced to the terms of these three poles, we might be surprised to find that some critics accept him because he is metaphysical rather than legal, for instance, while others find just the opposite, with neither side recognizing that the source of the difficulty is methodology.

Criticism of Hauriou's work nearly always has an anti-metaphysical character, even when it purports to call him a "mere" jurist or social scientist. The first anonymous responses to his work and those made by René Worms (1894, pp. 395–399; 1896, p. 399) and Henri Bouasse (1899, pp. 226–241) characterize it as traditional metaphysics masquerading as new positive science. Recall that François Geny's (1915, p. 110) chief complaint is that Hauriou speaks a crypto-Hegelian metaphysics by identifying the real and the rational and that Georges Renard offered a Thomistic interpretation that approvingly appraised the methodology as philosophical. Achille Mestre (1929, pp. 272, 278) and Jacques Chevalier (1929, p. 132), in the year of Hauriou's death, interpreted Hauriou's work as a philosophy, but found his philosophy to be a Bergsonian experimental metaphysics [*métaphysique expérimentale*] and a Platonism, respectively. Chevalier held the concrete ideal of justice up as the benchmark to which the jurist had to adapt facts. Julien Bonnecase made the unfavorable identification many others hesitated to state, that Hauriou was not only metaphysical but "mystical" (1931, pp. 161–185, 241–254; 1932, pp. 1–12; 81–108, 160–178, 241–263).

Georges Gurvitch's disagreement was not that Hauriou was philosophical, but that he chose the wrong philosophy. He never excluded all philosophy, nor did he accuse Hauriou of that, a crude sense of positivism. Phillip Bosserman's *Dialectical Sociology: An Analysis of the Sociology of Georges Gurvitch* clearly recognizes throughout, summarily, how vigorously Gurvitch rejected the assimilation of sociology to statistics in American fashion, and thus how squarely his normative facts [*faits normatifs*] stand within the Continental tradition of social philosophy (Bosserman, 1968, esp. p. 305). Again, Julius Stone's criticism was that there was a hidden and metaphysical criterion to the directive idea of the institution.

Another common criticism of Hauriou is that he is guilty of excessive legalism. From his ideological standpoint, Georges Platon found Hauriou started on the right path, but was unable to escape established law enough to become truly scientific and truly Marxist (1910, pp. 83, 85). In Chapter One, we learned that Joseph Thomas Delos was dissatisfied that Hauriou, by distinguishing law and science, was unable to make of institutional theory more than a partial legal theory—unable to make it the whole of law identified with the total social phenomenon. Similarly, Gurvitch later in his own career remarked that Hauriou lost his spontaneous sociological viewpoint to a formal juristic one because Hauriou sharply distinguished between social and legal reality.

Surprisingly, out of this formalistic critical background are a good number of critics who find Hauriou much too scientific to be adequate either as philosopher or jurist. Thus, at the start, Pierre Aubry reads Hauriou as confusing sociology and law. He says that Hauriou first becomes overly logical and then discards logic for spontaneity of society (1911, pp. 3–11). Interestingly, an anonymous reviewer, who once finds Hauriou too metaphysical early in his review; later in his review finds him a signal example of how modern social science corrupts law ("Review of *La gestion administratif*," 1899, p. 192).

A curious criticism is that of Georges Davy: Hauriou refuses sociologism for metaphysical reasons, but nonetheless falls into it because he insists on observation, namely, of ideas and of legal promulgations (1922, p. 158). Joseph Declareuil sees Hauriou's scientific way the only one possible in an anti-metaphysical age. Carlos Ruiz del Castillo approves his "psychological" study of ideas—studying persons, versus the formalist legal method. Marcel Waline approves Hauriou's start with the personality of groups, instead of with the original but less scientifically available personality of individuals

(Declareuil, 1929, p. 173; Ruiz del Castillo, 1929, pp. 98–99, 102; Waline, 1929, pp. 59–61). Frederick Hallis saw Hauriou as an observer of data who failed to synthesize it in a legally useful way.

Charles Eisenmann believed that to support law on history, as Hauriou did, was to lose the human subject; only Kelsenian absolutes preserve humankind (1930, p. 256). Two decades after Eisenmann, Hermann Dooyeweerd was to say the same, but from totally different sympathies. For Ivor Jennings, Hauriou's "sociology of law masquerading as philosophy of law," or rather as its support, was inadequate even as science. André Desqueyrat is willing to grant that Hauriou has matched Delos' desires closer than Delos thought.

Benoit Jeanneau (1954) disapproved of Hauriou making the general principles of law more a function of sociology than of judges. Lucien Sfez, anxious to show Hauriou as the enemy of "legal judaism," interpretation of texts by texts in a perfectly self-governing textual world [*interprétation des textes par les textes dans une parfaite autarchie livresque*]), stresses the inductive nature of his work. Roland Maspétiol less approvingly holds to the final criticism like Jeanneau's from the perspective of forty years later: Hauriou was above all a scientist of society, in the sense of being a close observer (1968, pp. 250, 261–262); but without a methodological framework, for example, of phenomenology, he mistook the accidental and passing notes of pre-1914 liberalism for the essential nature of society.

2. Technical Methodologies

The philosopher and the lawyer tie for first place in the popular mind for technical obfuscation. Both have recondite vocabularies, both have the temerity to claim that they speak for all other disciplines with regard to anything worth saying; many a sociologist will repeat this temerity, for example, the sociologist of knowledge. It would be rash for such tangled webs to be mutually comprehensible, especially to the student of one with no formal training in another. But in common use, law and philosophy speak realistically, for "philosophy" is used for the most pragmatic of lived opinions, too; and law enters most intimately into the fears and hopes of people.

As a less intuitive consideration, philosophy never appears in pure form bereft of contexts that do not understand themselves as being philosophy. The development of a philosophy, which is only philosophy and nothing else, turns out always to be minimally the capitulation to the demands for some medium of its communication, such as the language philosophy employs. Even further, philosophy needs a subject matter of inherence as well as a medium. Philosophy never speaks just about itself; for philosophy is the thought about everything, including itself but only among others. The discipline proper to a material object of study will always be in phase with a philosophy of the same; and if each discipline excludes all but its practitioners, then philosophy is bodiless, non-existent. Since this conclusion is professionally unacceptable, I will consider the allied disciplines, including law, open to philosophical treatment.

A third consideration about the relationships among disciplines is the following: The object of this volume is such that lay readers understand its study without comprehensive technical training or extensive background in law or philosophy. Method can be seized only by closely following every step of an argument; method is the way a worker does what he does. Methodology is the way the worker claims to do it, implicitly or explicitly, the doctrine underlying the reasons the work is done in this way. If, in the theoretical order for Immanuel Kant, the method precedes the content, concretely the methodology precedes even the method. We can criticize the content in terms of the method, but the method most properly must be criticized in terms of our methodology. The methodology may be subject to criticism itself for its coherence or its results, since it may be partial or ill adapted; but the methodology comes first. The technical legal method does not exclude a philosophical approach to the methodology.

Finally, Hauriou's work is so structured that theoretical writing is clearly demarcated from the technical. Between both types of writing is a constant interplay, but generally, the different editions of *Droit administratif*, the *Nôtes d'arrêts*, and related studies are further from our purposes than are *La science sociale traditionelle*, the editions of *Principes de droit public*, *Précis de droit constitutionnel*, and many essays that expand them. Thus I will exclude such considerations as the correctness of Hauriou's comments upon the *Conseil d'État* decisions, the history of French institutions he studies (the administrative law itself, decentralization, Roman law and the *Institutes*, the development of management [*gestion*], the differentiation in appeals to the administrative courts, and the French governmental institutions addressed in the final parts of the public and constitutional law books), and even the concrete theories of government, which apply his more fundamental ideas (public service, public function, public domain, responsibility and risk of civil servants, the organizational chart of the government, and delegation of power). I will reintroduce any of these topics, however, as they elucidate the primary topic.

3. Methodology of the Present Study

Hauriou's clearest statements about the relation of law, sociology, and philosophy occur at the earliest and at the final stages of his work. Comparing these, we need not worry about any strict delineation of the periods of development of his work and career, for the content of the key concepts remains remarkably similar, as do the concepts he considers to be the key ones. Concepts or preoccupations from his early sociological career, which appear to be long gone, reappear in very similar form during the 1920s. Thus, we need not use a genetic approach to start at his earliest work and interrelate all of the key ideas there, and then move on to do the same with each successive writing. Such an approach is also unable to synthesize his thought, since there are gaps found at any one time, which have to be filled in from works that appeared before or after.

For this reason, a safe approach is to collect the treatments for each of the unmistakably important concepts from over the fifty years of Hauriou's career together under one head. The individual concepts then can be set in a systematic order as close to that of Hauriou as possible with only slight attention to chronology. My arrangement of topics bears only a loose resemblance to an outline of Hauriou. Hopefully, he would not have fought such an arrangement; even his son, according to Sfez, freely rearranged his classifications in posthumous editions. Sfez illustrates how André Hauriou is a "gardener in the garden of my father," but a garden in the French style (*jardinier du jardin de mon père à la française*) in, for example, the complete recasting of the posthumous twelfth edition of *Précis de droit administratif* according to Hauriou's definition of institution (1966, pp. 358–362).

The scope of the present study of Hauriou's methodology is solely his explicit methodology, what he claims that his method is. It must be left to future study to develop his implicit methodology, which requires first the construction of systems for his non-methodological concepts; for example, his epistemological, cosmological, anthropological, evolutionary, and theological concepts, and then positioning of his explicit methodology in terms of these systems. Before continuing, I will clarify this concept of implicit methodology, which I have placed beyond the scope of this study.

Implicit methodology is the interpretation and evaluation of one category, clearly and exclusively defined, by the category or categories over and against which it is so defined. It would be an investigation of the ways in which the models an author uses are categorically commissive, and how the categories used are theoretically commissive. It would align the distinctions and interrelations an author makes with logically discriminable forms of propositions. From this alignment, implicit methodology derives deductively the methodology appropriate to each, finally proceeding to test the given author's explicit methodology in terms of these requirements placed implicitly by his conclusions.

This study, on the contrary, will only discriminate the categories as the author, Maurice Hauriou, does himself; it will only attribute to him the commitments he recognizes that he makes. It will interrelate only as he interrelated categories, insofar as this better defines them but not insofar as it tests them. It will not go on to develop the formal logic required for the use of each concept. Even the final chapter, the most constructive in this study, builds a metaphysics, which Hauriou does not build, but does so only because he demanded that it be built and provided some materials at hand with which to do so. It remains, then, on the explicit side.

The distinction of implicit and explicit is not dependent upon the way particular authors structure their work; the materials covered by either form of methodology will shift between implicit and explicit. Authors may, and probably must to some extent, test the logic of their categories, recognize their commitments, and analyze their results against their purposes. When and to the extent that they do this, they develop their explicit methodology. But there remains undone, in turn, the development of implicit categories, relationships, and commitments even in authors' extended efforts. Insofar as authors' intentions surpass their speech, and even more, insofar as their universe of discourse surpasses even by their intentions, always more remains to be said.

This study does not attempt to satisfy that shortfall between speech and intention or between intention and domain regarding Hauriou. The scope is modest; it is always desirable to clarify what is basic. Chapter One made clear the special need for basic research on methodology in regard to Hauriou, and the dire effects of substituting assertion about him for research into him.

I begin this study with Hauriou's comments on the ways of proceeding in any human pursuit and on the different kinds of pursuits that people undertake (Chapter Three). The next two chapters examine Hauriou's explicit methodology in law (Chapter Four) and in sociology (Chapter Five). We need to see not only how he says we should progress in any particular study, but also how we should describe and differentiate its object, and what its roots and distinctions are. The confrontation of these distinctions takes place more directly when, in the following two chapters, we will study the interplay of methods (Chapter Six) and apply them to the study of larger human groupings (Chapter Seven).

I attack the third prong of Hauriou's methodology in a study of his philosophical methodology (Chapter Eight). Hauriou simply says less about the manner of philosophizing. As a result, this chapter is more heavily doctrinal, attending to the philosophical doctrines Hauriou accepts or rejects, since this is nearly the only philosophical comment he makes. I will also pay some attention to the manner in which Hauriou says the philosophy of other disciplines is to be approached. Following this, I will define the nature and scope of philosophy as a discipline relevant to Hauriou insofar as it differentiates itself from law and social science (Chapter Nine).

Three

HAURIOU'S GENERAL METHODOLOGY

1. Introduction

This chapter examines the ways Maurice Hauriou had available to him to carry out human intellectual pursuits. The first section is concerned with Hauriou's conscious use of analogies and his appreciation of this usage. Other sections concern his relating science and art, theory and practice, and the several ways he characterizes his overall method.

2. Analogies

Late in his career, Hauriou stated a key rule for a legal researcher as "in the presence of a novel decision, the interpreter should always look for analogies" (1927b, p. 247). The same is true of scholars standing before any newly born science: in understanding, they cannot help but use analogies relating to older sciences. The reason that this can be done is that the older ones are not foreign to the newer ones. They are related by a "feeling" for the continuity among them. As the "touchstone" of the new, older sciences help determine its content, elements, and categories (Hauriou, 1899d, p. 2).

An analogy, however, never assimilates the material it analogizes, not even implicitly. It can never give the essential nature of its analogate. Requirements for their identity may be common to both, but they are never implemented alike. Any analogy is restricted and partial, excluding other analogies that may be equally explanatory. In such cases, a third, bridging analogy is needed. In this way, analogies can be corrected by using further analogies (ibid., pp. 5–6).

Social science, a new science in Hauriou's day, is especially sensitive with regard to its analogies. It is possible to throw the whole of its scientific activity to one direction or another by changing analogies. Thus, a biological model will imply mechanist expectations from the science, while a legal or logical model will lead in a libertarian direction, presumably because therein the thinking is rational and voluntarist. Because of the proximity social science has to decision, practice, and action, it is all the more important to get its analogies right (ibid.).

The point-by-point accuracy of the analogy is not most important here, but the character of the total analogy. Even inexact metaphors of society form reference points by which we can compare different societies. Thus, Hauriou will say of the first major metaphor of thermodynamics he uses, that its redeeming quality is to keep organic and inorganic realms of being—from being either completely different or completely identical (ibid., pp. 14, 35).

A. Material Analogy

The dominant analogy Hauriou uses from the sciences of inorganic matter couches the whole of *Leçons sur le movement social* in terms of the science of thermodynamics to illustrate his conception of society. His purpose is to show similarities between social and physical movement by juxtaposing the science of the one with the science of the other (ibid., p. 6). Because Hauriou is interested in society in terms of its power, the transition to the science of chemical and physical power is easy for him (ibid., p. v). Physics and sociology both have as their objects something with mass; for example, in society, mass is embodied in the number and bonds of its members. Thus, the laws of inertia, relativity, equal action and reaction will apply to both (ibid., pp. 12, 17). At different places, Hauriou also employs the laws of conservation of energy, of parsimonious activity, and entropy.

The danger of a mechanistic social science is closer, however, with a mechanical analogy than with a biological one. Hauriou's chief task is to avoid the reduction of human energy to chemical energy. Within the analogy, the way he does this is by rejecting the vision of society as a hermetically sealed container [*vase hermétiquement clos*]; freedom is a corrective to the principle of constraint (1896, p. 19). To continue the analogy, Hauriou has to find something in physics approximating liberty in social science; this he finds in the free movement of energy from physical movement to thermal phenomena, and back. This is to parallel the discontinuity between social stimulation and human thought; the thermal phenomena and the thought are the "representing" element, the physical movement and the social movement the "represented." Thus, the physical structure of thermodynamics is meaningfully representative, humanized; it becomes the fundamental analogy [*analogie fondamentale*] between society and the natural world (Hauriou, 1899d, pp. 7, 57, 62).

From the scientific viewpoint, another analogy Hauriou uses, even more pervasive and consistent albeit less dramatic is that of matter. In this case, we speak of a scientific matter, not the matter of form traditionally addressed in classical philosophy, matter and form will be addressed in the later chapter of philosophical methodology. He uses matter as his explanatory tool in *La science sociale traditionnelle* (*Tradition in Social Science*) (1896, pp. 1–25); it is a substrate, it has three dimensions (group, individual and their mediation), it is not abstract and geometric but expandable while limited, it allows commonness among parts as the place where [*le lieu ou*] characteristic social events take place.

But it is in his 1894 article, *"La crise de la science sociale"* ("The Crisis in Social Science"), where Hauriou explicitly attributes the notion to Gabriel

Tarde, that he most clearly elucidates the analogy (1894c, pp. 301–305). There he postulates a peculiarly social material as essential a base to its realm as is living matter as distinguished from inorganic matter to its proper order. The never-expressed reason for this presumption is apparently a logical or systematic one: Hauriou appears to hold that a starting point appropriate to its future developments exists for every order of being.

Hauriou's basic analogy here, then, is matter—physical, living, or social. Each is necessary to its respective order. Each has a more radical tendency to expand and disperse than to organize, although the tendency to organize is by no means negligible. To achieve likenesses among the parts of each is what makes possible its expansion, its formation of larger wholes: atom to atom, cell to cell, and human being to human being by the imitation of geniuses peculiar to the human order. Incorporeal matter vibrates, living matter procreates, social matter imitates; for likeness is a fact of activity, not a fact of static essences. Likeness is the stimulus for expansion, and is the end result of expansion. Parts that are ultimately discontinuous and heterogeneous begin to act alike. Parts form a temporal association able to do duty as an explanatory mechanism; driving toward likeness explains action both bodily and corporate.

The initial state of matter at every level is radical diversity; no isotope is numerically the same one as another, however much their chemical descriptions coincide. Diversity excludes one from the other, a primitive mode of privacy. Any harmony and grouping that it may become is identified with action toward likeness. Taking a cue from his thermodynamic analogy, Hauriou is willing to claim that action is voluntary. Universal repetition [*répétition universelle*] is the principle of action for this likening; Hauriou's more suggestive way of putting it is that, at bottom, on every level and in every order, a mighty love [*un immense amour*] is the principle of change (ibid., p. 304n2). While this sounds like a theological principle, the likenesses are acquired by action, not an endowment innate by creation (ibid., p. 303n1).

An equally persistent expression of this same vision is found in the notion of fabric or tissue (*tissu*). It is early found with the analogy of material [*matière*], as another means for expressing the unfamiliarity of social reality with more common physiological terms; but its clearest statement, as to content and origins, comes only much later:

> If we compare [society] to a fabric, the metaphor dear to Plato, we can say that its warp, representing the element of order, is made of objective ideas, while its woof, representing the elements of power and liberty, is made of wills and of the subjective passions of the human individual. [*Si on la compare à un tissu, ce que était la métaphore chère à Platon, on peur dire que la chaine de ce tissu, représentant l'élément de l'ordre, est faite d'idées objectives, tandis que la trame, qui représente les éléments du pouvoir et de la liberté, est faite des volontés et des passions subjectives de l'individu humain.*] (Hauriou, 1923d, p. 66)

B. Vital Analogy

Social analogies from the vital order may be left unexplained because of their brevity, for example, the metamorphosis in the insect world to the contrast between latent, unconscious and absolute political life and explicit, conscious and representative political life (Hauriou, 1929c, p. 118). It is still clear that the fabric and matter analogies, and even the thermodynamic one, lead to the living order as the most appropriate location for available analogies to society. "Life" and "energy" are social analogies we find in Hauriou's writing as early as the 1892 *Study on Decentralization* [*Étude sur la décentralisation*], throughout. Even better is the Bluntschli model of state construed as the course of a personal life (1896, p. 196).

An early and more suggestive statement of Hauriou's feelings on the analogy between human being and society concerns Portieux de l'Oise, who tried to develop administrative law upon a life-to-death human history. Says Hauriou, "This might have been a spiritual pamphlet; but all it is a bizarre labor" (1893d, p. 9). His own insightful pamphlet [*pamphlet spirituel*] was to be his *"La théorie de l'institution et de la fondation"* of 1925, as much committed to the metaphor of humankind as was the *Leçons sur le mouvement social* of 1899 to thermodynamics.

Some very striking features are evident in Hauriou's use of the overworked "man writ large" analogy. First, Hauriou states bluntly that some authors make of the human being and the social entity only a comparison, what we might call in English a "conceit"; for Hauriou, however, this comparison is a reality (1916c, p. 100). This must mean that both terms are real, that their structure is not just similar but actually the same, that the activity of each is identical. To support such marked claims, Hauriou lays down the postulates for this new comparative method [*une méthode comparative nouvelle*] (1933g, p. 107).

First, society is a psychological feat. Next, within it exists a reciprocal action and reaction of the human spirit and objective ideas; these are the foundation of the institution. Then, corporate personality is a social creation made largely in the image of human personality. However, since corporate personality is made in an unconscious way, it can reveal depths of the human personality that conscious introspection cannot. Finally, since in corporate personality the details of organization are blown up as on a screen, the observation is so much easier.

Hauriou presents this so that each form of personality is needed to clarify the other; he finds the reality of the one as hotly contested as that of the other in the public forum. But the direction of the comparison is already clear from his last postulate and it was stated unambiguously nine years earlier:

> I do not believe, however, that legal analysis can draw any profit from psychological analysis, here; and I am tempted to believe, on the con-

> trary, that it is the psychological analysis, which is called to profit from the results of legal analysis. This is because the personality of social institutions is seen as through a magnifying glass and elements show up there, which can remain deceptive in the human personality. (1916c, p. 285n1) [*Je ne crois pas toutefois que l'analyse juridique puisse ici tirer aucun profit de l'analyse psychologique, et je serais tenté de croire, qu'au contraire, c'est l'analyse psychologique qui serait appelée à bénéficier des résultats de l'analyse juridique. Cela tient à ce que la personnalité des institutions sociales est vue comme au travers d'un verre grossissant et que des éléments nous y apparaissent qui peuvent rester dissimulés dans la personnalité humaine.*]

Once again, the reason for this comparison is that human personality itself is known only by an analogy; we do not know it directly if we say it is an idea realizing itself in the common will of the nervous centers, that consciousness is a phenomenon resulting from the simultaneity with which the nervous centers react in the interior of the idea (ibid.). What results on every side is that society is the analogy by which humankind comes to know itself, rather than society coming to be known via human personality. This is a direction truly unique to Hauriou; Plato suggested it in introducing "justice writ large," but successors quickly took the introspective route.

The analogy of society to human being proceeds on two levels, on a transcendent one of the body-soul relation, and on an empirical level of observable action. Continuing the line of thinking in our introductory chapter on the "transubstantiation" of group individuality into group personality, Hauriou finds a "sort of union of soul and body" in the appearance of the personality as the State only at a later historical stage than the appearance of the national institutions. Though the analogizing factor is transcendent, Hauriou insists that the decision on its historical succession, soul to body rather than body to soul, is a matter of positive method, a decision based on observation (1912d, p. 9).

The structure of soul and body in human beings and in their societies is, however, yet more complex. The synthesis of a unique composite is not formed in one single movement of soul to body. Prior to this, a work-idea to be accomplished and a will to accomplish it are synthesized into a soul. Only after this union is there synthesis of this soul into the body, namely, to the will as a powerful force capable of realizing the aspirations (Hauriou, 1916c, p. 297).

Hauriou also tries to establish the elements of the corporative organism in an order which parallels the elements of the human spirit, eternal object of any philosophy [*objet éternel de toute philosophie*]. In this three-part schema, Hauriou sees that the statute of the corporation is the objective form, in which its peculiarity is organized. Parallel to this, he discovers the characteristics of difference, originality, particularity in every human being outweighing the likenesses among them. Unfortunately, the parallel ends here, although Hauriou goes on to claim law as the general rule in which the group becomes conscious of itself by attending to its internal likenesses. But the parallel ends because he claims that the government is the mediating factor that proceeds from statute and law to balance them. He does not draw out the factors in soul parallel to law and government (ibid., pp. xxx–xxxi).

The body of the institution itself, as the human body, is of a psychophysical nature, is a spiritualized body, even prior to its becoming a person because in both, all of the elements of body are more spiritual than material: the group of members is absorbed in the idea of a work to be done; the organs of the corporation are swept up in the willpower of realization; and the psychical manifestations of this communion are embodied in an idea (Hauriou, 1933g, p. 98).

Changing to a more empirical standpoint, Hauriou explicitly subtitles his *"Théorie de l'institution"* an essay in social vitalism [*vitalisme social*]. The two parts of the study concern the "anatomy" of the institution, its elements and structure drawn from the observation of human structure; and the institutional "physiology," its function through birth, life, and death drawn from historical analogies (ibid., p. 119). Such "birth" occurred for private institutions by the Waldeck-Rousseau bill of 1901, making older communities the product of contract; and for public ones by the treaties of peace in 1919–1920, establishing new countries. Such "death" occurred for private religious congregations suppressed by the legislation of 1 July 1901, and for public institutions by, for example, the eighteenth-century partition of the Polish state by Prussia, Habsburg Austria, and Russia.

There is direction by a discursive consciousness and by an intuitive consciousness, waking and in sleep, in parallel to the direction by State and by nation to their achievements (ibid., p. 112). Discursive consciousness reaches achievements with an awareness of its steps, even foresight of them. Intuitive consciousness reaches achievements with awareness only of the outcome, not of all the steps that make up the process of reaching outcomes. Directive ideas are the meaning of these outcomes, and can be achieved discursively or intuitively. They are the vital principle of social institutions because they pass from one to another person without losing identity due to their similarities to each other.

The irreducibility of directive ideas provides them the objective identity that is recognizable in different institutions. They identify the distinctive form of life that each institution has, separable from individuals' lives, insofar as these ideas are separable from us and act upon it. Hauriou calls this vitalism [*vitalisme*] of social institutions their physics [*physique*], the empirical availability of their living structure parallel to that of the human being. This means the "physics" of these bodies, not their "physique" (ibid., p. 128).

Much the same in elements, but slightly clearer, is the analogy of human and social will to public law. The pre-personal and sub-personal legal realities of the State are related to State legal personality in the same way as objective and subconscious human psychological realities are related to the human person. The three forces of governmental will are also powers of will crucial to the human individual faced with the need for action. These powers are implicit will—intuitive, instinctive, and unreasoned—whose organ is the electoral body; explicit will—reflective, deliberate, and reasoned—whose organ is the legislature; and the executive will, ready to pass into operation. These are detailed as a will for existence, a will for action, and a will of free submission. It is up to positive, observational psychology to take advantage of these indices supplied by the study of public law, for they are just the way for psychology to reconstitute the unity among various forms of human will.

> They are [important] in the human person; they are to be so also in the individuality of the state society, which is necessarily built on the model of human individuality. (Hauriou, 1916c, pp. 75, 664n1, 695) [*Elles le sont dans la personne humaine; elles doivent l'être aussi dans l'individualité étatique, qui est nécessairement construite sur le gabarit de l'individuale humaine.*]

Hauriou holds that this is the only way to insure liberty for political liberty is obtained by an organization, which gets its inspiration from human psychology (ibid., p. 115). "Political liberty is like the internal liberty of man, in that both are conditioned by organization and by structure, by the balance and adjustment of powers, are conditioned, in brief, by an objectively internal constitution" (Hauriou, 1918b, p. 815).

This fact of liberty justifies the postulate that the constitutionalism of politics simply reproduces the constitutionalism of the human being. This postulate, in turn, justifies the assimilation of corporate personality and human personality. This in its turn is a necessary program because this assimilation is the only way "instinctive and anthropomorphic man" can solve the relations between power and law, namely, by a personal structure that facilitates the distinction between justice and injustice. Hauriou believes that one of the most desirable features about this procedure is that it avoids entering a psychological discussion, which is out of place in politics. Here the evidence comes from the social and political order (ibid.).

The only deficiency in this comparison of the State person to the human person stopping the exercise of his power by a decree of personal will, is that within the moral person, the psychological operations are unknown, while in the State person, the constitutional operations of limitation by balance are known explicitly. Hauriou refers to "man rendered more understandable by the striking grandeur of his social dramas" (1912d, p. 146; 1901b, n.p.) [*"l'homme rendu plus sensible par la grandeur emouvante de ses drames sociaux"*].

Ultimately, this attempt to project human beings into the social group is anthropomorphic. There is no embarrassment in admitting to anthropomorphism; the projection is only a projection of the concept of being, which only goes to prove that human beings conceive of themselves, too, as beings—an excellent point of departure, being that of René Descartes (although this same passage in another work drops the reference to Descartes) (Hauriou, 1923c, pp. 346; 1923d, p. 724).

C. Other Analogies

Maurice Hauriou employs several other analogies to focus his work that augment the physical and psychological ones, but these others either are not as forcefully directive or are limited to only one stage of his thinking. Those worth considering are the historical, military, and capitalist analogies.

The advance in science evident in civilization is not proper to any one individual person; all people advance together. So the history of humankind as a whole comes to reproduce the ages of any one of its number. Quoting Blaise Pascal, Hauriou (1896, p. 46) sees the whole of humankind "as a single unique human being who subsists forever and learns continually" (Pascal, 1651, p. 46) [*"comme un même homme qui subsiste toujours et qui apprend continuellement"*]. This goes beyond the static structuring of man writ large, the passions of any single person, to something temporal and moving. In view of Hauriou's spiraling of history in two ages (medieval and renaissance that keep returning but at a different level), three cultural characters (religious, metaphysical, positive), and three political forms (aristocratic, democratic, executive-administrative), the analogy of human beings and history is bound to have decisive consequences. For, juxtaposing Hauriou's insistence on the reality of the analogy in terms of structure with his transformation of the structure into an active analogy, we have an affirmation that human and institution are both historical. The stratification of law at any time—civil, public, administrative—reflects the structure of the human person; with our new analogy, it also reflects the individual history and social history.

The historical analogy is also reflected in the thoroughly polemical character of Hauriou's writing, a character that allowed calling his antagonists "influences" in our introductory chapter. The historical forces of power, contradiction, and equilibrium [*pouvoir, contradiction, et équilibre*] are as active in the activity of individuals as in the movement of their society.

Hauriou calls the mobile order that a society effects equilibrium [*équilibre*] as opposed to the static balance of equality [*égalité*]. I will return to the topic of *équilibre* shortly; but at this point, suffice it to say that the analogy Hauriou uses to express this, nearly the only useful sociological concept he presents to some ways of thinking (cf. Siorat, 1969, p. 58), is the model of a line of march [*agmen*] (Hauriou, 1909a, pp. 8–11). Hauriou repeats this treatment in the first edition of *Droit public*, and the second edition of *Droit constitutionnel* (1910, pp. 7–10; 1929c, pp. 75–76). This military notion is that of troops in marching order [*la troupe en ordre de marche*]: not a preestablished movement or order, but one with some direction to it—movement as a whole, stable, and uniform movement, which is quite a modest notion [*toute modeste*] as it strikes Hauriou; it has for him several useful roles, and he repeats it often. It protects against surprises, from within and from without. It allows controlled output of energy so that the finite supply of energy is not dissipated in idiosyncrasy. It makes the multitude more effective by prohibiting variations; it allows organization of functions, and this seems to mean planning, here. Finally, it allows the choice of direction on the basis of information as a whole, not completely at hazard.

The differences between the 1909 and the 1929 accounts of *agmen* are worth noticing. In 1909, this order is a guarantee of liberty, in 1929, Hauriou supplies a fifth advantage of *agmen*, namely, that it elucidates the subordination of the march, as such, to necessities, that it is not itself any person, that it requires some chief director to maintain cohesion, to decide on functions, and to choose the direction. It is a leader's role and experienced strategies—"sometimes we march and sometimes we stop"—which are the rules insuring stability, and thus the freedom, native to *agmen* by itself in the earlier analysis. This conceptual tool used by Hauriou is the same one used by Aristotle to explain universality and by Thomas Aquinas to explain transcendentality.

A final interesting analogy Hauriou uses quite often throughout his career is that of "social capital." At the earliest stage, he speaks of the categoreal deposit for a society [*le fonds catégorique des sociétés*] (1896, p. 33), meaning the same by it as did Tarde, namely, the ensemble of traditional beliefs—religious, artistic, moral, legal, and scientific, to which one adapts in acting socially. If individuals do not use this capital, they play a shifty social game; and if there are enough others who refuse to act straightforwardly [*franc-jeu*], society is not possible.

The analogy reappears occasionally and suffices for Hauriou to operate not only as an understanding of society but also of the economy, such that the economy is more spiritualized than it is material for him. But as for the use to which we are attending here—the capitalist analogy for society Hauriou first noted its consistent importance in a late footnote (1916c, pp. xxviii, xxi, n1). There Hauriou is giving an example of what he means by the operation of the experimental method in his works. He tells how he early felt the need to sharply distinguish the subjective personality, referent of civil and economic law, from objective individuality, the category used for public law.

Next Hauriou came to identify only legal personality with private possession, while allowing the category of moral personality or subjectivity to be used in conjunction with the idea of social work, the category of institutional formation. Finally, in his late work, he came to realize, as a result of World War I, that political centralization is dependent on a form of social capital.

What Hauriou means by this is shown somewhat less tolerantly by his "God-is-on-our-side" attitude suggesting that the French simply had a greater social capital in the war:

> The Allies won only by their moral superiority. Their moral values and their power of sacrifice is what enabled them to hold on for these four

years, while they knew that they no longer held material superiority. On the contrary, the enemy had no moral tenacity, and did not hold out even five days after they were sure they no longer held material superiority. [*Les alliées n'ont vaincu que par leur moralité supérieure. C'est leur valeur morale et leur puissance de sacrifice qui leur ont permis de tenir pendant ces quatre années, ou ils savaient qu'ils n'avaient pas encore la supériorité matérielle, et l'adversaire, au contraire, n'ayant aucune tenue morale, ne résista pas cinq jours après le moment ou il eut acquis la certitude qu'il n'avait plus la supériorité matérielle.*] (1927c, p. 66)

Hauriou realizes, after the long use of an appropriate analogy, that a nation is centralized by a patrimony [*fonds*] of ideas and powers, that property and personality, and thus institution, are different ways of being each other. The living being spends resources and reconstitutes itself with the exchange. The late re-appreciation of economic factors by Hauriou was in part only the penetration of a long-familiar analogy.

3. Science and Art

In the coming discrimination of law, sociology, and philosophy as they appear in Hauriou's work, we will see a key distinction between science and art. Hauriou devotes little space to the differentiation independent of its use in discriminating law and sociology, however.

In science, individuals adapt themselves to what is, because of their need for knowledge. In art, individuals adapt what is to themselves, opposing their reaction to what is, because of their need for imaginative activity. Science employs an objective representation of things, reflecting them, expressing them; while the representations of an art express human beings, instead, with embodiments of the human tendency to react to things. Scientific representations are more objective than artistic ones and so approach mechanism more closely. Science does not coincide with mechanism, however, because human beings do not give up their demand for happiness and their actions to obtain it for the sake of their need to undergo the action of an environment. The very belief fondly harbored that the environment acts, fatally or freely, for their happiness, is already a reaction upon it. It is these ideals, systems, plans, and projects, which are artistic and which relate more to human freedom than to mechanisms. If one radicalizes both tendencies, it appears that science is mechanistic and art is libertarian (Hauriou, 1899d, pp. 44–46).

The chief characteristic of an art is to arise from creation, while that of science is to arise from experience, and subsequently from law and procedure, a way of acting directed by law (Hauriou, 1892b, p. 157). Science is less noble than art; for science teaches us how to live, but it is art that we do live. Science tells nothing of the origins, destinies, and substance of things; its laws are crude, approximate, and phenomenal. If any substantial truth—truth regarding not phenomenal manifolds but some single truth (echoing Pascal's "Is there no substantial truth, there being so many true things without the same truth?")—exists, then art brings human beings closest to it; for the efforts of art toward the ideal are living creations, and substantial truth would have to be living. Science cannot, then, take control of art; this is not their natural relation. Rather, the arts use sciences as auxiliaries; fine arts use history, anatomy, mechanics, and law uses sociology as well as political economy (Hauriou, 1893c, p. 8).

The most succinct and accurate statement of the relation of art and science Hauriou gives is, "the means to be used in any art are the essential object of the science relating to that art" (1909a, p. 25) [*"les moyens à employer dans un art quelconque sont l'objet essentiel de la science afférente à cet art"*]. Analyzing this, art appears to have the priority. From it derives a science. The objects of the two are not the same, unless we are to consider art and describe it in terms of its means instead of in terms of its goal. Science does not study the goal of art; it studies the means to the goal.

However, both arts and sciences are divided into types along the same lines. These are the organic, the representative, and those for control of action [*conduite*] (Hauriou, 1899d, pp. 163–165). The first is a matter of empiricism in science, examined inductively, upon the presumption of mechanism; in art, it characterizes the form of primitivism. Representational science and art escape the throes of organization on which we focus in organic modes, to gain distance by using a representative in lieu of the object. In science, this results in deductive sciences, such as mathematics, logic, and metaphysics; in art, it yields the form of classicism.

The final stage, of behavior, looks to the direction of action—not the mechanical action of organisms, not the abstraction of representations, but human or human-like action performed by deliberate choice. Its procedure is both inductive and deductive; it combines both biological needs and rational ideals. In science, it yields thermodynamic disciplines, and in human sciences, it yields moral disciplines.

In art, its form is the artistic finesse, which is a combination of classical ideal with artistic need in a uniquely personal way, as in romanticism. Notice that the human sciences are not relative only to human conduct; neither are the inorganic sciences (under a different mode of discrimination) relative only to the level of an organism. Rather, we see organic sciences applied to human conduct just as performative and representational sciences are applied to matter. Thus, three forms of physics—observational, mathematical, and thermodynamic—parallel three forms of sociology—observational, mathematical or metaphysical, and moral. Neither are sciences and arts differentiated by the amorality of one (or both) as against the moral involvement of the other; both sciences and arts enter into conduct.

So the relation of a science to an object and an art to a use of means does not exclude either one from any of the three levels, organizing, knowing, or acting. Science is active in transforming reality, while art is equally a means for achieving knowledge. Nonetheless, the distinction between them must be rigorous, since confusing the two is Hauriou's accusation against some aberrations which offend his ideas greatly as shown in the section, "Sociological Influences on Hauriou" in Chapter One.

The distinction is not as clear-cut as this demand for rigor and integration of disciplines in Hauriou, though. The answer stems in part from Hauriou using the term "science" in two ways contingent on whether he needs it as a whip to beat opponents or as an appeal to support his conclusions. In the one case, he identifies science with stretches of systems [*archipels des systèmes*], disparate abstractions where one becomes easily lost (1896, p. xii). In this lifeless sense, science concerns *facts* and is uncontrollable, while conduct concerns *acts* and is therefore controllable (ibid., p. 164). As such, science-as-theory is inadequate to account for art-as-life or law-as-practice (Hauriou, 1899d, p. 137).

On the other hand, Hauriou is just as willing, when the need arises, to call by the name "science" something that is a matter of practical ends [*buts pratiques*]. All sciences are founded on practical ends; even scientific determinism is only a category of our thought, which is employed only for practical ends. They are relative to each other (1902b, p. 358). Even all of the sciences of observation explain the synthetic organizations they study in terms of elementary finalities. This remains true since the rules of such elementary science, which at first appear to exclude purposes, really only ignore them: these rules admit only direct evidence, not preconceived evidence; they keep separate in analysis what is distinct in the given; and they abstain from questions about origins and ends, which are too abstract (Hauriou, 1896, pp. 18, 25). The ends excluded are the ends of processes independent of use, simply as mechanical processes; the human purpose of the study about these processes is an issue to be treated in what follows in this chapter.

We have no choice but to do science in the light of purposes. For science can be built neither upon the excellence of reason nor upon the reliability of nature. Immanuel Kant shows the limits of one; Charles Darwin the malice of the other (Hauriou, 1894c, p. 297). We ought to be well warned about this character of science; for science is not harmless without any moral impact. Hauriou sees science as a conscience and a consciousness in society, as is the individual human mind for each person.

As a conscience, science poses problems of conduct faced by society, and can give wrong answers; as a consciousness, it knows the reality of things, and cannot know everything about reality. If this, completed science, is dangerous because practical, then scientific research is much more dangerous. Therefore, Hauriou admonishes, "construct your science in the laboratory, work it out in seminars or independent courses, discuss it in the periodicals; but be careful of its promulgation in official courses" (1894d, pp. 392–393).

4. Theory and Practice

The issue of science and art is evidently tied to that of theory and practice, however difficult it is to say precisely what that relation is. The starting point is the same as in the previous question, namely, the identity of life and practice. It then is necessary to see that life needs a pragmatism or a positivism. Finally, Hauriou finds theory to have a more intimate bond to practice than when first broached.

Life makes practice all-important; the practice of liberty, renunciation, and belief energizes society to survive (Hauriou, 1899d, p. 137). To understand anything at all, it must be placed into its lived milieu; so we must understand it in terms of practice (Hauriou, 1879a, p. 2). But, because of the inherent impossibility that intellectual methods reach living reality, and because of the divisiveness that life forces upon action, the best that we can do in defining and understanding is to make an approximation (Hauriou, 1905, p. 12n1). For a one-sided stand is always in some way unfaithful to reality; but life always forces us to take sides, to judge which side the demands of life lie upon. So the application of some general method is a matter of prudence and of the personal professional sense of the specialist (Hauriou, *L'introduction à l'étude du droit administratif français*, n.d., p. xx).

The action which life demands is always a cause of division, for it forces us to take initiatives; it is inevitable that there always remain within knowledge adequate to life what Hauriou calls "ordinary deformations in an optic adapted to the needs for action" (1912d, pp. 39, 54) [*"les déformations habituelles de l'optique adaptée aux besoins de l'action"*].

Life refuses to allow the persistence and canonization of any divisions. Thus, life cannot be closed up into the tight viewpoints of categories. This is no reason to suppress the category, but only to examine it closely and to expect all its exceptions (Hauriou, 1927a, p. 763). This explains the strong statement refusing specialization.

> The division of work is dangerous for the individual, and imposes endless effort: effort not to let oneself be absorbed by the specialty, effort to resist invitations to laziness toward the mediocrity that becomes the professional type, effort to work outside one's function so as to keep up one's likeness to other humans, to remain a person, and not to become a machine. It takes no moral effort to become specialized, that is something easy and agreeable; that makes us smile. The moral effort lies in struggling against the dangerous consequences of specialization. Such an effort, how few make it! We fantasize only about highly productive specialists who can inspire the division of labor; and we pay no heed that their superiority is almost always due to their knowing enough to maintain a very broad culture. No one notices the defective set of incomplete results that their culture produces. (Hauriou, 1894c, p. 320)

[*La division du travail est périlleuse pour l'individu, elle lui impose un effort constant: ne pas se laisser absorber par sa spécialité, résister aux invites de la paresse, à la médiocrité commode du type professionnel, travailler en dehors de sa fonction pour rester semblable aux autres hommes, pour demeurer homme, pour ne pas devenir une machine. L'effort moral n'est pas de se spécialiser, c'est chose facile, agréable, souriante; l'effort moral est de lutter contre les conséquences dangereuses de la spécialisation. Cet effort, combien peu le font! On ne songe qu'aux spécialistes prodigieux que peut susciter la division du travail; et encore on ne fait pas attention que leur supériorité est due presque toujours à ce qu'ils ont su garder une culture très général, on ne fait pas attention à la foule pénible des incomplets qu'elle produit.*]

From this grounding in life comes the refusal to accommodate vast conceptual schemes. Life does not force them upon us; we force them upon ourselves. As Hauriou says catchingly, "We must never be the slave of formulas, but especially when we have made them up ourselves!" (1913b, p. 286) ["*Toutefois, il ne faut pas être esclave des formules, surtout quand on les a posées soi-mêmes!*"]. The only interesting feature of a classification is its psychological significance, what motivations lay behind it (Hauriou, 1887b, p. 18n1). This is not the kind of basis that should cement a category or theory indefinitely. We can use such solidified categories only as bins in which to set aside matters that have no practical use and so are not worth studying (Hauriou, 1879a, pp. 11, 68).

This is not just a preference for one over the other, practice over theory, with a basic harmony existing between the two. Rather, Hauriou says clearly that an unavoidable difference between theory and practice [*différence inevitable entre la théorie et la pratique*] exists (1933a, p. 40). The difference is that the practitioner knows reality is complex, while the theoretician wants reality to be reduced to simplicity, to a single principle. Hauriou knows his attack is that of the practitioner, displeasing theoreticians who desire the unity of abstract principle by his practical synthesis (1909a, pp. 74–75). Simplicity is itself a warning; as Hauriou says of one sample synthesis, "as all systematic constructions, this one is probably too simple to be completely true" (1899d, p. vii). A correlate of this drive for simplicity of logic is to make theory for a closed circle of initiates; for such constructions contain a subtlety, which excludes the public. Hauriou offers as the alternative to this clique "simple ideas"; but he means readily available ideas, rather than logically concentrated ones. Their rightness [*justesse*] (close in meaning to his word *"équilibre"*) breaks open the closed circle of initiates (1912d, p. 153).

This theoretical character is the deficiency of the Enlightenment democracy. Simple and logical, it cannot have the patience to endure through the chaotic disorder of political life (Hauriou, 1908a, p. 585). The French Republics, in particular, although Hauriou finds "parliamentary republic" a contradiction in terms, are prey to this theoretical simplicity of logic. Only when the French build something provisory, do they make anything durable; only when pressed by circumstances do they escape excessive logic and contrived posturing: "Logic is our national defect" [*"La logique est notre défaut national"*] (Hauriou, 1923d, p. 373).

In following the canon of practicality, the way appears to be the way of fact. This is the way to avoid vast social systems and preconceived ideas (Hauriou, 1906b, p. 26). Hauriou excludes the dialectical method as a means of proving his beliefs; the only method he will use is one that is as positivist as possible [*aussi positiviste que possible*], meaning to uncover and indicate the fruits that some beliefs have produced in civilization (1910, p. 42). He finds late in his career that this continuity has penetrated all his work: "the continual employment of the same method of observation applied in the same direction." This "positive method—sincere and practical" French style [*à la français*] positivism—can put us outside the influence of speculative doctrines, from whatever source (1916c, p. vi).

Thus, Hauriou rebuffs the Conseil d'État for continuing to use the theoretical terminology when it has rejected the logical consequences, the facts that derive from that theory (1927b, p. 26). Often, what "facts" means is the indisputable presence of clear texts in legislation; adherence to these facts is what makes a course of action "practical" (Hauriou, 1879b, p. 59; 1923d, p. 707). The obvious procedures of law also figure as facts, facts that often surprise logic, for example, the act that is part administrative and part not (Hauriou, 1891a, p. 230).

Above all, facts are going to mean the historical events that cannot be overlooked; these are the truly practical facts of Hauriou's type of positivism. Thus, conscientious administrators can only dream to reform administration by transforming bad practices to good ones, unless they have the help of a powerful and well-adapted institution (Hauriou, 1913a, p. iii). Such historical resistances [*résistances historiques*] are what we must observe, for it is those that can posit principles, which are just the inverse of a logical solution (Hauriou, 1902c, p. 249).

It appears that factual positivism coincides with social pragmatism. But such a facile coincidence is not all. For Hauriou, something fictive can have its factual effects dispensed with in an equally fictive manner if we find them not useful. The usefulness and the fictiveness in this association surely depend upon something more than simply the presence of facts (Hauriou, 1879b, p. 90). For example, the legislative fact that parishioners can be questioned on the political advice given to them in the church confessional, may perhaps best be ignored if the effects are inconvenient: "it is with certain abuses as with certain incidents on the frontier—the best solution is not to see them" (Hauriou, 1893b, p. 271).

The solution to this dissonance between facts and practice, then, is not that we should identify pragmatism with positivism, in any simple sense.

Theories are elaborated only long after the practical achievement of systems, but historical continuity does not fail for Hauriou (1912d, p. 3) merely because of its extended length. Theory follows fact afar off, but follow it does. A newly fashionable idea may be impractical, but what Hauriou does find practical is another idea, an older one (1900f, p. 247). If useless concepts are prevalent, which we must destroy, other concepts are available that are necessary, which we must conserve, because they are the sole support possible for the essential social realities (Hauriou, 1923c, p. 341).

The most practical hypothesis is what should play the preponderant role in determining rights (Hauriou, 1904, p. 606). The most useful theory is to be employed. The relation of theory and fact is far from being exclusive of theory; fact is invisible without theory. But to use an ill-adapted theory, one which is practically useless, is to condemn us to overlooking critical facts, which with a better adapted theory, we would see. For the theories themselves rest on real facts and are only the focused light [*foyers de lumière*] that we project upon things, facts, to make them appear for our best purposes (Hauriou, 1912d, pp. 11, 12n1).

What Hauriou takes as a scientific classic is no simple repetition of fact. It is eminently theoretical, in such a way that from it, the facts themselves gain their meaning. Scientific classics are "intuitive hypotheses, verified by critical experience and admitted by common sense" (1927d, p. 65) [*"Ce ne sont que des hypothèses intuitives, vérifiées par des expériences critiques et admises par le sens commun"*]. Even less fact-dependent, surprisingly, are classics of another sort:

> statistical truths which rest on averages and from which some rebellious facts always escape. But their precision *is* sufficient to let us act back upon nature; and it is this reaction, this form of creation of the world that people continue as a demiurge, which becomes the really classical work of science. (Ibid.) [*Ce sont des vérités statistiques qui s'appuient sur des moyennes et auxquelles échappent toujours quelques faits rebelles. Mais leur précision* est *suffisante pour nous permettre de réagir sur la nature et c'est cette réaction, cette sorte de création du monde que l'homme continue comme un démiurge, qui devient, en réalité, l'œuvre classique de la science.*]

Much of the falling out between theory and practice seems to be the discontinuity that so often appears in them. Even early Hauriou found the distance between the generality of the theses of a particular lawyer and the particularity of his conclusions to be ridiculous (1893d, p. 14). Thus, the excesses of logic are at fault: to draw from a fact, that in itself is true but the scope of which is limited, conclusions that ignore the limits. To introduce either a true fact or a true theory is insufficient; we also must be concerned with limiting it to its proper domain (Hauriou, 1900b, p. 373; 1912b, pp. 4–5; 1917a, p. 616).

Hauriou admitted to a strong attraction toward tight logic and coherent theory, such as Léon Duguit's, which he constantly had to resist (Hauriou, 1902b, p. 349). Occasionally, Hauriou could fall into systematization without wanting to (1899d, p. ii), or could work solely with principles (1912d, p. 136). His normal relationship of fact and theory can be generalized from the "rigorous method" where it appears in four steps: disengage the problem from every preconceived idea of a general system; examine it as a matter of fact, an independent and observable matter; distinguish and categorize all the relevant facts from each other; distinguish and categorize all the syntheses from each other (ibid., p. 4). Thus, using hypotheses is always permissible but we must use those that best accord with the facts (Hauriou, 1921, p. 9).

To explain a singular fact by another singular fact is to explain nothing at all (Hauriou, 1882b, p. 5). We cannot coordinate facts without directive ideas, and these ideas cannot help but become in their turn a kind of theory once their correctness has been verified by observation (Hauriou, 1916c, p. vi). Individual examples, passionate affirmations, and accurate instincts are worth nothing in refuting doctrines. "To one doctrine it is necessary to oppose another. . . . If the doctrines . . . are heresies, in the name of what orthodoxy are we to condemn them?" It is remarkable to see such a neutral methodological statement in an article that is, on other counts, perhaps the most passionately vituperative one Hauriou ever wrote (1933a, p. 20).

Hauriou speaks of the need for a system that is simultaneously practical and legally coherent (1907b, p. 764). This reflected and lived legal policy [*politique jurisprudentielle réfléchie et suivie*] must be penetrated (1922b, p. 658). He speaks of it in terms of meeting the logic of things [*la logique des choses*] (1923d, pp. 233, 234n2, 414, 432; 1929a, passim), a characteristic of facts, events, and institutions, which is to be duplicated and furthered in formal logic. It is not an assurance that "things" are as they should be; it is not a cynical despair of them matching ideals, no retreat to realpolitik. It is the recognition that some structures demand and initiate particular directions, which further initiative must carry out. For example:

> We do not pretend that these interferences by the elective power are completely regular; but they will become regular because the logic of a democracy demands it. It is not necessary to deny them, it is necessary to organize them. (Hauriou, 1912d, p. 57) [*Nous ne prétendons pas que ces ingérences du pouvoir électif soient toutes régulières; mais elles se régulariseront parce que la logique démocratique le demande. Il ne faut pas nier, il faut organizer.*]

The materials furnished under the pressure of practice must be organized into a theory (Hauriou, 1904, p. 615). Also, the corresponding forces must be organized into a living institution, a fact (Hauriou, 1912d, p. 2).

The way of organizing is what is at stake, both for theory justified in practice and practice justified by theory. No contradiction follows if we observe that a fact has a one meaning or value only when tied to a particular postulated situation, a postulate which itself is not absolute. For no institution has an absolute value. The truth of practice lies in the practical balance it achieves (Hauriou, 1923d, pp. 283–284). Practical arrangements do not always end up with the elements in the same respective positions; thus, it is prudent not to take a correction of boundaries between forces [*une rectification de frontières entre les forces*] for a definitive direction of evolution (Hauriou, 1911a, p. 20; 1912b, p. 5). The organization must, then, be one of tolerance: not only of opposed external parties, but also and especially of the divergent internal parts (Hauriou, 1895a, pp. 546–547). As theoretical elements, the parts exclude each other. Their combination can succeed only if it is practical, if it is fitted to bring about the desired evolution of each individual system (Hauriou, 1907a, p. 3).

5. Practical Synthesis of Factual Elements into Theory

The synthesis of these factual elements into a theory cannot be monistic or deductive; but neither is it simply a heap of elements, a "primitive disorder." For the elements are already methodically catalogued (ibid). It is no opposition of forces at random, not a sterile opposition, as when forces are simply coupled, two by two. This is a theory of the practical life; it is for the sake of the living movement of a system. The movement is the "given," not the theory; and the synthesis that fosters movement is the adequate one. "But the social system is in movement, and this movement constitutes a postulate" (Hauriou, 1909a, p. 63) ["*Mais le système sociale est en movement et ce movement constitue un postulat*"].

By means of the concept of *équilibre*, the practical synthesis can enter the logical order. "This idea lets us push the data of practical combinations right into the domain of logic; combination by *équilibre* becomes associated with order" (ibid., p. x) ["*Cette idée permet de pousser jusqu'à la domaine de la logique la donnée des combinaisons pratiques, la combinaison équilibrée devient de l'ordre*"]. The order is founded on equilibrium. It is a combination that becomes logical; it does not start as something logical. Equilibrium is the catalyst making the combination no longer eclectic, particular or illogical; for equilibrium creates order, and order is the sure sign that something has become logical.

Early attempts to characterize the theory acceptable to Hauriou went little further than the concept of an ensemble, for example, of administrative law: "a body of organized doctrine and an ensemble of administrative theories, connected between each other and gravitating around a common center" (1893d, p. 3) ["*un ensemble de theories administratives liées entre elles et gravitant autour d'un centre commun*"].

Hauriou will continue to detail this initial concept for the remainder of his career; but the most substantial attack on its difficulties comes in the first chapter of *La Science sociale traditionnelle* of 1896, where he deals with the practical theory under the name of transaction [*la transaction*], right after the preliminary chapter on methodology and just preceding the chapter in which he first introduces the concept of institution. He has posited universal contradiction [*l'universelle contradiction*], and society as the place of their resolution, but postulates the impossibility of their definitive resolution. He then offers three forms of provisory resolution—elimination, synthesis, transaction—but rejects the first two, retaining only transaction. He details this form of practical theory here and later.

"Contradiction is everywhere, in beings, in things, in facts" (Hauriou, 1896, p. 84) [*"La contradiction est partout, dans les êtres, dans les choses, dans les faits"*]. Human beings carry contradiction within themselves: consciousness or unconsciousness, body-soul, desire-belief-will, being or becoming in will, affirmation or negation in belief, weakness or strength in desire, religious-metaphysical-positive ways of knowing. In the social milieu, man stands contradictory to woman, the individual to society, collectivist socialism to corporate socialism, and feudal individualism to democratic individualism.

"Social life is made up of the solutions found to contradictions" (ibid., p. 107) [*"La vie sociale est faite de solutions trouvées aux contradictions"*]. Social matter absorbs the individual's problems, the interplay of need and reform work toward the resolution of social contradictions; we find the completed works of resolution embodied in institutions. But none suffice to end contradiction, for each completion forces its own contradictory into existence. In addition, life is made of struggle and competition [*de la lutte et de la concurrence*]. Contradiction is indispensible to any life that continues to be dynamic. Thus, the process of resolving contradiction is more interesting than the resolution itself.

One way of resolving contradiction is by eliminating one contradictory element. This is the way of natural history, but also operates occasionally among human beings, societies, and ideas. However, this is not always possible or desirable (ibid., p. 112). Instead, the contradictory elements often form an accord by synthesis: "a more comprehensive idea uses for its ends two partial and contradictory ideas, or a more general interest uses for its ends the particular contradictory interests" (ibid.) [*"une idée plus comprehensive utilize à ses fins deux idées partielles contradictoires, ou qu'un intérêt plus général utilize à ses fins des intérêts particuliers contradictoires"*]. For example, a foreign war has often united opposed internal interests.

Two forms of the synthesis are available. The evolutionary form is that in which the contradictory elements pre-exist the forthcoming synthesis, as thesis and antithesis. A political illustration would be a confederation. Another type, the ideal synthesis, is one in which the synthesis is first produced and the contradiction of its composing elements is not at first seen. The contradictions develop after the synthesis has been posited. Religious and metaphysical systems are of this type; posited all at once, they succumb to heresies, schisms, and schools adhering to one side or another of the contradictions that appear out of the whole. Socially, decentralization exemplifies this (ibid., p. 114).

The subhuman elements, which appear in elimination of contradictions and the human intellectual types of synthesis, evolutionary and ideal, leave room for another type of resolution. Human beings apply will to their activities. Free or not, it is as irreducible an influence as the other two, nature and mind. Its effect is to draw forth the individual being that underlies the sweep of mechanism and of logic, to attach fact to the being that lies at its root.

This is the meaning of transaction. It is a matter of tolerance, reciprocal concession, compromise, a dividing up between pretensions. "To transact is to cut the difference in two, to make one part equal to the pretensions of both parts, thus to accord them equality of power" (ibid., pp. 116–119, 128) [*"Transiger c'est couper le différend en deux, faire une part égale aux pretentions des deux parties, par conséquent accorder à celles-ci égalité de pouvoir"*]. Transaction is found everywhere: any generality, whether of logic or fate, finds a limit in facts; recognizing this limitation elicits transaction. Even regimes that pretend to be absolute are transactional, for they demand what Hauriou will call the "sovereignty of submission" from their citizens (ibid., pp. 116–117, 126–128).

The relation of this form of theory and practice with the other two is to be a relation of combining. Transaction occurs at the moment when the evolutionary synthesis rising toward synthesis and the ideal synthesis falling into contradiction cross each other (ibid., pp. 126–127).

The situation that renders transaction possible is the presence of a mediator, a third who intervenes to settle a contradiction for the two contradictories. "*The mediator is he who has no self-interest*" (Hauriou, 1896, p. 119) [*"Or, le médiateur est celui qui n'a pas d'amour-propre"*]. The mediator is not an agent in the contradiction, only a spectator who can act without taking sides to discover the "just" transaction. Because of the structure of being, the mediator's role is as universal as that of transaction itself. Syllogistic middles and chemical bases or catalysts, Christ-Son in the Trinity, and Christ-Redeemer in the position between God and creation: these exemplify the universality of mediation (ibid., pp. 119–122). Even the divine range of this doctrine is as much a matter of cosmogony as of religion [*autant cosmogonique que religieuse*], for it follows from "one of the most attractive theories of the world" [*"une des explications du monde les plus séduisantes"*]:

> Suppose that under phenomena there are everywhere beings hidden, of the type of monads. Under social facts we see beings, which are human beings; under biological facts we again find them, but now cells; and under physical facts we suppose them, this time atoms. The continuous series of phenomena is explained by the activity of these monads, but

> there is a difficulty: although the series of phenomena is continuous, or seems to be to us, the series of beings is vigorously discontinuous, for a being is an individuality separated from others. How do beings form a chain? This could not happen without an accord of their activity, but this accord presumes transaction and without doubt mediation; so we end up with universal transaction and universal mediation. (Ibid., pp. 120–121) [*Supposons que partout sous les phénomènes se cachent des êtres, des sortes de monades. Sous les faits sociaux nous voyons ces êtres, ce sont les hommes; sous les faits biologiques nous les voyons aussi, ce sont les cellules; sous les faits physiques nous les supposons, ce sont les atomes. La série continue des phénomènes s'explique par l'activité de ces monades, mais il y a une difficulté: tandis que la série des phénomènes est continue, ou nous parait telle, la série des êtres est forcement discontinue, car l' être est une individualité séparée des autres. Comment les êtres font-ils la chaine? Ce ne peut-être que par un accord de leur activité, mais cet accord suppose transaction et sans doute médiation, nous aboutissons ainsi à l'universelle transaction et a l'universelle médiation.*]

The insistence on reducing a composite to its parts is accepted method; but in social science this will be all the more important.

> But, we have already said that it is an axiom of present-day method, established in all the sciences of observation, that we must consider groupings that have been synthesized as the product of the activity by their component parts, in such a way that these elements are what are the location of action and the synthetic grouping is only a reaction. It is the part that makes the whole, not the whole that makes the part. (Ibid., p. 29) [*Or, nous l'avons déjà dit, c'est un axiome de méthode aujourd'hui établi dans toutes les sciences d'observation, qu'il faut considerer les ensembles synthétiques comme le produit de l'activité des éléments composants, de sorte que ces éléments ont une action et que l'ensemble synthétique n'a qu'une réaction. C'est la partie que fait le tout, non pas le tout qui fait la partie.*]

In social science, this will free the parts, which in society are human beings, to become self-determining.

This rich beginning is just that: only a beginning. Hauriou's treatment is no fuller than the above synopsis; he mentions it thereafter only sparingly in the remainder of this book and hardly ever mentions it thereafter. Transaction as the form for practical theory cedes later to other descriptions and titles.

A description for practical theory, which Hauriou will use as the usual accepted name, appears with a title of practical synthesis [*synthèse pratique*] in the watershed edition of *Précis du droit administratif* in 1907. He describes *équilibre* under this title:

> In other words, the equilibrium of the institution is a practical synthesis based on power. One of the forces present dominates the others, its power is moderated by the resistance of these others, but it determines the structure and direction of the whole. (p. 14) [*En d'autres termes, l'équilibre de l'institution est une synthèse pratique à base de pouvoir. Il y a une des forces en présence qui domine les autres, son pouvoir est modéré par la résistance de celles-ci, cependant il détermine la structure et la direction de l'ensemble.*]

(The term *"synthèse"* in the above quotation does not carry the technical meaning it had in Hauriou's 1896 work, *La science sociale traditionnelle.*) The acceptance of domination is conditioned proportionately to the necessity that it be given, in terms of a conscious and reflective judgment of how much acceptance is necessary to keep the institution going.

Hauriou's study of national sovereignty (1912d) details the model further but under the name of the method of composition of forces [*composition des forces*]. The "composition" becomes necessary when the practical and theoretical demands of a situation differ: when logically either of two theories encompasses the whole of a situation equally as well as the other, but the practical advantages to be attained demand that the two be combined:

> and for me the combination consists in making first one then the other move into the first place, depending on the different areas of law and depending on the greater or lesser usefulness which one or the other presents in these different areas. (Ibid., pp. 11, 12n1) [*et, pour moi, la combinaison consiste à faire passer au premier plan tantôt l'une tantôt l'autre suivant les provinces du droit et suivant l'utilité plus ou moins grande que présente l'une ou l'autre théorie dans ces diverses provinces.*]

We can extract some essential points of the method from the case in which Hauriou uses it here, namely, the general and national will: the representation (of the general will) by diverse powers (of government); the spontaneous convergence of these representations; and the achievement of this in view of reconstituting the composite unity of the matter under study, namely, the commanding national will (ibid., p. 153). The unity of action achieved by composition of forces is not the result of some initial stimulation or initial impulse, but is a natural phenomenon of tending together and convergence (ibid., p. 89).

Since this unity of composition of forces is an active unity, the intervention of all the forces composing the unity is required in every manifestation of that unity. The way in which this participation occurs can be either that all forces intervene in a way that is simultaneously present, formal, and positive, or in a way that they do not all intervene in a present and positive way in the same activity, but those that do not will act in cooperation [*de concert*] with those that do, by virtue of a previously established solidarity. Each is a possible mode, but the latter is more efficient. For example, executive power is more efficient than referendum for making decisions, when put in political terms (ibid., pp. 124–125). Each element in a composition of forces participates in it differently; both as to the extent and the manner of its participation. That difference depends on the condition in which one practices a composition of forces, for those conditions, in turn, determine what the practical difficulties are that arise (ibid., p. 86).

The analogy of *agmen* we considered above is suitable material for the development of this practical theory model through 1909 also. In addition to this analogy, the most interesting later development of the methodology for developing an acceptable theory occurs between the two editions of the *Droit public*. In the first edition, Hauriou recalls the methodological developments we have just described. He calls the new method for the "new discipline"—public law—a method of "practical combination," meaning a "practical synthesis of a certain number of elements, each of which is incontestably one of the constitutive elements" of the whole. Its advantage is that it possesses great objectivity, which means that it avoids logical theory, the subjective and personal constructs unusable to anyone but their author (Hauriou, 1910, p. ix).

Hauriou's second edition repeats the above definition of practical combination, not to accept it, but to claim it less a logical theory (what he wanted to avoid!) than a coordination of the materials for a theory (1916c, p. v). This he hopes to remedy in the second edition. But when we come (in the second edition) upon his description of a practical synthesis [*synthèse pratique*], it appears not too divergent from the content Hauriou employed before this point. It is not a logical unity, but a practical one, a unity of results. It is not reduced to one single form, but is a composite unity of elements. Again, in terms of national sovereignty, Hauriou details several aspects in the functioning of *synthèse pratique*:

(1) All the elements must be joined into the unity, seen to be part of it, since they do make it up.
(2) The elements in the synthesis are in a hierarchy, one or more subject to another or others; thus only those which dominate are unlimited (for example, in the nation this is the constitution or the power of existence) while the subject powers are limited (for example, the powers of government, the power of action).
(3) The synthesis comes about in the acts it executes, namely, acts of management by the dominant power and the acts of trust or guaranteed submission by the other elements.
(4) The synthesis is rendered possible by an interpenetration of the action by the elements; each reacts upon the other to define it and thereby limit it.

(5) The unity is facilitated and symbolized by the existence of an essential organ that participates in each of the elements' character; as a representative organ of the unity solely, its sole role is representative, to regulate but not to govern [*régner sans gouverner*]. (Ibid., pp. 662–676)

6. Classical Method

The method of developing a practical synthesis as the form of theory develops imperceptibly into what Hauriou calls the classical method. This is not an innovation only of his later career; it had been present from the period of his social science. But in his later writings, it took on the stature of a total method, supplanting practical synthesis. It affects the whole scope of human activity, offering proofs in morals and religion as well as in social and physical science. It is the interpenetration of physical and intelligible worlds, which led to the formulation of practical synthesis and now leads on to classical method.

Hauriou's dissatisfaction with the results of intellectualism, which I remarked upon in my introduction and shall reappear in my chapter on philosophical methodology, led Hauriou to stress, as he had done earlier, the faculty of intuition. This faculty is not its own guarantee, however; it needs to be confirmed if we are to accept that an idea sensed by intuition brings a new truth. The sciences are said to confirm intuition by experiment; but social, moral, and religious intuitions present difficulties because we cannot confirm them by experiments designed in the tradition of scientific method: We cannot specify their origin since their founders and reformers are in advance of their time; they are discontinuous in the sense that the intuitions as responses are vastly out of proportion to the stimulations.

Intuitions retain a content of mystery or they would cease to be of the character they are. Generally, they come from an intelligible world that penetrates the physical world. The only source for verifying intuition of this kind is historical experience, negative and positive; this plays a role in these matters similar to that of scientific experiments studying the physical world (Hauriou, 1929c, p. 63). Nothing shows the truth of a doctrine better than history; it has the value of a lesson in reality [*une leçon des choses*] (Hauriou, 1912d, p. 107n1).

When set in this way, scientific truth ceases to be so alien, because it also benefits from this method of historical verification. Scientific evidence is sister to artistic or humanistic evidence since the evidence for both is "the classical" (Hauriou, 1927g, p. ix). Scientific classics depend upon the moral classics, the real classics of our civilization. Discovery of truth is the result of a virtue just as much as it is the result of a method. Scientific method demands sincerity in observation and humility in accepting the correction that facts give to preconceived hypotheses. Aristotle postulated and used the scientific method but it bore fruit only over the course of history. Before that came to pass, the moral formation introduced by Christianity had to intervene (Hauriou, 1927e, p. 65).

This historical method is Hauriou's classical method, "proof by classics." It is not a variety of pragmatism but a method the evidence gathering of which is a slow procedure. The evidence unrolls over the course of centuries witnessed by an entire public as opposed to being examined only by specially trained observers, members of the "scientific community." The classical method begins with creation of some work—artistic, literary, or scientific—in which the intuition of a genius uncovers some of nature's secrets. It continues in the work of criticism, which a work in any of these types undergoes. This methodology is not done publicly for the most part. It culminates after a long time and much criticism in the admiration by posterity. Such a proof, which uses every form of reason, each in its appropriate place, is the most fit to produce in us that evidence, which marks the true: intuition for invention and creation; discursive reason for the criticism; and common sense or prudence for the definitive judgment.

This evidence and the synthesis of activities it implies is not peculiar to any exclusive group of individuals, national or professional. It is universally human because in it, humanity recognizes the characteristic elements of the human type. All the elements of the human type are in this methodology, although balanced and weighted differently in different studies perhaps. It expresses the simple and common leanings that dominate all human beings and that conform to human nature.

All we need for this methodology to overcome the arguments of any skeptic is that the human beings must have reached a sufficient stage of civilization and be of good will. By sufficient civilization is meant that they have passed from a nomadic to a territorially stable mode of living, which is the present situation in the West (ibid., pp. 64–65; Hauriou, 1929c, p. 56).

This stability is the condition and goal and, as will appear shortly, its ending of classical doctrine. For example, public law refuses to continue following and justifying arbitrary decision that has always had a place in public law. It seeks stability by adopting the categories of subjective law, especially those of the legal person and of the legal thing. They are fundamental legal categories and are the essential conditions for stability. What Hauriou (1914b, p. 334) says of public law here well describes the attitude of practical theory as it tends toward classical doctrine and becomes acceptable: it needs to come to rest [*il demande à s'asseoir*].

7. Dualist Method

Hauriou affords classical method, synthesizing theory and practice successfully, ample scope as being "clear, concise, logical, certain, optimistic, definitive, intelligible for all" (1916c, p. 242) [*"de la clarté, de la netteté, de la logique, quelque chose d'assuré, d'optimiste, de définitif, en même temps que d'intelligible pour tous"*]. But one gets weary of so much perfection; concentration on a unique object prepares our sensibilities to become attuned to new melodies and harmonies. Classical thought, while appreciating the value of unity, must bow before the limits of human thought. What this means in practice is that the dualism of matter and form, irreducible to each other after four thousand years of philosophy, forces anyone dealing with reality to acknowledge it (1929c, pp. x–xi). This preface to the second edition of *Droit constitutionnel* is dated 8 September 1928.

Although completing classical method temporally as well as logically, Hauriou explicates the dualist method much earlier. Before the turn of the century, Hauriou (1893e, p. 3) had been calling lawyers "pragmatic dualists" because they stood in law while trying not to prejudice the premises of social science. Later (1912d, p. 8) he finds only one satisfying solution to the problems with which he is dealing, and that is to admit two parallel syntheses, each presumably of the character worked out above.

These two syntheses react one upon the other. They do this in their entirety, by a sort of pre-established harmony. Finally, they are two aspects of the same reality, surely; but they are two aspects that cannot be confused one with the other.

The most thorough treatment of dualist method, however, appears in four pages of Hauriou's *L'introduction à l'étude du droit administratif français* (Introduction to the Study of French Administrative Law), an unedited short brochure, which can be approximately dated anytime after 1903 by examining it in terms of the dates noted in its references (pp. xx–xxiii). In a section entitled, "Some Observations on Dualism" [*"Quelques observations sur le dualisme"*], Hauriou describes dualism as the practical synthesis of two elements inspired by the necessities of life and by the procedure of combining a principle and its exception. In prior works (he later identifies these as the *Science sociale* and the *Leçons*), he explains that he has used the method but not explained it, but does so now in three maxims:

(1) Admit that the unity of any fact is the result of a purely practical synthesis worked out by life, and that on analysis every fact breaks down into complex elements. This is as true of individuals or physical facts as of social facts. As an example, we consider the simple result that a tree is struck by lightning: this is a single fact only insofar as it endangers our safety or destroys our property; but scientifically it is a manifold of elements studied by a spectrum of sciences, none of which can reduce their respective materials to less than two elements (force-matter, heat-movement). The unscientific monism of attitude is to conclude from the practical simplicity of a fact to the simplicity of its efficient cause.

(2) Place yourself at the dynamic point of view, to pick out the elements composing a fact, admit that the more important composing elements are forces that act one on another.

Of these two, Hauriou attaches the most importance to the second maxim. It is necessary because, once we open our eyes to the evidence and risk being swallowed by the vast scope of practical synthesis, we need rules for discernment, ways to choose and select. Toward this purpose, the point of view of confronting and reacting forces becomes evident for several reasons: we can easily observe opposing forces since the fact of conflict reveals them, usually much more clearly than their occasional cooperation; and when these forces are in conflict, they are independent of each other and are significant for the institution, the institutional balance they strive to achieve. The principle opposed social forces in every area are power and needs; these take their respective roots in the basic individual or psychological forces of belief and desire.

(3) Still from the dynamic point of view, admit that every system of forces in movement seeks its state of equilibrium, and that the most stable equilibria are those based on the predominance of the most subjective forces. This helps to discern which among the composing forces is dominant over the others, and thus which imposes on the social institution its practical unity. This in turn shows the direction of the evolution of the system. The development of this idea is lengthy: in the *Leçons*, Hauriou showed that social equilibria based on idea, subjectivity, and representation are more stable than those based on combinations of purely objective forces. In *La Science sociale traditionelle*, the analysis of institution showed that rudimentary balances based on the predominance of objective forces evolve toward more subtle and more solid equilibrium based on the predominance of subjective forces.

Other than Hauriou's admitted forebears in dualism (Tarde, Auguste Comte, Descartes), its best recommendation is common sense. Long experience has taught that, in social matters, no theory can be deduced to its logical extremity without concern for its dualist limitations. No rule can be posed without admitting exceptions. Practitioners who actively respected this rule because of the requirements of their situations were creating a dualism without knowing it. They, as Hauriou in his conscious dualism of theory and practice, had to respect the underlying complexity of facts [*complexité souterraine des faits*].

Four

LEGAL METHODOLOGY

1. Introduction

This chapter considers the argument Maurice Hauriou makes for law as a science and as an art. The chapter also studies the several sources from which the discipline of law develops. It also looks to the existent law and the two directions this takes, a dualism that has some effect upon the discipline of law.

2. The Discipline of Law

A. Law as Science

Hauriou calls law—organized and codified—and the work of developing a doctrine from it, which academic lawyers perform, theoretical law—or better, law as a science [*le droit théorique—mieux scientifique*] (1967, p. 17). This scientific frame of mind [*esprit scientifique*] is not reducible to a positivist frame of mind [*esprit positif*]; the first is a free movement of ideas while the second is sheer textual commentary (1893d, p. 21). The task of doctrine is to make a choice from the conclusions of jurisprudence and to organize conclusions rationally (1897b, pp. iii–iv).

Doctrine is meant to look for the essential reason for subordinating secondary justifications of jurisprudence. Simply to juxtapose the different reasons given in jurisprudence without hierarchizing them is not acceptable (Hauriou, 1922a, p. 150). The theory of law must be systematic and reasoned (Hauriou, 1907a, p. vii).

Case law is never a final appeal for Hauriou. A legal theory is necessary for jurisprudence. It is not sufficient to say of an issue that it has its special rules, which change with the needs that appear for service to the public. The special rules, rather, derive from a principle, and even the variations in application follow some barometer. The theory is to be disengaged from the jurisprudence. So firm is this disengagement that the cases from which the theory is drawn can in turn be criticized by reference to that same theory. The Lepreux case is remarkable for the model it gives of how Hauriou develops a complete theory from the recognized need for one (1899e, p. 517).

Casuistry, or the resolution of cases simply by reference to other cases, is undemanding and subjective; its contours are indeterminate. The correct legal procedure is to ignore the bulk of material objects, the lines of jurisdiction, and the hierarchies and structures, to concentrate upon the legal objects: the cases wherein these material objects have been at issue. These are the theories jurists must study. This is their work. "The essential is that minute analyses be made and that a synthesis result from them: this alone is the work of the jurist, the work of theory construction, and this is what it is necessary to learn" (Hauriou, 1901a, pp. 556–557) [*"L'essentiel est qu'il soit fait des analyses minutieuses et qu'une synthèse en résulte: cela seul est travail de jurisconsulte, travail de construction d'une théorie, et cela seul est ce qu'il faut apprendre"*].

A purely dynamic construct such as Léon Duguit's is unsatisfactory. That is a repetition of the movements of social energy, and this is not law. Law is a kind of static state (Hauriou, 1916c, p. 172), a matter of classification as opposed to pure legal technique (Hauriou, 1892a, p. 61¶132). What must be done in law, instead of repeating legal technique, is to track down the "secret logic" of analogy, which makes rules once posed extend to all analogous cases (ibid., p. 60).

So insufficient to the law is legal technique and practice by itself, that they would have nothing at all to do with law except that legal theory gives the techniques a legal effect. Although subjective constructs of reason can have no legal effect, on the level of facts there can be no clarity or foresight, both necessary to law. So the science of law has the effect of making practice more secure by anticipating it, and of making theory more effective by putting it in contact with the process of determining the conditions for action (Hauriou, 1909a, p. 60).

Hauriou finds the development of legal theory and science, as distinct from legal practice, to take place in what he calls the interval between executive order and its execution (1923d, p. 438). Historically, it develops from a primitive condition of society in which the function of judges was to look at facts of settlement already accomplished and then to render their opinions regarding them. The parties to the settlement were not required to abide by the judge's opinion because they voluntarily submitted the matter for judgment while under no duress to do so. Over time, judges came to look at the facts of a situation before its resolution, and to render decisions prior to settlement.

The full development of this process was to create a place for reason separate from the place for acts—a decision-making process and implementing the decision, implementation being a pure executive technique (Hauriou, 1909a, pp. 59–60). The rationality of legal science derives from the abstract, rational model of the human being it presents. The human form that the state guards is the ideal that the law expresses; this is as true for the feeling for law as it is for how people appreciate law as in the texts of the law. Different legal systems differ by how far they have progressed in forming this abstract and rational model of human beings (Hauriou, 1897b, p. 15).

The abstract rationality of law also comes from holding equality before the law as an ideal, an ideal implied by the very concept of law. This ideal demands an abstract character to law, for human beings, by nature, are unequal (ibid., p. 14). Law is tied to a group of ideas current in its epoch of history; by taking up these ideas law advances: for the sake of method, order, simplicity, clarity, and, toward these ends, decentralization (Hauriou, 1916c, p. 238).

In a general system of law, then, concepts are indispensible; law cannot be reduced to practice. Concepts constitute the essential support of a legal system. The concept of the person is more essential than are the legal regulations (Hauriou, 1923c, p. 341). The authority of law lies in the truth of its representations, how accurately it represents the relations existing among people; the source of authority is in truth. Just as heat cannot be passed from a colder to a warmer body, so a less adequate truth cannot give validity to the representative authority over a community (Hauriou, 1899d, p. 130).

The science of law develops along autonomous lines, which are distinct from the study of morals and of religion (Hauriou, 1967, p. 181). Hauriou praises some jurisprudence for refusing to accept moral arguments. "The weakest legal argument seems to him better than the best moral argument, and from the point of view of a judge this is perfectly correct" (1916a, p. 334) [*"le moindre argument juridique lui paraît préférable au meilleur argument moral, et de son point de vue du juge juridique, elle a parfaitement raison"*]. He condemns other jurisprudence for acting on moral rather than legal grounds (1879b, p. 17).

The science of law as we understand it today, as an organized system, does not predate modern times; so primitive eras are matters for legal archeology, not for the science of law (Hauriou, 1929c, p. xiv). Therefore, even early in his career, Hauriou identifies the subject matter of legal science as institutions; the study of institutions is to law as the study of sociability is to social science. Institution is the material object of law (1894c, p. 310). Equating the material object of law to the common interests of a legal group, he explains this object by saying that law does not fall into a world of fragmented individuals [*poussière individuelle*]; it attaches to a world of solidarity (1902a, p. 305).

Law is a social science, and like every other social science, it deduces conclusions peculiar to itself—based on its exclusive principles that would not be derived from the principles of any other social science. For example, from law we may deduce that taking bread that does not belong to us is a legal infraction, while, based on the principles of ethics, taking the same bread might be considered the morally right action under certain circumstances. Law deduces its consequences because representation is the final cause of social movement (Hauriou, 1899d, p. 133). That is, law must be rooted in the freedom manifested by the fact of representation, and directed to the maintenance of conduct [*conduite*] toward which representation by concepts is directed.

Hauriou identifies three elements of law in order of importance: the institution as an objective individuality (as distinct from a subjective personality), the legislative texts, and power (1906a, p. 135). Elsewhere, he finds all law to be made up of a set of social elements: oral conflict, acceptance of solution, and a public judge, meaning a judge with more authority than that given him by only the will of the parties (1905, p. 17). The second set of elements is more a question of the accidents of law, while the first are the properties of which the formal object of legal science—representative solidarity—is composed.

The science of law is necessary for the practice of law and it cannot dispense with theory. But, says Hauriou, it is "a theory which has the pretention of resting on ever more analytic observation of the facts" (1916c, p. 605n1) [*"Une théorie qui a la prétention de reposer sur une observation de plus en plus analytique des faits"*]. Many fail to grasp the demands of this method of observation, observational, rigorous, and transparent. Most want finished systems, but Hauriou's work is plagued by incompleteness because of its observational character. He builds ensembles, and then continually rebuilds them, so that his works are only "successive bulletins of a research laboratory" (ibid., p. xxvii) [*"bulletins successifs d'une laboratoire de recherches"*].

This ideal of the "legal laboratory" was behind Hauriou's entire conception of what a law school should be (cf. Hauriou, 1901a, passim). But the laboratories, which law has at its disposal, come down to only two: History shows that legal systems move in a closed circle between the pole of the institution and the pole of the contract as supreme explanatory phenomenon. Comparative law shows Western legal systems to be the most interesting ones because they are the most personalizing. These two laboratories are successive in importance; for together they show that the direction of law goes beyond individualism to personalism (Hauriou, 1969, p. 131).

The circular way in which laboratory procedure moves is due to the uncertain results of inductive research when it is pursued honestly, without having already decided on the outcome to which it will be directed. Pursued honestly, inductive method in law finds us often ending up right where we began (Hauriou, 1923d, p. 75n1).

This observational method is conjoined and perhaps identified with the experimental method. Experimentation is required to control the observations in any scientific research; this is also true of free scientific research applied to law. "*But experimentation here means the adjustment of particular institutions to a comprehensive construct*" (Hauriou, 1916c, p. xxvii) [*"Or, l'expérimentation, ici, c'est l'ajustement des institutions particulières à une construction d'ensemble"*].

Thus, Hauriou studies particular institutions; to him they have a particular significance. He puts them with this significance into a total social grouping. The entire pattern of institutions in society that Hauriou developed depends for its mobile balance upon observation. But observation depends upon facts and their interpretation; the interpretation of facts can always progress. So we begin by fitting facts together satisfactorily; then, as we continue to observe and reflect, we must continually fit new facts into the scheme, continually rebuilding the complete picture. The result may be different from the first trial, but each successive approximation comes closer to reality.

Building the ensemble of theory for legal science, then, is not done from above with sure strokes of first principles. It is done from below by repeated observations. It is experimental, constructed by a method of combining forces with their directive ideas. It is not inflexible, for it has only the form given it by its fitted parts; it is nothing but the synthesis of these, but these can and must change. The only demands of principle upon the comprehensive construct other than to assemble the facts are that it must develop a balance of forces and it must stick to reality (ibid., p. xxviii).

In the laboratory of law, the fund of history offers institutions as the formal object of law. The historian of law finds all relevant material to be comprised of institutions. But this calls into question the principle that in a legal formula only legal elements have a place. Some believe that the institution would have to be viewed as having legal effects to be a legal entity, and this view is a priori excluded.

Hauriou finds this way of thinking the antithesis of the experimental. For him, if we accept as true that history offers institutions as the appropriate category, and we accept that history is the source of legal facts, then how could we not accept that institutions constitute legal facts? Methodologically, the only reason for excluding them would be that, if institutions were admitted as legal, the method of law would become descriptive rather than deductive. The formula that legal doctrine can contain only legal elements appropriates formulas used by legal normativism that Hauriou criticizes. The descriptive method in law is exactly what Hauriou is aiming at; but it is unacceptable to those he calls ideologues of law, who demand that law be deductive (1907a, p. 5).

The "realistic" point of view Hauriou claims to be developing in law opposes the aprioristic and deductive drive to simplify theory, a drive he believes can be satisfied only at the cost of opposing real needs for the sake of principles. Practical motivations surely can be criticized in terms of principles; but practical reality nonetheless bursts those categories and principles wide open. Principles for Hauriou are but the syntheses of facts. The power of realities [*la force des choses*] is the material of which principles are made. Thus, because facts constantly change, principles are relative and we must constantly check that our formulations still adhere to facts. Living institutions are formed only by the combination of principles and facts (1905, pp. 2–4).

The principle for the classification of public law is order. Hauriou takes the standard concept of legal order to be that "there exists an order of things, and law is conformity to this order" (1909a, p. 3) [*"Il existait un ordre des choses, et le droit était la conformité à l'ordre"*]. On the contrary, Hauriou believes this order is not pre-established, offering two reasons. He holds that a pre-established order can be validated only on the theological basis, but is then inappropriate to law; and the method used to arrive at the conclusion is too descriptive, not taxonomic or classificatory enough (ibid.).

Hauriou believes that pure description—simply repeating the facts described, with no reflection and synthesis—is not sufficient of itself to justify legal systems. The order required is not pre-established but constantly in motion: "it is the movement of social transformations that it is important to observe" (ibid., pp. 7–8) [*"C'est le mouvement des transformations sociales qu'il importe d'observer"*]. Progress has a direction, it moves toward a social ideal; but societies do not know that they pursue it, "only that they move" (ibid.) [*"qu'elles marchent"*]. This is the sense of the *agmen* already studied in Chapter Three.

Hauriou recognizes that his method of legal science can give the superficial impression of a subjective thought searching agonizingly within itself for its true essence. He opines that François Geny's reading of him as an Hegelian metaphysician was such a reading. To an astute reader, however, the reworking of the same ideas gives the impression of a laboratory. Hauriou believes that he always works with the same method and with the same directive ideas and in the same direction. He can publish only the successive results of his legal experimentation. Some of the earlier ones are destroyed in doing this, but the great majority of them accumulate in a coherent fashion (1916c, p. xxviii).

B. Law as Art

As everywhere, art is much closer to life than is science. But, as Rudolf von Jhering said, in law, life should not have to strain; it is up to legal thought to follow life (Hauriou, 1911a, p. 24). This is why civil law is of central importance in law, the transposed image of life [*image transposée de la vie*], just as it is in life (Hauriou, 1916c, pp. 386–387); and why institutions, which represent continuity and action, are more important in law than the legal rules of continuity alone, because our environment is a world that strives to become vital and active (Hauriou, 1933f, p. 127) [*un monde que veut vivre et agir*].

It is well known, says Hauriou, that legal constructs done in too scientific a manner, meaning conducted using distinctions drawn too radically, always turn out to be unfit for life (1909a, p. 23). Thus, the sin of Revolutionary law and its normativism was an excess of logic. This sin was a sin against life, for life is not logical. The norms of social order and justice are rational notions. However, they are not in the order of logical reason but of intuitive reason, of skill and experience. We can use principles, but only sensitively and sparingly (Hauriou, 1929c, pp. 234–235).

General systems of law, though modish, commit this sin. They have to combine varied theories—of public law, private law, and sovereignty—into complicated systems. Each of these, in turn, is a composition. So general systems cannot be directly constructed or they would be inappropriate to life, which develops the subsystems' requirements separately (Hauriou, 1912d, p. 4). This emphasis upon lived demands is what justifies Hauriou's claim, "Ultimately, my frame of mind is the same as that of the ordinary jurist" (1916c, p. xxvi) [*"Mais, au fond, mon état d'esprit était la même que celui du juriste ordinaire"*]: rigorous method of observation, applied to the struggle of forces, to combat tendencies to immoralism. The difference is that, in Hauriou's day, this could not be done instinctively, but required a conscious insertion of self into the project of moralizing life. Toward moral life, or toward the normal, is the congenital orientation of the legal system. Jurists who establish theories on the basis of accidents or of the exceptional are doomed to refutation by life (Hauriou, 1923a, p. 659).

So, to indulge in academic science, for example, to seek the ultimate origins of power instead of the daily ones, or to discriminate legal constructs from legal "givens" when the two eventually merge anyway, are questions that Hauriou says are "tiresome" to law (Hauriou, 1916c, p. xxviin1; 1929c, p. 30). Hauriou is concerned in this part of the *Principes de droit public* with refuting François Geny's criticisms of him. The distinction of the phenomenal given [*donnée*] from the construct that in time becomes as phenomenally basic as the natural given [*donné*] is Geny's. Formal science, in this sense, excludes from use any of the proofs in law that are now used daily, and revealingly tends toward the law of least effort. Formal science completely insures judges against every contingency of ad hoc decisions, thereby putting them beyond the demands of life itself (Hauriou, 1929c, pp. x, xi).

This orientation toward life, the creating and maintaining of life, takes law out of the realm of science, even observational science. Hauriou completes the definition of law as an art with the ideal of a natural law realized progressively in classical works. His denial of a fixed order in nature, however, leaves the definition open to investigation independently of the alleged source of law in nature.

There is a science of law and sciences auxiliary to law; but, as a creator of social order and justice, law is an art. Every legal theory is a work of art and the legal system in its entirety is an imposing and noble work of art. It is the art of the good and the equitable [*ars boni et æqui*] and the art of the settled and the secure [*ars stabilis et securi*]. The purpose of the science of law is to clarify this art (Hauriou, 1927d, p. 70; 1929c, p. 61).

By stating in positive terms Hauriou's denials of Hans Kelsen's formal science of law, we discover these further dimensions of the art of law. Law is the science of an art, irremovably tied to an artistic formation. It is not an ordinary science, even insofar as it is a science, since it does not have knowledge as its unique object. Its object is not the knowledge of existing law; it does not reduce to an organized system of technical and formal notions, carefully articulated to combine one with the other, without the insertion of any non-formalized base. To say that legal science cannot create is false (Hauriou, 1929c, pp. vii–ix).

However, making law an art does not reduce it to mere practice. The non-formal elements of law (court practice, politico-economic-historical materials, moral ideas, preoccupations with social order, and with justice and natural law) are not simply part of the practice instead of the science (ibid.). Hauriou does occasionally call the system of law a matter of legal technique to distinguish it from the preoccupation that legal philosophy has with principles of justice, whose every application is the same. Justice explains nothing because it explains everything by the same principle. Legal technique, on the other hand, instead of giving ultimate causes, gives proximate causes, the cause and effect relation between each right and its peculiar explanation, because each right is specialized in purpose (Hauriou, 1909a, pp. 83–85).

The word "technique," however, is reserved only for certain procedures of the profession. The lawyer, no more than the sculptor or architect, can be confused with the practitioner, and law is no pure practice. Practice simply follows directions; this is the technical act. But law and jurisprudence discover social truth precisely because they construct the social order. Construction requires more than technique, it requires artistic intuition, the source of truth appropriate to life. The construction is a work of art, not just mastery of technical tools (Hauriou, 1927d, pp. 70–71). The hypothesis upon which the artistic edifice of law is built is not that of blind activity, of determined or chance movement. It is based on the hypothesis that social relations are analyzable into will-acts formulated by responsible persons (Hauriou, 1893c, pp. 6–7). This is not the basis for technical engineering.

This distinction from science and from technique locate law as an art for Hauriou. It is for this reason that he refuses to allow his legal ideas to be made into a general system, philosophical or sociological. Law can only organize positive or observational realities, and so it remains case law. It cannot grow unfertilized and theoretical by intellectual parthenogenesis (1903a, pp. 560–562, 562n1).

The artistic construction law makes is something Hauriou calls a semi-metaphysical construction. It creates a continuity of will-acts from erratic and occasional individual acts. This means that the legal will is artificial in that it possesses not the subjective traits of the individual wills but the objective character of legislators, their legislation. It is nonetheless non-arbitrary for two reasons. First, the creation is a result of social necessities; law does not create these social necessities but is only their interpreter.

Second, the social will and the individual will do tend to merge, turning some of the artifice into fact. Social will gradually becomes less monolithic as needs are satisfied, and individual wills become less erratic as good laws direct them (Hauriou, 1898, p. 20). The creation of social will, ever more realized, from individual wills and for the sake of individual wills constitutes the artistic endeavor of law. So Hauriou sees evil not just in institutions but in individuals, with the consequent task of law not satisfied by the empty creation of an abstract capitalism or an abstract socialism. "It is people that it is necessary to reform by an effort of moral education. This is one of the tasks of jurists, and it is not the least important one" (Hauriou, 1966d, p. 15) [*"C'est l'homme qu'il faudrait réformer par un effort d'éducation morale. C'est l'une des tâches des juristes et elle n'est pas d'une petite importance"*].

For Hauriou, the issue of creativity in law restores legal investigation to the right track. He views the crisis in legal thought among his contemporaries as a result of their confusion of the moral and physical worlds, of liberty with matter, under the infatuation with science (1919b, pp. 691–692). Hauriou tries to identify law not with merely an event occurring at some locale but with the human service it renders (1891b, p. 473). The justification for doing so is his relocation of the creative power in law from the legal rules to the institutions.

Locating law in rules instead of in institutions is the whole problem of law in Hauriou's day; mislocation is a result of confusing duration with creation—confusing the reaction of texts with the action of institutions and ultimately confusing material endurance with spiritual active creation (Hauriou, 1933f, p. 94).

The spiritual ideal of justice is in contradiction to the elements of material reality. Only the creative and spiritual power of law can realize justice. Law does not arise, then, from simply drawing a rule from concrete political and economic life by generalization and abstraction (Hauriou, 1916c, p. 8).

Creation, and hence spiritual qualities, is what distinguishes law as an art. Such spiritual qualities characterize the law at many places in Hauriou's writings. Thus, the three elements making up law are all spiritual: an interest to be pursued, a power of decision manifested in risk taking, and a social function to be fulfilled (Hauriou, 1909a, p. 45). The goal of equilibrium [*équilibre*], which penetrates all law and social science, ends in the highest and spiritualized combination of objective individuality with subjective personality (Hauriou,1916c, p. 298).

Legal power is the combination of three elements: the majority power of domination, which is relatively brute and material, with the two minority powers of authority and competence, which are both spiritual powers, of will and of intelligence respectively (Hauriou, 1923d, p. 162). As a final example of law's spiritual qualities, even the power of property, the center of bourgeois life and the central conception of the legal system oriented toward bourgeois life, is spiritual and not material. Property is a question of speculation, risk, and enterprise; it is focused not on the present but on the future, not toward enjoyment but toward acquisition, not toward consumption but toward production. All these orientations of property make of it a spiritual element of law (Hauriou, 1927d, p. 58).

The art of law or law as an art, directed upon life and centered in creative spiritual power, is essentially active. It is no passive, social result, or a mirror of tranquility. Law is essentially conflict, the unity of which is a synthesis of contrary principles, not a single principle. It meets not its own demands but those of the forces seeking synthesis. We judge its worth by how well it brings us "the good life." Does it meet the demands of good sense, take a stand at the mid-point [*stat in medio*]? With these goals, law cannot be formulated, it does not immobilize life in a formula. Its being is an active one (Hauriou, 1902b, p. 359).

The role of law is not to mirror social relations in a receptive manner alone, although it must in justice reflect what exists; it is also an instrument of social change, actively ordering, modifying, and reforming social relations (Hauriou, 1896, p. 379). Law is intended to institute society, a task that is improper to morals or even to statecraft. To institute is "to establish within, by internal resources," this in the interest of persons. This means, then, "to infuse within it an internal principle of life," which, quoting the poet Terence, is "to implant in its heart a more lively affection." Even more accurately, the active role of law is to reorganize and reform institutions, for they are originally organized by individuals' initiatives. The action of instituting which law has comes down to this, that law "orders them toward an objective of order and justice" (Hauriou, 1967, pp. 269, 281).

Essentially active, law could have no other source than power, making it a falsehood that power could do nothing legal without law, since power creates law. "Power is law in potency or act, and law is power in act" (Hauriou, 1923d, pp. 252–253) [*"Le pouvoir est du droit en puissance ou en acte et le droit est du pouvoir réalisée"*]. Powerful interests do not end when law begins. Some needs are always at stake in law, "so that law does not rule, but struggles" (Hauriou, 1892b, p. 4) [*"que de droit ne régne pas, qu'il combat"*].

Hauriou refers to "philosophers" in general to support his idea of law as essentially a matter of action. What creates individual rights is not just "the eminent dignity of the human person" [*"l'eminente dignité de la personne humaine"*]; this is powerless without the process by which it affirms its place in society by risking itself for society, namely, legal conflict. "Law arises only from action" (1916c, pp. 194–195) [*"Le droit ne nait que de l'action"*]; a mere definition cannot evoke it.

Besides this more analytic way to his opinion, Hauriou also calls on the history of law to show that the procedure of direct action is the fundamental legal procedure (ibid., p. 21). The theoretical demand or claim of a right is negative: the demand not to have action abridged. But only a power that is customarily recognized in practice, that realizes itself upon something or against someone, is positive. This simple interest in practice is necessary and sufficient for jurisprudence to recognize a right (Hauriou, 1905, p. 33). Jurists can make the idea of the just precise only in the execution of work, in the laying down of laws, in rendering judgments, in resolving actual cases (Hauriou, 1927g, p. vii). Legal rules themselves refer to nothing but action:

> Altogether, what is a legal rule except a rule for acts? The legal rule is a limitation of activity, it has reality, then, on the occurrence of acts; it is administrative acts only which can manifest the administrative rules. The great advantage of litigating administrative acts is to put the judge directly in the presence of what contains the majority of legal rules in potency. (Hauriou, 1897a, p. 49) [*Car en somme, qu'est une règle de droit sinon une règle des actes? La règle de droit est une limitation de*

l'activité elle se pose donc à l'occasion des actes; c'est des actes d'administration seuls que peut se dégager la règle administrative. Le grand avantage du contentieux de l'acte d'administration est donc de mettre le juge directement en présence de ce qui contient en puissance le plus de règles juridiques.]

According with this specification of law as a matter purely of action, Hauriou stresses that law is basically a system of means and not of ends; for example, of individual rights and not the purposes for which those rights are exercised; seldom does law attend to motivations (1967, p. 182). Thus, in a "realist" method of law, we do not search out the objective of judging, the purpose of the goal of the act of judging [*la fin de la fin de l'acte de juger*], to find out what role a judge plays. Instead, we look to the way the judge came to be, historically, and this tells us the practical value of the institution of judgeship (Hauriou, 1905, pp. 3–4). The only way to justify a principle of classification and organization in law is by the number of elements it explains and coordinates (Hauriou, 1909a, p. 13). Although any classificatory system is a matter of motivation, the motivation here is the practical but immediate one of coordinating disparate elements.

The accomplishment of an end by lawyers is not by appeal to abstract legal principles, but to a formula, which they both compose and interpret to bring about that end; there is no appeal to abstract notions of cause or of objectives (Hauriou, 1882b, p. 14). We become a "prisoner of logic" when, by accepting a rational model of legal operations, we are led to deduce from a complete theory a particular conclusion according to the motivation alleged. Once we accept this model, the motive cannot vanish from the analysis and we cannot attend to the nature of the act or operation independently of the motives (Hauriou, 1890, p. 406). The notion of law as action, however, demands that we do address the nature of the action independent of its motives.

The loosing of law from its rational conception in favor of the practical art is the key to understanding law. The only "given" for law is that it is an excellent vehicle for the frontlines in the battle between the just and the unjust. It is a useful tool, and this fact determines the approach to the study of law, namely, how to organize the tool. Practical direction gives custom a great role in law of creating the system of legal expectations, of "superlegality," since the question of such ends is not the question inside of law. It makes legal personality available as an efficient type of organization apart from requiring any position on its reality or unreality, its literal or figurative nature (Hauriou, 1916c, pp. xxvi–xxvii). This practical point of view also allows unprejudiced definition of facts. From the practical point of view, liberty is equally as factual as social mechanisms, as opposed to liberty being the ideal with the mechanisms as the only facts (Hauriou, 1899d, p. 129).

The practical question comes down to *équilibre* as the manner of organization. Order founded on equilibrium is the legal base for the method of practical combination in law. It is the criterion of the stability needed for ordered movement; the external and constitutional balance of powers in government is the sign of ordered movement (Hauriou, 1909a, pp. x, 10). These, in law as in general theory, must have one power taking the initiative and setting the conditions, and the others submitting to them; this is not subordination, but it is an inherent inequality (Hauriou, 1916c, p. 214).

Law as an art—living, active, creative, spiritual, and practical means—is good for free scientific research (ibid., p. xxvii) [*bonne pour la libre recherche scientifique*], for it does indeed supply a principle: relativism, the principle of dualist method. "Dualism has been formally raised to the level of a necessary principle first by M. [Gabriel] Tarde, and then by M. Hauriou" (Hauriou, 1902b, p. 359n1) [*"Le dualisme a été formellement érigé en principe nécessaire par M. Tarde d'abord, par M. Hauriou ensuite"*]. Gabriel Tarde's contribution was that of Hauriou's precursor in dualism [*précurseur du dualisme*], in a note two pages earlier than the last citation.

Dualism, or more widely pluralism, is a practical necessity in law. If we follow only one theory, and that theory is not completely true, everyone will be probing into it and progress will be held up for a long while (Hauriou, 1899a, p. 37). From a more theoretical point of view, we do not know whether one or several systems and foundations for law exist (Hauriou, 1912d, p. 5). This is not to say that the legal techniques must be extremely diversified; not every distinction, even if psychologically well founded, must be mirrored in practice. For the need of practical simplification abolishes all psychological distinctions, reducing them to legal archeology (Hauriou, 1912a, pp. 418–419) [*archéologie juridique*]. But Hauriou's point is that simplification of the law [*droit*] into laws [*loi*] is wrong for misrepresenting the law (1914a, p. 375). This self-acclaimed "realism" or hard-minded approach is realistic only in that it deprives interests of all protection. The reality of law must always be complicated by the idea of guarantees; in social matters, everything needs a guarantee, and every guarantee for its reliability is a complication (Hauriou, 1919a, p. 141). The monolithic and simplified legal system is not true to action.

Hauriou's dualism in law is a dualism of matter and form. The content of rules and the legal acts is tied essentially to human liberty conditioned by social order and justice as the matter, and the formal texts of these as the form. Classical legal method accords equal importance to matter and form, defining one only in terms of the other and pursuing a balance, which preserves both. Although the primitive formation of a legal system emphasizes formalism in the codification of laws, shortly after and thenceforward an evolution toward the spirit of the law occurs, a notion that is material and not formal (Hauriou, 1929c, p. v).

The duality of matter and form Hauriou postulates in law is the dualism of subjective law and objective law. In objective law, what is independent of subjects is not admitted to be legal; what seems to be independent of subjects is maintained in reality by subconscious ideas. So the objective in law is what is maintained by subconscious ideas. This is the first of the three meanings in Hauriou of the "objectivity" of law that Thomas Morris Haynes distinguishes (1949). The first refers to the fact that law grows out of balances, which do not involve high degrees of self-consciousness among the persons concerned. It also refers to the institution as internally integrated, and not considered in the context of other relatively independent individuals to whom it is related. Finally, it refers to the fact that many phases of law deal with juridical acts and care nothing for the kind of personality at its source.

The subjective in law is what is maintained by conscious wills (Hauriou, 1925c, p. 90). This is a relatively neutral position, which meets the demands of romantic requirements for contract and of collectivist reliance on social facts. To attempt purposefully to reduce these two to one is revealing because it does not work. The facts show us the opposition of tendencies and of methods, which is overall and persistent. The lawyer is obligated to accept the duality as a hypothesis, to suppose that it corresponds to some profound psychological necessity and that it is instinctive, and then to clarify the reasons and the results (Hauriou, *Introduction à l'étude du droit administratif français*, n.d., pp. xiv–xx). It is not enough, however, simply to say that both parts of the duality must be used. For the lawyer's acceptance of dualism comes down to a very practical question of method. So to say both must be used, a little of each, is of no help at all. One must outweigh the other, for things cannot be parceled out equally (Hauriou, 1916c, p. 1). One or the other must dominate, depending on the different branches of law (Hauriou, *Introduction à l'étude du droit administratif français*, n.d., pp. xiv–xx).

Objectively, we can consider legal facts as the result of forces in which no conscious will acts, and behind which there lies hidden no responsible personality. Hauriou tells us that this is the way we should view constitutional law and the relations between public powers. These are objective because they do not presuppose the action of subjects, resting instead in the manifest facts. The reason responsibility is absent from this area of law is the vast disproportion between the political fault a civil servant commits and the tremendous financial loss that may follow from it. Civil servants put their honor, ambition, and reputation at risk here, but not their wealth. The constitutional dimension of law is immersed in the objective play of powers (excluding the power of property); for other than the power of property, which meets our private needs, power comes to human beings from outside of choice and so is independent of will. It is the force of realities [*force des choses*] that counts here (ibid.).

In summary, in public law, those who start to build legal theory with the subjective method never make a real passage out of subjective data, remaining limited to purely subjective givens. The way to proceed even in studying the legal personality is to explain as much as possible by the objective method, and use subjective data only for whatever remains unexplained. This way follows the precept of moving from the more, to the less known. It follows the method of modern psychology, starting with states of consciousness and only finishing with the subjective ego. It also follows the movement of the scholastic definition of person, beginning with the "indivisible substance" and then modifying it as "of a rational nature" (Hauriou, 1916c, pp. 84–85).

On the subjective side, conventional wisdom views legal acts as the exercise of conscious wills belonging to responsible persons. Civil law or commercial law fit in this rubric, since they are the relations between particulars, social relations between responsible subjects. These are the areas of commerce and exchange and such rest on a number of postulates—needs, desires, pleasures, passions, appetites, speculation, debt, compensation—each of which, in turn, postulates the subjective personality. So the subjective method is the natural and necessary procedure in this kind of situation (Hauriou, *Introduction à l'étude du droit administratif français*, n.d.).

Hauriou defends subjective law before the increased popularity of objective social approaches in his day. Even if no logical reconciliation exists between the two, a truly positive science of law that excludes any metaphysical preoccupation with logical unity, must recognize the practical unity, which only the two together constitute (1912b, p. 4). He is always drawn more toward the subjective side, justifying this tendency by professing that objective law is almost entirely a law the only purpose of which is to prepare the organization for personification. Therefore, Hauriou concludes that objective law is entirely oriented toward the moral person and toward subjective law (1914, p. 337).

Having parceled out public and private law to the predominance of objective and subjective legal methods, respectively, Hauriou also addresses the direction of administrative law. As an observed fact, the administration acts more in a managerial capacity [*gestion*] than in an authoritative manner [*autorité*]; it tries to satisfy needs and assigns responsibilities to administrators. The logical consequence is that it moves more toward subjective law; it is not all subjective, but the subjective appears as the principle and the objective as the exception. Whenever we exercise rights and the rights have practical consequences more than our merely enjoying or possessing rights, subjective law dominates. This is the way the two must be combined: since the law demands both, and since they cannot simply be juxtaposed—"for law, a living work, like life, demands syntheses" (Hauriou, *Introduction à l'étude du droit administratif français*, n.d., p. xix) [*"le Droit, qui est œuvre vivant, a besoin des synthèses, comme la vie*"]—one of these must act as the principle (subjective law) and the other as the exception (objective law).

C. Plural Sources of Legal Disciplines

The status of an action in law is dependent upon the subjective character it possesses or aims toward. In turn, Hauriou sees this character manifested in a spectrum of methods: classical method—formally outmoded, the classical principles of subjectivity can be readapted; evolutionary—the general movement of an existence is from inorganic to organic; subjective—the more evolved something is, the more subjective it is; and the explicitly historical—objective procedure comes first in law, and only later the subjective foundation for it (1916c, pp. 41–43). In sum, the ways to the legal essence of something are historical; history will be the source of the legal discipline, science, and art.

Historical method is the method most appropriate for law studies. Everything makes its life's journey in "time." An article by Pierre Hebraud studies Hauriou's sense of the importance of time as a category functioning in law and social science (1968, pp. 179–208). Social stability of law results from a slow, uniform movement of transformation in an ordered social system. Hauriou tells us that this conflict of forces of stabilization and of movement, in which some break down and others maintain themselves, is the perspective he adopts from his earliest to his latest works, and that we see the same conflict in physical systems as well as in social ones. Everything happens in time, but time does not appear to be moving when social change and individual change keep pace. In these circumstances, we integrate time into our social geometry and relativize society without consciously realizing that we do so. The forces of movement are dominant over the forces of stabilization, but only slightly so, since movement does not run free. Human beings create most of the institutions that retard movement. The forces of movement are not necessarily forces of disorder, however; for changes can yield a better order as well as a worse one (1933f, p. 77).

In law, then, history is the perspective closest to the real. Law unrolls on the historical plane: one state of law prevailed yesterday, another today, and a third will prevail tomorrow. These are steps in the evolution of the same body of law. Relations of sequence attach these steps to one another, and relations of coexistence attach the contemporaneous different parts of the system at any point. The past of law explains its present and illuminates its future (ibid., pp. 77–79). Historically enduring in law, and therefore real, are the institutions. Thus, their act of founding is the legal foundation of society and the state and the theory of law, in a broad sense, closely follow the history of institutions. The history of institutions, then, is the proper way to study law and the source of legal disciplines (1925c, p. 89). From law, we can understand community the way our forebears did, for law stores up the definitions and concepts of tradition (Hauriou, 1879b, p. 71).

Hauriou suggests three starting points of law: the concept of the intelligence, the moral rule or will, and a consensus (1884, p. 9). Stated differently, law begins as a simple concept of intelligence and ends in its practical realization by means of force; intervening between these two is customary consent, manifested in legislative law, and its jurisprudential interpretation (ibid.). In other words, to reduce the whole system of law to legal rules is anti-historical and anachronistic, for law begins in the one-sided sacrifice of individuals for an ideal, followed by voluntary submission to a judge. Only then does law yield legal rules and written laws (Hauriou, 1909a, p. 53).

These several alignments of history appear to be fairly consistent despite the changes in terminology. What might appear to be inconsistent with these, however, is their historical arrangement as Hauriou details in his posthumous final work, *Introduction à l'étude du droit* (1969, p. 132). There law moves from the voluntary to the intellectual. The intellectual goal is the directive hypothesis of his research, his researches to verify that goal. The movement from voluntary to intellectual is spelled out as the movement from formal procedures towards their foundations, from the implicit to the explicit, from the discontinuous towards the continuous, from the particular toward the general, from the subjective toward the objective, from practice toward concepts.

Ways of reconciling this apparent shift in Hauriou's position are available; for example, the rational character of law that Hauriou admitted even in his early works, may be what he means by a movement toward the intellectual. This would make the rule and the intellectual coincide, bringing into harmony the earliest analyses with the final one. But difficulties still remain, such as what he might have meant by saying that the movement is from the subjective to the objective. This changes Hauriou's terminology in his last years; for he had referred to legal rules in earlier works as the objective element in the legal system. But he had long since begun to represent the objective element by the objective institution.

Whatever the role of the intellectual element in law, whether initiating or culminating legal evolution, it remains true that in Hauriou's classical position, ideas make civilizations and are not the product of them (1916c, p. xiv). The intellectual character of law is not a rationalization of an existing organic structure; representation and not organism must be made the basic legal category (Hauriou, 1899d, Appendix 1, pp. 132–143). Just as concrete human beings do not exist as an assemblage of organs but exist by the medium of their functions and only then have organs to fulfill functions, so "the legal body of an objective institution would already be an abstract reality of the purely psychological order" (Hauriou, 1916c, p. 122) [*"le corps juridique d'une institution objective serait donc déjà une réalité abstraite d'ordre purement psychologique"*]. All that is concrete and material is the numerical population, since the organs of a legal institution are essentially abstract systems of functions in which individuals are submerged.

The intellectual element is of the general order; this is the genius of law, to rise from the particular to the general, from the ordering of details to general principles at last, principles whose limited scope have been established in advance by the details (Hauriou, 1929c, pp. 235–236). These general principles are to be identified with the common ideas; this is the intellectual material of law (Hauriou, 1916c, p. 235). The common ideas so affect the process of law that the assimilation of individuals to them pushes forward the growth of law, and that the law in turn is an instrument for better assimilating individuals (ibid., pp. 232–233). Only one way exists in which the form of law and the result of it could have such a connection: if the content of law expresses humanity and for Hauriou, that is just what it does. As with everything classic, law expresses humanity in brief [*humanité concentrée*], what there is in human beings that is general and abstract and that is extremely durable, possibly eternal (ibid., p. 242).

This way of positing a prime element of law demands that we supplement it by asserting that this abstraction is not impractical. On the contrary, it is the special tonality of "legal" law [*loi*] rather than *droit* to be vigorously centered on common ideas. Legal texts are a clear, logical, and classic law, and because of this profoundly human (ibid., p. 241). It is not an ideal rule of law society seeks. Texts are, instead, the very elements that make law concrete—authority of the legislative, judicial, and administrative varieties that depend upon the intellectual element (Hauriou, 1911a, p. 5).

The intellectual element, which founds concrete existence, also perpetuates it. This element assures continuity of action from the authority pursuing such a directive idea. Because of this idea, moving about within the confines of a system of legal institution becomes extremely advantageous (Hauriou, 1925c, p. 114). A second element in law and consequently a second source for the legal discipline is will or, more specifically, liberty. The idea of necessity is not a properly legal idea (Hauriou, 1912d, p. 103). The maxim of law is the paraphrase of the individualist Revolutionary maxim, "whatever is not prohibited by law is permitted" (Hauriou, 1925c, p. 95). No permission need be given for will to achieve a legitimated exercise. If individual liberty is not creative of law by some sort of transposition of spontaneous moral activity, then no other source can be adduced to supply for it (Hauriou, 1929c, p. xi). Necessities do not produce freedom. This is why law needs free will or something like free will, but it does not need a universally free will (Hauriou, 1893c, p. 7).

Just as science needs determinism (not an absolute determinism, but a relative determinism), in the same fashion, law needs free will: not an absolute free will, but a free will related to its conditions for exercise (Hauriou, 1933f, p. 172). Although necessity is not a properly legal concept, giving an essential feature of law, it plays a part. For the content of the written law is not willed in full; it is largely determined by social necessities. Even what is willed is partly the result of natural inclination (Hauriou, 1902b, p. 355, 355n2). Although the legal value of acts rests upon the disciplined autonomy of will, self-discipline is not a matter of subjective and internal whim but a result of the objective organization of the self: the check on will by intelligence in the person and the habitual check exercised by the division of powers in the social person (ibid., pp. 30–31).

The will that is the source of law is not only relatively free will, but also a manifested will. For this reason, it can be the source of legal science as well as the source of legal facts. The element of the manifested word [*parole donnée*] in the contract is an original element of social life since it produces legal effects (Hauriou, 1916c, p. 198). We have already seen oral conflict as an essential component of law and part of the analogy of social "matter" was that language is the "space" wherein legal facts come about.

Agreement upon a legal formula by the parties to an organization, their logical connection [*enchaînement logique*], is of greater weight as a proof in law than the way the facts independent of the formula seem to stand (Hauriou, 1882b, p. 19). The legal judge is not concerned with the real and psychological will of the parties in a contract or an institution, only with the legal and manifested or declared will, because only manifest will is available to observation. Any legal use made of the entity of a subjective will must be such as accords with the roughly average will of the collectivity manifested in their practical business (Hauriou, 1903a, pp. 570–571).

Manifest free will as a source of law attaches law to the existential context. Liberty is related to being a state or a contract; for, in organizing liberty into a constitution or in achieving it into a contract by organizing our decisions to secure it, we organize at the same time a being. This is the product of the relation of law to liberty. For "being and liberty are at the center of everything" (Hauriou, 1923c, p. 345) [*"L'être et la liberté sont au centre de tout"*]. From their relation comes the inherent antagonism Hauriou discovers between law and any theory that reduces individual beings to their appearances for a subject; for law demands a philosophy of singular existences, whereas nominalism demands a philosophy of a theory of subjective appearances (1916c, p. 58).

To have to say that "law" is a source for legal science and art may sound ludicrous; but law does have to share its prerogatives with the other candidates for sources of law; for example, history and ideas can occasionally be in conflict with the law. Law is, however, a third broad source of legal discipline for Hauriou. Written legislation is most prominent among the possible meanings of law in this claim. In the modern state, says Hauriou, *loi* has centralized all of *droit* and all of its sources, the rules of authorities, and the customs of the populace (1916d, p. 46). The existence of a relevant text is the condition for the survival of any institution into a changed era (Hauriou, 1916c, p. 83). Written law arises as a matter of convenience to allow situations of dispute to be considered in advance of actual disputes instead of creating the need for sudden rulings with many unanticipated factors. "In this practical necessity, this convenience, lies the whole concept of law" (Hauriou, 1909a, p. 54) [*"Dans cette nécessité pratique ou dans cette habilité pratique gît toute l'idée de la loi"*].

In relation to jurisprudence, legislated texts dominate even if they are obsolete, even against the body of standard authors and jurisprudence (Hauriou, 1879b, pp. 24–25, 37–39, 52–53, 71, 74). "Jurisprudence avails nothing, for it cannot contradict the law" (1899n, p. 48) ["*Le jurisprudence ne peut rien, car elle ne peut pas contredire la loi*"]. In a conflict, jurisprudence can develop institutions that are contrary to the law only on condition that the principle for the contradiction is located in the law (Hauriou, 1899b, pp. 47–48). Hauriou rejects a legal education that looks only to jurisprudence instead of to legal principles. The law then disappears beneath the jurisprudential gloss, since the future judges and businesspersons never learned how to redact laws. This is a deficiency with which Hauriou taxes American legal education (1923d, p. 313).

Legal sanction as a source of law is closely tied to legislated text. While not defining law as sanction, Hauriou still says that law without sanction is only moral rules. Law becomes living, an event, only by violation and subsequent enforcement (1884, pp. 8, 12).

Legislation cannot monopolize the sources of law, history, and ideas, however. For law is equally the progress of jurisprudence. The proper legal task always has as its goal to bring harmony to growing activities; the relevant legislated texts always lag behind. Practice keeps on moving, and jurisprudence can follow it, while "the laws cannot be remade every day" (Hauriou, 1879b, pp. 11, 17) [*"La pratique marche tous les jours et la jurisprudence peut la suivre, tandis qu'on ne peut refaire les lois tous les jours"*]. Jurisprudence must follow closely upon unlegislated practice and must continue even if the laws are silent. Legislation is not perfectly in accord with the facts, but jurisprudence works to put itself in accord (Hauriou, 1891a, p. 232). If the legal rules were to be taken as ultimate and independent, they would obscure the law; the necessity for the rules being as they are becomes clear only in jurisprudence (Hauriou, 1884, p. 12).

Jurisprudence has a significant power of evolution in the application of texts by adapting them to new situations. It is not held to the primitive hypotheses of legislators. In abandoning their spirit, however, the lawyers must respect the letter of the law; otherwise, it is not interpretation but correction. "By the letter, we mean the literal sense, which results from the faithful recognition of the words" (Hauriou, 1900c, p. 533) [*"Par lettre, nous entendons le sens littéral, celui qui résulte du rapprochement loyal des mots"*].

Literal interpretation is even suppler than interpretation by the spirit. The motivations of the legislation may have been cramped and rigid, while the texts give ample room for adjustment. The suppleness comes from the disassociation of one textual passage from another within legislation, which must be presumed for any interpretation. This presumption is explained by the following principle: "The first rule of interpretation becomes this: there is not a law, there are only isolated legislative dispositions" (Hauriou, 1893a, pp. 94–95) [*"La première règlè d'interprétation devient celle-ci: il n'y a pas de loi, il n'y a que des dispositions législatives isolées"*]. Legislative texts being assembled together in one place, one statement in a text, means nothing. The justification for this presumption is that legislative assemblies are too vast to be capable of making a tightly unified and coordinated law. So the logic from the middle of his career that guides interpretation must be a logic that depends upon the demands of the law and not a legal one, a logic that looks to *droit* and not simply to *loi*.

Apparently contradictory to this early set of Hauriou's directions is the succinct logic from the middle of his career that takes legislated texts to provide a complete meaning:

> The legal scope of any particular law is something already inherent in the text: this is not an isolated text, but is the totality of the texts codified into a given law. The structuring of a law is very precise, resulting from the entirety of the texts of the law, even its title and the headings of its chapters, a structure which has the effect that a law on bordering roads [the type of case Hauriou is analyzing] constitutes a logical system on a determinate matter . . . , and that the matter for which it is made cannot be modified by a simple administrative decision. (1913, p. 227) [*Le régime légal d'une loi déterminé, c'est encore quelque chose qui est inhérente au texte: ce n'est pas un texte isolé mais c'est l'ensemble des textes codifiés dans une loi donnée. Il s'agit d'une ossature très précise de la loi, qui résulte de l'ensemble des textes de la loi, de son titre et des rubriques de ses chapitres, ossature qui fait qu'une loi sur les chemins vicinaux constitue un système logique s'appliquant à une matière determine . . ., et que cette matière, pour laquelle elle est fait, ne peut pas modifié par de simples décisions administratives.*]
>
> Ultimately, this is the recognition of the legal value of codification, not the codification of the laws into a code but of the articles into a law; it is the recognition of the value of the fact that a law on a certain matter, even though divided into articles, is an organic whole. It is the recognition that beyond the signification of the parts, the articles, there is a signification of the organic whole, a signification, which has just as much textual validity. [*En somme, c'est la reconnaissance de la valeur légale de la codification, non pas de la codification des lois dans un code, mais de la codification des articles dans une loi; c'est la reconnaissance de la valeur de ce fait, qu'une loi sur une matière donnée, quoique divisée en articles, est un tout organique, et qu'outre la signification des parties que sont les articles, il y a une signification du tout organique, signification qui a, elle aussi, une valeur textuelle.*] (Ibid.)

Nonetheless, Hauriou notes the play of jurisprudence even in this, a continuing demand that leads him to continue asking, even ten years later, "What text in law has no need of interpretation?" (1923d, p. 84) [*"Mais quel est le texte juridique qui n'a pas besoin d'interprétation?"*] The principles for interpretation are the principles of liberty and equality. Liberty according to the law means that the only effect law has on liberty is to command and forbid; law is the limit of freedom and the guarantee of it. Law is rooted in self-mastery, conformity to order in the individual, which requires law even less than does the legal community.

Equality before the law does not mean a sentiment but an objective idea based on observed likenesses. To attain equality, it presumes an absolute centralization of the power of law's domination over individuals. The solution to the apparent inconsistency in Hauriou's doctrine depends, then, upon just what role jurisprudence plays in a particular situation. In circumstances that carry greater occasion for mistake and error, jurisprudence must care that much more for the rigorous logic of its solutions. This jurisprudence then becomes the foundation for the constructions of legal theory and doctrine (Hauriou, 1899h, p. 404).

This high respect Hauriou gives to the action of judges in court he justifies in terms of the voluntary acceptance of their decisions, which law demands. Since law is not a matter of constrained force, since the entire legal system is a mutual acceptance of mutual decisions, individuals cannot therefore claim that the only role of the judge is to restore violated rights. Instead, the judge has a more creative role in guarding legality, and can be considered a source of law (Hauriou, 1905, p. 2). Judges create law more than they serve it. They harmonize the legal expression of the national consciousness—law—with the natural expression of the same—the declared will of parties. Judges make the law live by modeling it on the needs of the collective, but only according to the ideal—the objective ideal of the social environment given in terms of manifested wills (Hauriou, 1903a, pp. 383–384).

The method of legal procedure that Hauriou sets up for the judge to follow has three phases: First, apply formal logic to the fullest on the texts of decisions, to determine the exact object of the most recent one. Second, determine the milieu external to the legal action, which gives it bearing; declared acts of will alone suffice as a relevant milieu. Finally, fill in the gaps of declared will when the coherence of the decision demands it (ibid., pp. 577, 579–582). This is the free scope the judge has in creating law and which demands that the judge's decisions be considered as a source of law. Judges in the administrative courts, in particular, make of law a question chiefly of judicial decision. Their decisions absorb authoritative rules and legislative laws, and surpass them both as a source. The final thrust of administrative law is to make the active power in law the judge instead of the written texts (Hauriou, 1897a, pp. 30, 32).

The sources that make law existent and available for study have been moving toward the increasingly personal, from text to jurisprudence. The extension of this movement would locate one end of the spectrum of sources in the individual lawyer, which is what Hauriou does. He believes that the professional sentiments of other good jurists are the prime matter for theories [*la première matière des théories*] and that even if unproven, these are trustworthy professional sentiments we should follow (Hauriou, 1907a, pp. xiii–xiv). The possession of this legal mind [*le sens juridique*], is the best guard against errors from positivist influences. Conversely, the positivist mind is the greatest danger to the acquisition of the proper legal appreciation (Hauriou, 1894d, p. 394). Jurisprudence is instinctive and manifests the legal mind's dominance over practical and theoretical disadvantages (Hauriou, 1891a, p. 231). The instinct of jurisprudence must be used to build legal theories. It is sure and it is profound (Hauriou, 1897b, pp. iii–iv). Legal theory must be constructed only by jurists, constructed as a whole and introduced by procedure (Hauriou, 1884, p. 12).

3. Forms of Law

Law as a discipline is a science and an art with numerous sources. Throughout the discussion of legal discipline, the unavoidable distinctions in existing law between *droit* and *loi*, and between the goal of justice and the goal of order, forced themselves upon the issue. These factors must now be dealt within their own right.

Hauriou's early description of law was a program for the development of a school of "representative law," which recognizes that the organic is greater than the representative, but is intelligible only through the representative (1899d, Appendix 1, pp. 132–143). Working from this premise, he sets up requirements for a good legal system. Such a system has an affirmation of natural law, an ideal of justice. It places the chief basis for positive rights in the representation people make of their interests. Its theory of the state bases itself in historical social situations, and distinguishes between the governmental organism and representation of it. Politically, it subjects the executive to the legislature, yet finds some way to free it from legislative oppression and stagnation. The foundation it admits for nationalities is the free will of the inhabitants. In international law, the school of representative law stands on the principle of non-intervention, but anticipates the day of European federalism when intervention will be legitimate. This is only an empty form to be filled in; during his career, Hauriou modifies even some of the requirements laid down here, for example, that of the executive subjection.

In mid-career, Hauriou is speaking of law in terms of a synthesis. The synthesis it pursues is an integral order in social affairs. Its distinctiveness is that, unlike the many other syntheses and balances, it is total rather than partial; it balances all the partial syntheses. Yet it is not just the assemblage of other syntheses, nothing over and above them; it also has a special character.

There are economic balances of interests with interests, political ones of powers with powers, administrative balances of functions with functions; law is special in that it balances interests, powers, and functions with each other, but total in that it preserves law as law only by preserving all three balanced strata. Law is total in that all parts of social order participate in it; law is special in that it is founded upon a feeling for justice, such that there can be no society at all without it. It is total insofar as it applies to and comprehends all persons from every one of their aspects; it is total to guarantee all their rights. This implies its special nature, too: that law envisages people as having rights, and lets them prove their rights in risking everything for the sake of rights (Hauriou, 1909a, pp. 37–39).

The definition Hauriou proposes at this point is a purely formal one, coinciding with his general conception of the legal system. It uses balances "to the second power," establishing first an equilibrium between the political forces and law, and then another between the different forms of law, such that the state of law is itself an objective equilibrium. He defines this state of law in terms of its conditions:

> Here is the definition: There is a "state of law" within political domination: (1) when the political power, which is at the same time legal, subjects itself to the rules of law, which it has itself made; (2) when the law which derives from governmental decisions and that which derives from the customary acceptance by the subjects are balanced in a higher form of law [*droit*] which is positive law [*loi*]. (1916c, p. 18) [*Voici cette définition: il y a "état de droit" à l'intérieur d'une domination politique: (1) lorsque le pouvoir politique, lequel est en même temps juridique, se subordonne aux règles de droit positif qu'il a lui-même crées; (2) lorsque le droit qui procède des décisions gouvernementales et celui qui procède de l' adhésion coutumière des subjets se sont équilibrés en une forme de droit supérieure qui est la loi.*]

Every form of positive law, then, is evaluated practically in terms of an equilibrium, as "a positive system of conduct destined to react against" (ibid., p. xxvi) [*"Un système positif de conduite destiné à réagir"*] some misbalance: administrative law, against the arbitrariness of the administration, constitutional law, against the power of political forces. Legal theory, broader in scope than either administrative or constitutional law, is intended to rectify the brutalities and the weaknesses between person and person, and by doing this to develop liberty.

Hauriou's final exposition of law in general, some of it as late as the end of 1928 in the posthumous *Introduction à l'étude du droit* (*Introduction to the Study of Law*) is the most explicit of all. It ceases to base law on balances to be yet more observational in its description.

> Law [*droit*] is a totality of the precepts of behavior for persons living in society, whose end is to maintain peace and to bring about a "social whole of personalities." (1966a, p. xii) [*Le droit est un ensemble de préceptes de conduite pour les hommes vivant en société, dont le but est de maintenir la paix et de réaliser un tout "social de personnalités."*]
>
> These precepts, whose content is taken from ideas of social order, morality, and justice, are elaborated by a technique adapted both to social

> realities and to legal ends. (Ibid.) [*Ces préceptes, dont le contenu est tiré d'idées d'ordre social, de morale et de justice, sont élaborées par une technique adaptée, d'une part, aux réalités sociales et, d'autre part, aux buts juridiques*.]
>
> Their rational efficiency is reinforced by the constraining influence of some power, which the subjects have accepted, on the condition of a judge's intervention. (Ibid.) [*Leur efficacité rationnelle est renforcée par la contrainte d'un pouvoir accepté par les sujets, sous la condition de l'intervention d'un juge.*]

Somewhat less full a definition, but containing mostly the same elements is that law is, "the law of a social system of conduct which tends to assure the social peace by regulating relations and ordering organizations; its prescriptions are sanctioned by social constraint" (Hauriou, 1967, p. 181n71).

Hauriou refines these definitions as follows:

(1) Positive law is an autonomous social discipline, which regulates voluntary acts of individuals. For the sake of these individuals, it institutes society, and does this in two phases: first, it creates a state of peace and then it organizes this state into a "social whole of personalities." It endows society with legal personality.
(2) The sources and the instruments of law can bring about this society only if they engage in a never-ending dialog between the commanding power and the subject power; both remain powers and limit each other. This is chiefly the extent to which *équilibre* remains as a directive hypothesis in Hauriou's final work.
(3) The proper matter of this discipline of law is constituted by the discipline itself; it is its choice of ideas and its choice of the ideals, social order, and justice.
(4) The discipline also constitutes its own proper form; this it does by its techniques of practice. The technical procedures of law adapt legal precepts to social realities and to its matter, the ideas it pursues (1969, p. 133).

Hauriou goes even further by making the concept of law he seeks to develop into a completely analyzed set of characteristics, ten in number:

(1) Law is a social discipline.
(2) Law is autonomous; its place is in the ethical and artistic order.
(3) Law rules people's acts.
(4) The end of law is to institute society for persons.
(5) This end of law breaks down into two: to make peace rule, and to make liberty rule.

(6) Law has its own matter; the matter consists of ideas and ideals, order and justice.
(7) Law has its own form, resulting from its technical tools.
(8) Law is effective even as reasonability; but it also profits from constraints placed by government.
(9) Law, including its constraints from the government, is accepted because of its subjects' obligation to submission.
(10) This obligation is accepted only on the condition that a judge intervenes in each particular case.

Hauriou does not detail the definitions of order and justice, devoting his efforts to their necessary conditions and their interplay, instead. Order is shown by peace; but instead of order being based on peace, peace is based on order, which itself is based on the belief of people in some ideas that Hauriou details. Justice is defined little more than by the Justinian precepts: live uprightly, harm no one, and give to each his due (ibid., p. 134) [*honeste vivere, alterum non laedere, suum cuique tribuere*].

Law is not an unequivocal term; dual in its end, dual between its matter and its form, the first distinction is between *droit* and *loi*. Laws are not the law [*La loi n'est pas le droit*]; *loi* is the work of legislators and is often impassioned. But *droit* is rational (Hauriou, 1897b, p. 41), the ensemble of rational likenesses among individuals, which the state must maintain (Hauriou, 1896, p. 378). Socially, legislative texts are necessary for group living; to live is to act, and to act is to decide and execute—to determine and to follow out a will. In this sense, legislative law is the subjective aspect of social existence; it is the exercise of will (Hauriou, 1898, p. 135). It is, however, an inferior mode of existence of rational law, *droit*. So the institution eventually comes to dominate written law, rather than vice versa (Hauriou, 1907a, p.16n2).

The distinction between order and justice is parallel to, and perhaps identical with, the distinction between *droit* and *loi*. *Droit* and justice are more comprehensive in scope and deep in meaning than their counterparts. The more primitive counterparts have a peculiar meaning and a special purpose, which, however, cannot be realized without their full development into their other. The relation is difficult to conceptualize; the least confusing approach is to trace the duality, whether under the order-justice rubric or some other category, through the works.

Even very early Hauriou was wary of confusing two directions in the study of law: the legal rules, based on internal evidence, moving toward ideas in the legislative realm and more akin to philosophy as a model science; and the legal facts, based on external evidence, moving toward the existent groups the judicial realm dealt with and finding a model in sociology (1884, p. 11). For a period thereafter, Hauriou's appreciation of law attends only to one side: law is an instrument of social conservation, demanding prudence; it is the creation of order by making use of the power of positive society. With this, the state maintains rational likenesses in the community and so the power is rationalized by being directed toward this end (Hauriou, 1893c, p. 4; 1896, p. 382). Law is identified with conformity to order. This means that law establishes the peace and that it contains a conception of social order. The order in question is one oriented toward and by the ideal of justice, one depending upon the members' sacrifice and so not closely tied to any natural law conception of justice (Hauriou, 1896, p. 356). The unity of social order at this time is, then, chiefly an abstract unity; the conflicts of rights in society are not resolved in the order created by law, but are instead sublimated and hierarchized before the needs of the group for peace (Hauriou, 1898, p. 139).

It becomes clear to Hauriou, however, that order is going to demand justice. Law has two ends: solidarity, and justice, which is the way to solidarity. This justice is not a priori and artificial; it is instead the concrete arrangement of right-living for society, for "if it is to endure, it must *live well*" (1902b, p. 475) [*"si elle veut durer il lui faut* bien vivre*"*]. Living rightly—according to justice—is needed for permanence of social order, and permanence is needed for law to achieve its goal of securing rights. For rights cannot be secured only temporarily; the stability of rights is not secondary to some other content, for stability is the very substance of rights. Without it, rights are only claims, not rights (Hauriou, 1899f, p. 475).

The terminology of objective and subjective law, which Hauriou broadly introduces in his *Leçons*, applies to this distinction of order and justice. Law is objective when it is seen as relating to the social needs and goals, subjective when applied to individual liberty, which allows the social ends to be attained. The subjective element is what properly constitutes the law, and by law (*droit*) here, Hauriou understands, first, rights, but also legislation, as Hauriou says explicitly (1899d, pp. 48–50). Whether subjective or objective law is that which Hauriou aligns with justice instead of order is not perfectly clear; but my reading suggests that subjective law does, since the objective law concerns social ends, as does order.

In his mid-career, Hauriou is still able to say that the whole question of law is enveloped in one imperative: peace must be attained. Earlier, this would have been equivalent to saying order must be attained and this is largely what he means here, too. He expands his thinking to hold that the primary role of law is to pacify conflicts by balancing them; and what balance achieves is order. But now, in saying that social peace is the supreme end of law, he refers to two states of peace: material peace, which is cessation of battles, and peace by law, which is a solution of the profound cause of battle by rules conformed to justice. We must maintain the first at any price, for only with that attained can we then establish the second (1905, p. 150; 1909a, p. 36; 1911a, p. 21).

This attainment of peace realizes a situation of law against the law [*droit contre droit*], for control of conduct by law and control of conduct by morals are not the same, and now even the control by law is manifold. The political sovereignty that attains the material peace is in conflict with the rule of law that establishes justice. Hauriou opines that the rule of law that establishes justice is more perfect, but both are indispensible (1911a, p. 19). The legal system places society and the individual in opposition at first, while collective needs counter the sense of justice. Later, when joined together in practical combinations, the legal system places individual and society back into equilibrium. Social rights are based on the protection of individual rights, and individual rights are based on faith in the institution, which has been proven by its self-limitation. Society then pursues peace, and peace is possible only by justice. The criterion then for deciding which one dominates which, social rights or individual rights, is a changing one: whichever realizes the greater dose of justice. Neither is absolutely dominant (Hauriou, 1909a, pp. 49–50, 64).

When laws conflict should we follow order or justice? "Our position," says Hauriou, is, "every positive law or order of the government is conformed to right order of some kind, and is to be imposed on citizens until it is proven contradictory to 'the rule of law' which is another kind of law" (1911a, p. 14) [*"toute loi positive ou tout ordre de gouvernement sont présumés conformes à une espèce de droit jusqu' à ce qu'ils sont en contradiction avec 'le règle de droit' qui est une autre espèce de droit"*].

The rule of law is a legitimate counterargument to laws because it is itself another kind of law, law as justice. So preliminary discussion of the legality of positive law is senseless; only the perfect clarity of human reason would make this non-anarchical. There can be proof contrary to the presumption of justice owed to positive law; but the presumption must be upheld until then. The source of this presumption lies in Hauriou's theory of legal acts, and more specifically in the conditions surrounding them. Some are conditions of the act—that the matter of the act is a declared will to produce a legal effect and that the form of the act be recognizable procedure. Others are conditions of the agent—that the agent is autonomous, has the capacity for the act, is disciplined, and self-limiting by placing structures and limitations upon the organization of the agent's acts (ibid., pp. 6, 9, 24–28).

In the second *Droit public*, Hauriou refers to the two forms of law as two sources of law, for they both come down to the same thing: written law. These texts then have two sources: custom and command (1916c, p. 27). The positive law is established twice, once when it is formulated and executed by political power, and again when people slowly accept it through a peaceful history by custom. The first is provisory and incomplete, only with the second does law become established and perfect. No formal criterion exists where one stops and the other begins.

A particular criterion can, however, be developed on the occasion of a particular legal question. For example, the superficial level of property law is mere possession, and the foundational level is rights, which are not actual possession but assure and lead to possession (ibid., pp. xx, 389, 390n2, 810–811). Respectively, the two sources relate to objective and subjective law, relevant respectively to things and to persons, to institution and legal personality (ibid., p. 172). They are related closely; Hauriou now describes order as an enduring stage, with a direction inhering to it, bringing it surely to the perfect stage of law (ibid., p. 22).

In an article near the end of Hauriou's career, devoted explicitly to social order and justice in relation to law, he still ranks social order as most important. In a given law, social order is more apparent than justice, often making the text appear formal and arbitrary. What it does accomplish, however, is to give the particularities to any legal system. Justice always acts in the same sense, the natural sense of the conscience and heart. But the intellectual prescriptions of order are categories corresponding with the categories of social relations, making one system of categories much different from another. Justice has no categories, for justice is unitary, unique; it is social orders that are diverse (Hauriou, 1927d, pp. 66–67).

In his final book, the second edition of *Droit constitutionnel*, Hauriou again places order over justice in importance to law. But he ties the sources of order not just to necessity but to several types of autonomy also—some individual autonomy, some belonging to the action of the political authority, and some proper to order itself. In spontaneity of liberty and power is a potential order. Order is a limitation on power and liberty but within its limits, they work spontaneously and autonomously. Their spontaneous tendency is toward order, this direction itself being an aspect of their autonomy. Institutions use their power to limit themselves, and use the need for order as an excuse to tie their own hands. So despite different ends, order and justice move toward each other. Justice is supposed to realize a proportionality among individuals in the enjoyment of what is good, and order is for the sake of assuring stability, rationality being the highest human type of achievement. But order is not possible without some justice, and justice, once established, is the best form of order (1929c, pp. 21, 35, 36, 22n9, 97n10; 1933f, pp. 72–76).

Raising the question of the place of social peace in law, Hauriou once again asserts that law begins not with rules but with particular decisions intended to end strife. But for the first time, he addresses the desirability of doing this. He questions whether an agitated and dangerous life in full political liberty is more advantageous to a country than the stagnation of complete social peace. This alternative has something to be said for it; but in practice, the life of political liberty is exhausting and the people then may aspire to achieve the profound peace of authoritarianism (1929c, p. 195). Hauriou continues to hold out social peace as the most desirable state but, without the development into a just society, "the populace races into slavery" (ibid.) [*"on voit alors les populations se ruer vers la servitude"*].

In his introduction to the study of law Hauriou restates all these themes concerning the social order and justice (1969, pp. 136–137). This double end of law continues to be demanding. Law seeks to realize them; when it does, they become part of law. Law nourishes itself on order and justice and they become its substance. At this late date, Hauriou identifies order and justice with the double origin of rules, *Themis* and *Diké*. He does not make this identification explicitly, but the description of the two makes the correlation clear. *Themis* is the *intra*group origin of law, it stems from the disciplinary power of the father of the family [*paterfamilias*] to distribute the goods to his household as his prerogative. This comes close to the idea of social order, which Hauriou had much earlier linked to familial power. *Diké* is the *inter*group or interpersonal forum, in which the relations of individuals to each other are those of free commerce, the relations of commutative justice. As each takes place in the movement of any society, law must follow them and does so by its sequence of order and justice. Joseph Albert Broderick has an extensive summary, analysis, and application of Hauriou on *Themis-Diké*; he considers it very important and helpful (Broderick, 1967, pp. 168–180; cf. Hauriou, 1929c, pp. 97–98).

The "dialogue" of order and justice again advances by self-limitation of the powers that command before the "sovereignty of subjection," that is its subjects' power to cease being subject (Hauriou, 1969, p. 137). This "transaction" or "compromise" between social order and justice aims for the best available solution, meaning the most justice reasonably attainable at any given moment, which may not correspond well with the ideal maximization of justice in society (Hauriou, 1967, pp. 165, 184). The limitation on justice remains the limits of social peace, of objective and rational solutions. Law cannot begin to do its work, then, until the population has reached its age of reason, whether from normal development or from fatigue at war (Hauriou, 1969, p. 135).

Five

SOCIOLOGICAL METHODOLOGY

1. Introduction

Maurice Hauriou's general dualist method has been pervasive enough to cut across the lines of science and art in law. Dualism is also a characteristic feature of social science, leading it toward both subjective and objective poles. Consequently, this science, while remaining truly scientific, is distinguished from other sciences by being practical and moral in its theory of progress and by being individualist and idealist in its tradition. The matter of social science—sociability—develops in two ways, economic and political, which eventually relate back to the basic social stratum, as we shall see in Chapter Six, on the methodological interplay of law and social sciences.

2. Sociological Dualism

The practical acceptance of dualism present in the universe requires that social science be dualist, not monist. Social science is a science of observation. This is the static factor it shares with other sciences. But it is also a factor in social progress, which makes it peculiar among sciences, which makes it an art. Social data are at the same time acts and facts, acts while being produced and not yet separated from their agent, facts when once separated and eliciting a further act. The acts are on the side of individual liberty, the facts on that of social mechanisms; this is the same dualism introduced by a priori political and moral theories, but Hauriou believes that it can and should be introduced instead by observation in sociology, a posteriori (1896, pp. 27n1; 155; 1912b, p. 11).

These two directions are the objective and the subjective. The objective aspect gives first place to reality independent of individual will; it is social reality realized by and for itself. The subjective aspect considers social reality as projected into the human subject, as realized by human beings and for human beings, according to their willed intentions. The objective study of society is structural and static, an observational study, focused by formal and material causality and relatively atemporal. The subjective approach is functional and dynamic, in view of the constructive tasks of society and so using the category of final causes in a temporally fluid environment (Hauriou, 1896, pp. 34–35, 43).

From the objective view of the individual as a creation of society and the subjective view of the society as a creation of individuals come quite different practical results: no liberty for individuals in the first case and an excessive liberty, a private dream world [*hallucination individuelle*], in the second. For this reason, an absolute and irreducible contradiction is evident between the practical correlates, the collectivist and the individualist systems of society. Both cannot hold the primary place in the study of society. To stipulate only that both must be used is insufficient; we must specify their mode of coexistence (ibid., p. 36).

Hauriou's approach to this duality is a practical one. In practice, we see a mixture of these ideals, and only the logicians of each system demand that the mixture cease on the grounds of a theoretical irreconcilability. The real balance of any moment, however, is one that cannot be transformed by abstract principles, because whenever opposing forces meet we always need to reaffirm the oppositions and to rebalance them in accord with the new situation. From the individual's point of view, either solution might prevail. Since the subjective approach would appear to demand penetration of human consciousness and intentions, which we do not in fact penetrate by our cognition, the scientific law of parsimony would recommend the objective approach. But looking at the nature of social evidence, the call from our unpenetrated awareness [*cri de l'inconscient*], which continually reappears in certain tendencies of society, indicates clearly that society is individualistically oriented. The condition inherent in social science is that it must continue to make law possible. This means that it must progress "in the individualist direction, which is that of law" (ibid., pp. 6, 36–39, 103–104; Hauriou, 1899f, p. 471; 1909a, p. 28) [*"le sens individualiste qui est celui du droit"*].

3. Discipline of Social Science

A. Scientific Discipline

Hauriou considers the study of society truly a scientific task. He means by science what we have seen elsewhere, not a hypothetical science so much as an observational one. He refuses "the ruining of many positive things for the pleasure of reconstructing society hypothetically" (1916c, p. 218) [*"La ruine de beaucoup de choses positives pour le plaisir de reconstruire hypothétiquement la société"*]. He can examine that which is in accord with "the nature of things," but this does not limit him to facts, the objective side. For only material forces are organizations of fact (1907a, pp. xiii, 13–14). The realism of sociology's origins is outmoded, the positivist realism that excluded dealing with any metaphysical data at all. A more mature social science can deal with the positive manifestations of such data (Hauriou, 1912b, pp. 8–9). The energies available for study in social science are chiefly representative ones, those that represent both organic and metaphysical existences. The energy is of the same sort as what it works upon, for the representative knowing in social science represents the beliefs and opinions, the representations, which are the largest portion of social life (Hauriou, 1899d, pp. v, 128, 136).

Because representation in social science is a matter of ideas rather than consciousnesses, it is possible to make society a function of mind without making it subjectively introspective and impenetrable to positive science. Sociology can retain the objectivity of the other sciences, although its object is subjective. Sociology cannot observe mental acts, but it can observe their manifestations (ibid., pp. viii, 42). By reason of this expanded scope social science provides the model for other positive sciences, instead of being less scientific than they are. The sociologist has the advantage over the physiologist, for example; in studying organizations, anything psychic that appears is fit material for sociological, but not for physiological, observation (Hauriou, 1909a, p. 19; 1929c, p. 72). Similarly, the psychological study of human beings focuses on the adaptation of consciousness to mechanism, meaning adaptation of the subjective to the objective. The social viewpoint, however, sees the adaptation of free consciousness to free consciousness, of the subjective to the subjective (Hauriou, 1896, p. 6).

Sociology is scientific precisely because it is open to these dimensions. Hauriou is willing to call only empirical sociology scientific, referring disparagingly to the positive and closed sociology as philosophically determined in scope. As a science, sociology has no need for a universal and thoroughgoing determinism; all it needs is enough determinism for its particular kinds of laws. No science needs more determinism than this relative and varying amount: less of it is needed the more a science's material is vital and spontaneous, and sociology's material is eminently so (Hauriou, 1893c, p. 7).

Whatever determinism sociology needs is satisfied by the category of imitation. Imitation is the disposition among individuals to follow a leader, giving a regularity to facts but with something saved for liberty and discontinuity in the original agents, in those persons of genius who are followed, and in the source of imitation, which lies within spontaneity rather than external, in the environment (ibid.). Imitation is peculiarly a social category: it occurs only in society and society does not occur without it (1896, p. 14). It poses for the sociological researcher a problem in the logic of ideas; for the idea that prevails in society is the one most conformed to the ideal that has formed the society at the start (There is grammatical ambiguity in Hauriou's reference to the ideal *que s'est formé la société*, the ideal which is found as? by? in? society). The deterministic and the idealistic aspects of society, which compose its scientific character, both derive from the process of imitation (1894c, p. 299).

The scientific stature of sociology is secured not just by ideas, however; in society, ideas are ineffectual without business and interests to stabilize them (Hauriou, 1916c, p. 227). The financial and business interests are a transformation of the qualitative and ideal aspects of society into a quantitative scale, and it is these interests that allow a quantitative treatment of the social. To start with mathematical methods in social sciences would be to presume social mechanisms. But Hauriou favors the introduction of quantitative methods once sociology has passed from its infancy. As a matter of prudence, the beginning science would be led awry by a mathematical model; but when experimental observation has allowed quantification to be seen as a transformation of the ideal elements, then it is perfectly permissible (1899d, pp. 8, 17).

The way of treating quantitative aspects of society is not that they be worked out like a problem, but that they be set up as imaginative structures or models to stimulate and stabilize thinking, not to do the work, but to foster the imagination [*non pas opérer mais imaginer*] because such quantitative aspects of society are not accurately measurable, only estimable not so much as measurements, but as objects of appreciation [*non point mésurable mais appréciable*] (ibid., p. 12). Statistics themselves do not prejudice the case, although objectively they must be interpreted to mean that something depends on something else and follows it as its natural consequence. Nonetheless, the subjective interpretation cannot be scientifically disallowed, that a moral reaction produced the effect. The subjective is preferable to the objective in social explanation, but the objective that is the ordinary interpretation of statistical analysis can be used as an exception to this preference by law and social science for their special purposes (Hauriou, 1900b, p. 37). Social science is different from other forms of science in that it is more practical, moral, individualistic, and traditional than the others.

B. Practical Science

In social science, the problem of knowledge is indissolubly tied to the problem of conduct. Human beings know society by science and must act in the society they help to establish. Knowledge cannot help but influence human action in society. "To the extent that science takes hold of its object, it modifies that object" (Hauriou, 1896, p. 28) [*"A mésure donc que la science prend connaissance de son objet, elle le modifie"*]. But in social science, this modification is even stronger than in other sciences, for in social science the study views society as the whole and the individual as the part. In accord with one of Hauriou's scientific laws, the parts act more effectively on molding the whole than that whole on its parts, although this also occurs. So social science, with individuals as the part, gives the social scientist much greater scope than other sciences, for example, biology, psychology, or physiology, wherein individuals are the whole (ibid.).

Equally, then, sociology is more dangerous than other sciences, because more effective. It demands social reform, social science verges toward radical science. Its rise, contemporary to the beginning of Hauriou's career, is for society what adolescence is for the individual. It is a crisis when clarity, with all its possibilities for error and fault as well as for truth and growth, succeeds upon the surety of instinct and tradition (ibid.; Hauriou, 1894d, p. 393).

To be put to social use, to be an action, social science must have a content appropriate to this nature. It cannot have as its object only objective facts, the theoretical way the individual stands with the group. It must include the subjective reaction, the feeling, stated in terms of "me and the others." It cannot have as its content knowledge of the past; the reconciliation of liberty and organism needed in social science is not just an historical one, but a present one. The content cannot be hypothetical states of affairs (for example, the objection that if social sacrifice were fully realized, then no violence would be left to be balanced by it) (Hauriou, 1896, pp. 5, 15, 196; 1899d, p. 101). Fact and theory are distinctions irrelevant to the content needed by social science.

Instead, the focus of social science is not upon truth but upon value. Falsehoods can be quite socially useful for a greater or lesser period of time, even if, on other grounds, we presume that they cannot ultimately be useful. Social science concerns not the truth or falsehood in systems of facts or ideas, but their social consequences, their power to bring people together (1896, pp. 26, 256). This is the sense of value in this science: that a "bad" fact is not a contradictory one but an inefficacious one. Thus, Hauriou can call his social science a positivism to the second power, because it is disinterested in positivism itself as a system and in its contradictions. His brand of positivism admits the good and the bad, and admits that they are in contradiction, but refuses to dub them good or bad on account of their being in contradiction (ibid., p. 27).

This line of reasoning raises the question regarding facts, "useful for what?" The goal of society is progress, and progress is identified with an increase in "social matter," sociability. (I will return to this point later in this chapter.) The goal is neither an increase in organization nor in accumulation (ibid., p. 23). Social science, in attaining this goal, makes a claim no other science can. For example, biology makes no claim to make life, but social science does increase life, social life (ibid., p. 39). On the other hand, organization is not irrelevant to social life; organized society goes beyond material peace and public order, which are negative ends and the precondition only for society, to the positive end of some social work to be done. This further stage spiritualizes society (Hauriou, 1916c, p. 53). Hauriou summarizes these tasks of social science: after the excessive socialism is used up in fighting its battles:

> it pertains to science coldly to discount these results and to indicate to men of intelligence the positions they ought to assume and the agitation they ought to stir up from now on, to act peaceably toward the best possible solutions. (1896, p. 390) [*Il appartient à la science d'escompter froidement les résultats et d'indiquer aux esprits sages, des maintenant, les positions qu'il convient de prendre, l'agitation qu'il convient de créer pour agir pacifiquement dans le sens des solutions possibles.*]

The recommendations in this revolutionary program contain the negative end of peace and the positive end of tasks, together with the active involvement Hauriou found inseparable from social science. We can judge events only on practical considerations: how well they serve to reconcile, group together, solidify, and develop the individuals and their group (ibid., pp. 25–26; Hauriou,1899f, p. 471).

C. Moral Science

Hauriou's escape from the rigor of exclusive mechanism in social science leaves him free to make sociology a moral science, for it is the monistic rigor of logical explanation due to a presumption of mechanism that excludes all contradiction of good and evil. If only the impersonal interplay of likenesses (Gabriel Tarde) or differences (Émile Durkheim) or even both together made human society, then no anti-social acts or doctrines could exist. But such acts and doctrines do exist, these work back in turn to manifest the presence of a level other than the mechanistic in human society. Likenesses and differences among individuals are not simply present; they are also put into service for or against society (Hauriou, 1894c, pp. 294–295; 1896, p. 15).

Social science cannot help but pronounce upon conduct; by reason of a mode of conduct, the life of nations possesses a scientific character, making possible a science not only social but also moral (1896, p. 29). Hauriou refuses to entertain complaints that conservatives raised during the origins of sociology, namely, that social facts are not observable, regular, or determined. In place of this hopeless way of preserving tradition, Hauriou asserted that, instead of sociology being unable to cope with moral data because it was observational, sociology on the contrary is required to embrace moral data precisely because it is observational. The impartial observation of facts has required social science to recover the moral questions and surrender moral indifference (Hauriou, 1894c, pp. 294–295). Because social science can remain scientific while becoming moral, Hauriou can say in mid-career, "I have tried to establish the rights of traditional moral beliefs *in the name of sociology itself*" (1916c, p. xxiv) [*"J'ai essayé d'établir les droits des croyances morales traditionnelles au* nom de la sociologie elle-même*"*].

How does this sociology, which is a moral science, function? It is not positivist, but it is observational. It observes that people living in society have moral feelings; it is not concerned with the fact that an isolated individual has such feelings and follows them, for this is the arena of religious and philosophical moral studies. The feelings of social people are manifested by indignation and approval; these responses are organized into moral ideals, which can in turn react upon their minds, for example, in systems of laws. These manifestations are *sui generis* in each society; they are useful for preserving it. But simply from the presence of this moral manifestation in a society, we can derive neither the fact that its moral ideal is limited to this society only, nor on the other hand, that it can be validly extended to all humanity. (Hauriou's phrase expresses the ambiguity even grammatically: "We know not if it can extend beyond one" (1894c, pp. 299–300) [*"On ne sait pas s'il ne le dépasse pas"*].) We can, however, make a comparative study of moral ideals in various civilizations, correlating those ideals with some judgment of the degree of development of the civilizations, creating a hierarchy from our results. The criterion of "higher" is notoriously judged by skeptics as an opening difficult to close; Hauriou handles it by couching the criterion as "a problem of logic." The problem is how to have the most life together with the most stability. The life in question here is individual life, the life of persons in the society. The moral sociology, which by comparative study will yield this answer, is social in origin, social in means, but individual in end. Because of this final characteristic, it can serve as a source for systems of law, since law depends upon individualistic presumptions (ibid.).

Social science is a moral science; society is a moral fact, and its essential problem is the problem of good and evil. The product of social science should be rules of conduct. The rules must be socially profitable and morally valid; one demand implies the other. The source of this optimistic conclusion is not itself optimistic. Time, patience, courage, and striking illumination of knowledge are lacking to society, perhaps; but gradually, societies build and secure social and political structure:

> That which has assured final success is this consoling reality, one without which there would have been nothing, namely that the good is more coherent than the evil; the evil is numerous, but the good is coherent. (Hauriou, 1923d, p. vi)[*Ce qui a assuré le succès final, c'est cette réalité consolante et sans laquelle il n'y aurait rien, à savoir que le bien est plus cohérent que le mal, le mal est nombreux, mais le bien est cohérent.*]

The condition upon which sociology will yield this result is that it admits the existence of a powerful social tradition containing the revelation of a moral system, and that it admits the linkage between the progress of civilization and the development of this tradition. This is what Hauriou calls "social revelation," "the revelation of rules for conduct by the moral and religious traditions of humanity as it progresses" (1916c, pp. xxii–xxiii) [*"la révélation des règles de la conduite par les traditions morales et religieuses de l'humanité progressive"*]. He considers this in no way an appeal to divine revelation; social revelation simply applies the maxim, "judge the tree by its fruits" (ibid.) [*"on juge l'arbre à ses fruits"*]. This type of revelation is possible because of the peculiar nature of socially available data. Social objects are effective and have worth primarily because people believe they have worth. Moral science is the detailing of what we believe to have worth, and for this reason, social science is subordinate to moral science (Hauriou, 1894c, p. 298). For instance, it matters little whether what is felt to be freely done really is the work of will instead of the result of mechanisms, because in social dimensions, the belief itself is sufficient to have effects that far outweigh any theoretically correct answer (Hauriou, 1896, p. 156). The moral science of sociology, then, has two levels of observation: the observation of organic and mechanical phenomena and the observation of the social representation [*représentative sociale*], the beliefs and knowledge that are current in society (Hauriou, 1899d, p. 163). As we have already heard Hauriou say, social science as knowledge does itself change society.

To introduce the moral dimension of sociology, Hauriou would be willing to have two schools of sociology exist, one with morality as an object and one without, as a last resort (1894d, p. 391). But the more likely result would be for the unity—not of social science, but science in general—to be broken, such that henceforth, some sciences would deal with morals (sociology among these) and others would not. This second state of affairs is not startling as a suggestion; many others have made it. What is startling is the immediately following third possibility, which, in the light of Hauriou's previous statements that social science is the paradigm for other sciences, seems more likely to have his approval. The third suggestion for integrating sociology as a moral science is that unity of science will neither be destroyed nor will it be preserved on the basis of an exclusion of moral concerns. Instead, the unity of science may arise based on moral concern in science, since even the physical and natural sciences do consider moral matters in a fashion proper to themselves, for example, decline, death, control, or progress (Hauriou, 1894c, p. 294n1).

From sociology as a moral science to sociology as an individualistic idealism is an easy passage when two final statements of Hauriou on the subject are conjoined: "The moral precept of sociology is 'be human beings'; it is not 'build a social machine'" (ibid., p. 321) [*"Le précepte moral de la sociologie est: 'soyons hommes'; il n'est pas: 'fabriquons une machine sociale'"*]. But the fundamental postulate of the social order is that human beings are spiritual (Hauriou, 1927g, p. v).

D. Individualist Science

From this individualist point of view, Hauriou explicitly claims that his social science is not at odds with non-deterministic characteristics: "I have thus reconstituted an individualism by social science alone" (1899f, p. 473) [*"J'ai donc reconstitué un individualisme par la seule science sociale"*]. Individualism depends for its justification in social science upon no external input, as from religion or philosophy. Even more clearly, he connects the historical fortunes of individualism in social science to this assertion: "Thus, a little sociology leaves the individualist tradition, and much sociology returns to it" (Hauriou, 1912b p. 11) [*"Ainsi, un peu de sociologie éloigne de la tradition individualiste et beaucoup de sociologie ramène"*]. Hauriou urges sociologists to believe in the sure instinct of the mechanists in social science; they attack the state, law, religion, and morals. Each of these is dependent upon individualism, which illustrates the importance of the doctrine in the heart of social science (Hauriou, 1896 p. 41).

Human society must be explained in terms of human beings; we must presume that they are its social finality (ibid., p. 18). Hauriou appears to favor Herbert Spencer's explanation of this fact on the grounds that the human species precedes human society, and therefore, human reason does also, making society a product of the human psychology. Hauriou accuses contemporary sociologists of reversing the roles, although he would not go on with Spencer to classify sociology as a branch of psychology (1923d, p. 44). Society lies somewhere between the natural given and the artificial product, it escapes both categories. Society is a product of evolution; but since this evolution is human evolution, the products and the evolution are self-made by human beings. Society, then, develops human nature and human individuality (Hauriou, 1896 p. 13).

The source of social energy is the individual person, just as in physics it is the individual atom. In social science, the rigidity of organic mechanisms and of intellectual logic play a part, yielding abstracted facts; but only the individual action under the spontaneity of the individual will can attach facts to existence, or existence to facts (ibid., pp. 115–116; Hauriou, 1899d, p. 34). Collectivism finds only the reaction, subsequent to the truly originating action, the individual's. Hauriou's social doctrine, which he calls an individualist pessimism [*pessimisme individualiste*], unlike collectivism, does not tamper with given facts. His doctrine does not divorce the social order from the fault-ridden individual members, leaving it open to unlimited progress. Instead, it continues to possess the same deficits as its individual source.

The distinctions of just from unjust and of good from evil are the death of any exclusively social theories of law and morals. These distinctions in the social climate revert to the individual person (Hauriou, 1896 pp. xi, 42; 1911a, p. 38). Nowhere else as much as in social science, do individual persons appear in their full potency for creating the changes. Other sciences see human beings as the whole with organic parts, which have the most profound effect upon them, while in social science, individuals are the part and consequently are the source of its variations. So even though the first step in sociology is to look at social facts without considering that social facts are the acts of human beings, the last step to which this process leads is to see them as the sentiments, concepts, and wills of human beings (Hauriou, 1896, pp. 5–6, 28–29).

The relationship of the social and the individual in science is complex. Individual evidence leads to collectivism; it is only collective evidence that leads to individualism. Individualism as an absolute starting point is dangerous; it misinterprets social situations and neglects collective reality. Individualism can correctly be the only conclusion derived from social research based on evidence (ibid., pp. ix–xi). Social science offers the only valid and non-contradictory support for the individual. It insists on the reality of social existence, and thus provides the security individual existence needs. For example, to justify individual property by individual labor is futile, for labor is essentially collective carried out in relation to other people. But the stability and repose of socially recognized possession of property gives the security required for individual liberty (Hauriou, 1899f, p. 476).

Thus, Hauriou's proposed defense of the individual's liberty before the exclusive social power of an overweening state, is an essentially social project. First, unionization [*syndicalisme*] must be extended through full liberty of association; then, groups must agitate for decentralized public control and for political representation of special interest groups. (Hauriou does not view this process as violence, but as the only alternative to violence.) Once achieved, this must be made international in scope, for positive society of the market is not a territorially conditioned unity in the way a political unity is. Only out of this is the state to be defined (as "political unity of the metaphysical social fabric"), defined by its constant struggle as an active defense against religious and economic power groups (Hauriou, 1896, pp. 391–395). No longer unique, it can no longer oppress the individual's liberty.

E. Idealist Tradition

The individualist unity Hauriou claims his social science has provided is due to the ideal element among the modes of existence it attributes to social phenomena, namely, movement, representation of movement, and direction of movement. Idea increasingly comes to dominate action; but idea is the individual element, relating to the individual mind, while action is the collective aspect, accomplishable only by groupings (1899f, p. 472).

By the same token, social science must be idealist equally as much as social action because it is practical and moral. As such, its effects can be disastrous if it is wrong; so its method cannot be hypothetical. It requires certitude, and certitude of all the facts, not of a selective few only. Its directives are total, concerning the whole range of practice. Its certitudes must concern even objectively and individually unobservable sentiments, those that are subjective and unconscious. These sentiments of society are observable only through collective evidence. This collective evidence is tradition (Hauriou, 1896, pp. viii, 29–31, 33).

This social revelation cannot be supplied even by internal observation of the individual, for the unconscious is invisible even to introspection carried out by consciousness. Social science cannot rest on the criterion of individual evidence as other sciences do, on what appears evident to the scientist inside his rational precautions. Rather, in social matters, the unanimity of belief is the authority, for society is felt, thought, and willed by human beings (ibid., pp. 30–31). Even for persons to know themselves, since they are in part unconscious, too, society must reveal itself. "For the human being to know itself, and society as well, society reveals itself to itself" (ibid.) [*"Ainsi que l'homme se connait, de même la société, elle se révèle à elle-même"*].

The truth of the social order is revealed by the idealist tradition. This tradition, namely, the tradition of sacrifice for the sake of ideas, is needed for progress. But since progress is identified with life, "logically this truth ought to be revealed by life" (Hauriou, 1899f, p. 473) [*"Logiquement cette vérité doit se révéler par la vie"*]. This idealist tradition, what Tarde had called the the categoreal patrimony of societies [*fonds catégorique des sociétés*], is an ensemble of traditional beliefs, religious dogmas, artistic ideals, moral precepts, ethical principles, and legal positions, which a society must admit or fail to achieve its successful establishment (Hauriou, 1896 pp. 33–35).

The elements in the tradition that we should prefer are those that have the characteristics of universality and symbolism; universal because, in practical social matters, beliefs are what have the real power—proof. The most universal are capable of the widest spread, have the most power, and thus have the most proof. They must also be symbolic; they must indicate a correspondence between the social truth and the intimate nature of human beings. Insofar as society is the synthesis of the activity performed by individuals, the social atoms, it is also in some manner the image of human individuals (ibid., p. 34). The persistent endurance of beliefs embodied in tradition is, however, a more primary criterion than these qualifying characteristics.

These traditional beliefs must be detailed by social science. It might appear contradictory that beliefs and rules of conduct be formulated while being unconscious, but even formulated in that sphere, they always imply a mystery, an unexplained imperative. They begin as the privileged intuition of a seer shining upon consciousness. If the seer were to disappear, the intuitions would become unknown again but for social preservation. Belief corresponds to the unconscious sentiments of the group; once the believing community is formed, it acts as an attraction and an authority to others (ibid., p. 32).

The use of social revelation, however, must be limited. As social revelation becomes a consciousness, once recognized, conscious social revelation must make consciousness prevail over unconsciousness. We cannot appeal to unconscious social revelation against the light of individual evidence. The unconscious must remain subsidiary. There cannot be formal contradiction; social revelation of the subjective side of social science cannot be in contradiction to objective observation. Consciousness is more comprehensive than reason, and so cannot renounce its right to control and synthesize both sources of social science. What contradiction does appear, such as between the pessimist viewpoint of social revelation and the optimist viewpoint of positive science, the individualist and the socialist points of view respectively, must be due to some tragedy. This is the chief point of revelation by society that Hauriou insists upon: the Fall interpreted according to evolutionary theory. He will only postulate Fall because of a contradiction that is not justified but is exercisable (ibid., pp. x, 33). He refuses to posit religious definitions or explanations for it in his social science. Even in one of his allegedly philosophical articles, he says of his relating of the natural law and the human species, "rightly understood, I am trying to make this restoration not as a theologian, but as a sociologist accustomed to the exigencies of the positive method" (Hauriou, 1933a, p. 27) [*"Bien entendu, nous n'entreprendrons pas cette restitution en théologien, mais en sociologue habitué aux exigences de la méthode positive"*].

4. Social Matter

Hauriou says that for social science to look—as the psychological school does—for a unique, essential social fact is an error. Such practice focuses on consciousness and ignores what Hauriou believes is crucial: that "body comes first." His preferred method qualifies as social all the facts produced in society as long as those facts are related to the group or to the idea of the group (1896 p. 302).

On the other hand, looking for the material proper to social science to map out or graph its events in physical space is also incorrect; for although the same social facts succeed each other and can be placed sequentially, peculiar social fact exists that is unique and unrepeatable: the event of social change, not as one event in a series, but as human input to the modification of the social state (Hauriou, 1899d, p. 11).

The object of social science is not political organisms. True, all social matter is organized; but to make social science the study of social forms, institutions, and organs is an error. Structure is key but secondary. Individuals are in the first place in society, their relations are more important than organizations. We must then visualize society without specification into any of its forms (Hauriou, 1896, pp. 4, 16; 1894d, p. 394). As common to all its organized forms, social matter must have potentialities of all the developed forms, not just one of them (Hauriou, 1894c, p. 301).

Herbert Spencer's law of complexity is an attention to social differences; the real oneness of society becomes clearer, for Spencer, as accidental likenesses are specialized off, then developed off into coordinate disciplines and then organized back into the whole. Auguste Comte and Tarde stressed social likeness; Hauriou agrees that similarities among individuals greatly enhance the strength of society. But human difference and human likeness of themselves fail to constitute social matter; since both are animal conditions; neither organization nor propagation explains the uniqueness of human society (Hauriou, 1896, pp. 14, 48–50). The higher the stature a society possesses, the less regular and the more discontinuous are its repetitions (Hauriou, 1894c, p. 302).

Even attention to action as the social phenomena is wrong. Action is abstract: it loses the human being, the concrete agent. It is not ultimate: for actions, in turn, must be defined as modifications of social matter; social matter determines the actions, rather than actions determining it. It is mechanistic: it reduces matter to phenomena, and phenomena to movement. All these approaches are legitimate, but not exclusive or basic (Hauriou, 1896 p. 2).

The specification of a social matter as the object of social science is, however, the most significant factor in defining social science. Giving it a matter means giving it a source for development. Hauriou goes about this by inventorying what elements are present in society, and then combining them (ibid., pp. 1, 4). Patent from the start is that a societal remainder [*residu social*] exists, which we cannot explain away by individuality; it is a resistant remainder [*residu réfractaire*]. It develops in and for itself; with nothing decided from outside in some universal way. It is an impersonal and objective collectivity. It is equally as real as individual reality, and eventually must be combined with it (Hauriou, 1899gf p. 467). Hauriou holds that a traditional definition of social life fits evolutionary theory perfectly; that society is the highest life is true now and remains true progressively, something that transcends psychic life. It reconciles the individual self in its unity, as a consciousness, to others like itself (1896, p. 6).

Succinctly, social science is the science of social matter. Social matter is society, or more correctly, the social state of being, which Hauriou defines as "a mode of existence in which the human group and the human individual are reconciled and in which people feel them to be reconciled" (ibid., pp. 4–5) [*"un mode d'existence en qui se concilient et en qui les hommes sentent se concilier le groupe humain et l'individualité humain"*].

This is the definition of the unorganized social matter. Hauriou defines organized matter as "a whole whose parts are in order or aspire to put themselves in order" (1916c, p. 9) [*"un tout dont les parties sont en ordre ou aspirent à se mettre en ordre"*], or as "a collective difference which brings itself about and reaches a kind of individuality" (1896, p. 333) [*"une différence collective qui se réalise et parvient à une sorte d'individualité"*]. The second definition takes up the viewpoint of the group's form, its function, since the difference in this form can be called an organization only because that difference provokes joint effort and action. Hauriou describes the form of a group curiously, in view of traditional usage. He describes its form as its material element, what comes first in them. By identifying this with function or end, a spiritual element as he admits, the material and the spiritual aspects of society are evidently closely tied in the very foundation (ibid., p. 340).

The close union of human beings and the exchange of their services with the goal of a common good cannot be called anything but society; the converging efforts and parallel action make society come about. It is a situation that is social [*pro socio*], a compromise that constitutes the basis of every society (Hauriou, 1899a, pp. ii, 46, 47n1). This develops from sociability [*sociabilité*]; sociability is a fact of cohabitation, ultimately dependent upon the fixity of the human species (Hauriou, 1899f, p. 470; cf. 1933a, pp. 32–35). It is produced by will internal to the group, and so the finality of this social existent should not be ignored in studying it, as Hauriou believes it might be in studying the individual human physical being. The motive for society is, at its most basic, to exist together [*d'être ensemble*]; but in terms of this, a group cannot be picked out and characterized. It is on the same level as historical facts, which are organized only later by the student into a unity, for example, migrations and wars; the unity that gives it existence is not understood. So for any society, something objective, an external end is needed: a philanthropic work or a commercial activity or a role to play, or at the very least, to live together in some particular circumstances [*de vivre ensemble dans de certains conditions*], which is adequate albeit amorphous (Hauriou, 1898, pp. 130–131). No society is founded without such an end, and it must be an announced end (although not a statutory one), since the society must remain faithful to it. The purpose eventually forms a closed circle outside of which there are only antisocial acts (Hauriou, 1900d, p. 334).

If the end must be announced, the feeling of solidarity need not be acute or explicit. Only the sentiment of a group, not the awareness of individuals within it, is necessary. "What the ego finds facing him is not a collection of individuals, but a collectivity, an ensemble" (Hauriou, 1896, pp. 7–8) [*"Ce que le moi trouve en face de lui à ce point de vue, ce n'est pas une collection d'individus, c'est une collectiveité, c'est-à-dire, un ensemble"*]. Its energy, the energy that makes it, is generated by the mere fact of being together. The fact of fraternity is exciting enough for individuals to stabilize and maintain it; so in some sense, this fraternity is itself the social matter (ibid., pp. 20, 48n1). On the other hand, and complementarily, the drive for equality is the agent for the progress of the social matter; the passion provoked to achieve this is the motivating force (ibid., p. 45).

Both of these sentiments on the part of member individuals are necessary to society, for society of itself has no power of creation, only of inertia. For this reason, Hauriou finds unworkable the ideal of practical positivism to exclude enthusiasm, and to run the human social machine more efficiently, on a minimum of energy. Excluding passion and suppressing enthusiasm makes society impossible (1896, p. 20; 1933g, p. 94). This enthusiasm and the will that it is rationalized to equate, are constant only by an artificial means, by the agreement of all the individuals. But the agreement is not arbitrary, though artificial, for acceptance by the individuals of the end is absolutely necessary for social survival (Hauriou, 1898, p. 136). Progress depends upon the stimulus of enthusiasm, and progress is the most important thing to know in social science (Hauriou, 1896, p. 24).

5. Differentiation in Social Science

Hauriou combines social matter with its structural organization to consider what he calls social fabric [*le tissu social*], a distinguishable configuration in society (ibid., p. 3). These three social fabrics are refinements of social matter. The positive fabric is of the material order in comparison to the other two;

there human beings exist and organize to pursue concrete interests, economic and partly political. This is the origin of societies; they are created from this fabric. The other two fabrics, the metaphysical or state [*étatique*] and the religious, are of the spiritual order; being of the realm of sacrifice and ideas, they do not create society but only redeem it from contradictions within it. The metaphysical fabric of societies is a part of the political society, that part which is idea-directed. It is not the nation, and neither is it the government; but it is the fabric wherein state governs the nation.

Unlike the religious fabric, the metaphysical is only human; because it is so, it must use power to achieve ends. The use of power is contradictory to its rational character (hence, it is called metaphysical). Because of this contradiction within itself, it must aim beyond itself to achieve even the human perspectives and goals it sets for itself. The religious fabric has a source of power beyond the human for use in organizing society, and so it is of use in enabling the metaphysical to reach the properly human ends. The positive fabric has no institutions that are properly its own and independent of the other two, which redeem the positive. The spiritual characteristics of the metaphysical fabric are that it operates in an abstract, reasoned, discursive, and consciously critical fashion. The religious fabric's spiritual characteristics, on the contrary, are to be concrete, instinctive, unquestioned, and traditional. The concrete nature of the religious fabric appears in its reliance upon land and social class structures, while the abstractly idealistic and fictive movement of the metaphysical fabric makes the introduction of money, credit and the state appropriate to it (ibid., pp. 197–200, 204, 211, 227–228).

A. Social Matter and Political Unity

The loose use of "social and the political fabric" are two states of the same social matter. Anything that unites people is a fabric, is social even if it is not political. Sociologists often confuse social groups and political unities. However, not all social relations are political. Political relations are more limited than social (ibid., pp. 295–296). It is not political unities but social matter that counts most in social science, for the element of progress is not in the political unity but in the fabric. Political unity is a necessary reaction to insure the preservation of acquired likenesses, but it does not have its own principle of movement. Rather, "political unity is a certain form given to a pre-existent social fabric, as a second stage of organization added to the fabric's organization" (ibid., pp. 297; also 300) [*"L'unité politique est une certaine forme donnée à un tissu social préexistant, comme un second étage d'organisation surajouté à l'organisation du tissu"*].

A constant internal struggle ensues between social matter and political unity, for the political is concerned to "run" the social while not destroying its supra-political drive. The social is indeterminate, unlimited, and supraterritorial, while the political unity must be defined, limited, and territorial. One person can belong to many different social groups, but to only one exclusive political group of any single kind. The fundamental reason for these differences is that the social fabric that is not political is built upon division into groups by the specialization of work upon the different and competing tasks a society needs done in order to thrive. The political unity cuts across dividing lines, making of a people a single whole sufficient unto itself (ibid., pp. 297–300).

Every social fabric can achieve political unity; all three social fabrics can do so at once. Thus, political unity is not limited to the metaphysical order. For example, corresponding to the three social fabrics can be political nations, political states, and political theocracies. On the other hand, there can be non-political groupings at each fabric: companies, literary movements, communities of the elect. In addition, some groupings can confuse the political and non-political at each fabric: pressure groups, corporative states, established churches (ibid., p. 298). Sometimes, however, Hauriou seems to use "social" to mean not the matter of society, but that unity of positive fabric that is economic. I will offer a treatment of the distinction resulting between political and economic entities shortly.

B. Political Science

Hauriou believed that he was the first to see the true nature of political and of economic science because no one previously had based them upon the *équilibre* of powers (1909a, p. 25). "Politics is defined as both the science and art of balancing power" (1916c, p. 52) [*"La politique doit être définie comme étant à la fois la science et l'art des équilibres de pouvoir"*]. The end of political persons is to work for stability and good functioning of government, and for the maintenance and development of national unity. Their means is the balancing of powers. This artistic means is, as in every science of an art, the object of political science (ibid.). The criterion for this balancing is whether the balancing neutralizes or energizes the powers balanced. The "divide and rule" maxim can, then, be a sign of either good or bad politics. To divide and thus weaken powers is a destructive politics. But on the other side, we can divide powers by balancing them, thereby creating a social organization. In practice, we cannot avoid attempting to balance powers and create social organization. This, for Hauriou, is *the* point of view in political science (1909a, pp. 25–26). He adopts Comte's definition of a political fact: the reaction of the whole on the parts (1902b, p. 358).

Hauriou refuses to place all political institutions on the same level under the pretext that in all, we find the same common traits. He finds that method sterile; good scientific method requires distinctions be made where they can be. There are resemblances that give political unity to a group of political institutions, but there are also differences (1916c, p. 303).

C. Political and Economic Unity

As we have seen, Hauriou often uses the social or the non-political when he means economic. These are two degrees of solidarity, two forms of society. The political order is that of juxtaposition, as in an enclosure of two contiguous inheritances; it is called *cohabitation*, and obliges us negatively, only to abstain from certain acts that go beyond our rights and damage others. The economic order, or *collaboration*, obliges us to perform positive acts toward the others (1899a, pp. 52–53). Political power is the power of authority to relate and order, the end being identifiable with power. Economic power is the power of special interest to affect or accomplish something (1892a, pp. 5–7). The political order is material for objective law; for example, constitutional and public law. Economic phenomena find individuals (physical or moral) facing one another, and are subjective phenomena being material for commercial and administrative law more properly (1911b, p. 215).

In the *équilibre* of the political order, each power strives for supremacy, while the economic powers strive for equality, the static balance of an intermediary between two extremes. Contracts may always be unequal, but their binding force can be explained only by reference to the equality of parties (Hauriou, 1909a, pp. 23, 33). In political society, people are held together inside the same group by their submission to the discipline of the same institution or by their participation in the same ceremonial procedures. By contrast, in the economic society people are held in relation to one another by their collaboration in the common work of satisfying human needs (Hauriou, 1916c, p. 174). If people in political life are unequal in authority, they are equated in the application of laws; they have equality of rights. But the economic order envisages individuals as unequal in terms of the profits and debits they incur before the community; in that, no equality of fact exists (Hauriou, 1923b, p. 722). The differences appear even in the nature of the corresponding disciplines: politics is the science and the art of balancing power, while economics is the science of balancing production and distribution in view of society's economic organization (Hauriou, 1909a, pp. 25, 32).

The ultimate difference is the kind of interest involved, public or private. Political society is disinterested and not profit-directed, while economic interest is both. Both render a service to society, but one is interested (Hauriou, 1927a, p. 762). The political and public life is the direct governing of people under sanctions of law; economic and private life is indirect governing of people under the menace of needs. The public protects the private, and the private nourishes the public (Hauriou, 1923d, p. 146).

Hauriou further explicates public life as having three phases: concentration of legal restraint in powers, which dominate free individuals; the transformation of these powers into services to these same individuals; and a disinterested passion of both for the public life itself as good. A public is "a crowd composed of individuals who can think together" [*"une foule com-*

posée d'individus pouvant penser ensemble"]. It is an area for discussion and opinion; "the essential value of a public is speech, language" [*"Le bien essentiel du public est le parole, le verbe"*]. It is a free space in which individuals feel unenclosed, whereas in private life, individuals know very well that they are inescapably imprisoned (1916c, pp. 396–404).

Hauriou may appear to evaluate public existence more highly than private; this is partly so. All sorts of opinions, including economic ones, become more firmly fixed in political opinion, legislative and that of political parties, where opinion finds its stabilizing location (1912d, pp. 64–65). Although neither order is viable without the other, the economic society is at the service of the political institution when the economic society constitutes a community within the political institution (1916c, p. 176). The factor that conserves the slow, uniform movement of a social order is not economic division of labor, but its political organization (1929c, pp. 71–72). Economic needs do precede the political needs; but the economic are not on this account superior. The development of ideas and the spiritual civilization flowing from it are conditioned by political, not economic factors, by political regimes, which temper the excessive domination due to primitive economic needs, thereby giving freedom to the spirit (1923d, pp. 617–618).

No one becomes part of a community to be a consumer or a taxpayer [*contribuable*]. The essential political fact for persons consists in this, to exist together, to live together, to inhabit together [*être ensemble, vivre ensemble, cohabiter*]. This life in common is the end, but power is the means whereby it is realized; these are the two axes of politics. On the contrary, the essential economic fact is collaboration in the production of wealth; production of wealth is the end, cooperation in work is the means.

Among the ancients, public life was dominant; Hauriou admits that in the modern world, economics appears to dominate public life. He refuses to accept this picture, however, because the question, "how can we arrange to live together?" always leads to the question, "how can we arrange to work together?" Work is not natural to human beings; so the organization of repose comes first. In normal times, the provision of subsistence is accomplished by social arrangements, and individuals can direct their attention to arranging their lives. In the modern world, especially, where the paternalistic relations are less dominant, community life narrows down to a community of inhabitants [*habitants*]. This is a quality that is equal for all, while that of taxpayer is not. Sometimes the two are not even conjoined, much less identical. Someone can be a non-paying resident, or a paying non-resident. In sum, inhabitants live together and thereby constitute the city, while economic persons only try at most to gain subsistence for the city, a secondary function (Hauriou, 1900e, pp. 222–224). Above all, this is true of the state:

> The state is not an association for working together in the production of riches; it is simply a certain manner for people *to be together*, to live to-

> gether, this is the essential political fact. (Hauriou, 1900a, pp. 416–417) [*L'état n'est pas une association pour travailler ensemble à la production des richesses, il est seulement pour les hommes une certaine manière* d'être ensemble, *de vivre ensemble, ce qui est essentiellement le fait politique.*]

This is, however, only one side of a social situation in which the economic society also has a certain form of preeminence. Economists usually consider economic phenomena as independent of political forms, although economic society is still social (Hauriou, 1896 p. 295). It succeeds to political idealism in dominance in the state. Political idealism was needed to begin the state, but only economic realism can continue it, because idealism, not a merely vacuous promise, is a promise of the real (Hauriou, 1927g, p. vii). Even the formation of political ideas depends on economics: the politician who proposes a social idea cannot fully comprehend its implications without confronting it with the economic reality of governing or forming institutions (Hauriou, 1907a, p. iii).

The political order by itself is non-individual and does not allow an environment for the fullest individual development (Hauriou, 1899f, p. 470). The economic order allows and demands relations among individuals for the satisfaction of the needs of life, making the true economic quality of the citizen to be that of a consumer (Hauriou, 1909a, p. 2; 1923d, p. 146). This does not reduce the citizen to a material mouth to be filled, for the economic order is broader than the merely financial, embracing also the political ordering of the satisfaction of needs (Hauriou, 1899a, pp. 4, 6). Both the economic and the political orders are "powers," energies of individual people who pursue their advantages. But neither is only a potential, an energy in an impersonal sense, irrespective of human reference. Accumulative material energies are only one form of potential. Other forms are energy from physical position, energy of tension between dialectically opposed poles, and the energy each individual can bring into play of his own spontaneity in will. Each of these potentials is political as much as it is economic, so economic energy as material cannot be opposed against spiritual and humane power (Hauriou, 1899d, p. 52).

With Karl Marx, Hauriou holds that economic phenomena precede political phenomena; his "body first" principle dictated that. He ranks economic phenomena as the most socially important; he says they constitute the axis of the whole system; political phenomena are at their service. Economic phenomena are not materialistic, however. On this point, Hauriou differs from Marx's historical materialism. The economic factor appears more spiritual than the political factor because economic facts are not dominated by the pure mechanism of the means of production, but by economic ends—wealth, property, and services:

> The economic factor appears to be more spiritual than the political factor . . . in sum, we conceive political economy to be dominated by social economy, which is the finalist point of view on life. (1916c, p. 108, 108n1) [*Le facteur économique nous paraît plus spiritualiste que le facteur politique . . . en somme, nous concevons l'economie politique comme dominé par l'économie sociale, ce qui est le point de vue finaliste de la vie.*]

With public and private life each having its dominant viewpoint and sphere, discriminating between the two becomes difficult. The fundamental distinction is based on the distinction between general interest and particular interest: "But nothing is more elastic than the notion of general interest" (ibid., p. 572) [*"Or rien de plus élastique que la notion de l'intérêt général"*]. Eventually, private life becomes more dependent upon continuous and regular public services, because only such services can furnish the security individuals need. The process seems inexorable: the more a political community, dissociating itself from economic society, transforms itself into a legal community, it must, for its protection and support, create a bulky administrative and fiscal equipment. This is nothing but an economic enterprise used increasingly in the free market. Once the free market has a lesser volume of business due to legal regulation, economic power has begun to become one with political power. Hauriou takes his analysis to be nearly fatalistic, since it is the only way to bring guarantees to every phase of people's lives (ibid., pp. 372, 574). Hauriou much earlier had expressed that when approximation of legal to economic fabrics happened, eventually a conflict would arise between general and particular economic interests, and the particular economic interests would win out, creating a dictatorship, another manifestation of individualist pessimism [*pessimisme individualiste*] in social science (1899c, p. 490).

Six

METHODOLOGICAL INTERPLAY OF LAW AND SOCIAL SCIENCE

1. Introduction

In a 1905 text, Maurice Hauriou summarizes the methodological interrelationships in his work that this chapter studies:

> All social institutions are painted over with law, but underneath this covering of paint they have a reality which is purely social, which is political, economic, or worldly; the institutions are for social needs, the law coats them and conserves them. It is indispensible for sociologists to take account of the legal coating; it is no less indispensible for lawyers to remember that underneath this outside there is a social flesh, living, suffering, and demanding. And this dualism is encountered even in those institutions, which are a part of the peculiarly legal mechanisms. (1905, pp. 10–11) [*C'est en effet toutes les institutions sociales sont peintés en droit, mais par-dessous le revêtement de cette peinture elles ont une réalité purement sociale qui est politique, économique ou mondaine; les institutions sont pour les besoins sociaux, le droit les recouvre, et les conserve. Il est indispensable aux sociologues de tenir compte de l'épiderme juridique; il est non moins indispensable aux juristes de ne pas oublier que sous cet epiderme il y a une chair sociale, vivante, souffrante, exigeante. Or, ce dualisme se rencontre jusque dans les institutions qui sont des pièces du mécanisme proprement juridique.*]

To fully appreciate this instructive passage we must compare sociology and law as disciplines, to define their scope, and compare and contrast their contexts. More than merely discriminating between sociology and law, Hauriou admonishes that we must provide for their interchange, the passage, or transformation from one viewpoint to the other.

2. Social and Legal Order

In some passages in Hauriou's writing, sociology and law neatly fit together as disciplines. The fact that makes sociology of interest to the lawyer is that social studies, when done in the way Hauriou considers correct, arrives at the study of progress, a point of view closely aligned with the legal one (1899d, p. vi). This is the material for law; law needs the material element from social science. Because no empty legal judgments exist, only judgment upon "something," law cannot eliminate the formalities of social science but can only simplify them (1896, p. 312). The legal constructions are themselves social data, and the most external of social data. Because of their presence among social data and their eminent observability, verifying social science as having its proper orientation towards individualism is easy (ibid., p. 39). As a result of their close tie, the same criteria for distinguishing better from worse apply to both studies. Stability and liberty grow in the better social climate and these same two are the ends of law. "To the superiority of the social state immediately corresponds that of the legal order" (1916c, p. 53) [*"A la superiorité de l' état social corresponde immédiatement celle de l'ordre juridique"*].

The relation of law and sociology is not nearly so amicable, however, as it appears on the face of things. Hauriou's "The Law Faculties and Sociology" was subtitled "The Necessity of Combining Two Antagonistic Conceptions" (1893c). The antagonism he finds is only an instance of the antagonism between art and science. The science of sociology is a method of objective observation, which disengages a law from phenomena taken as natural appearances without changing those appearances any more than is unavoidable; it presumes determinism. The art of law pursues a subjective ideal, establishing laws for free events, modifying and influencing—even creating—them, therefore presuming an order beyond and transcending the phenomena of society (Hauriou, 1893e, p. 1).

To take social phenomena as the object of social science invariably misunderstands law and morals, because it abstracts from the agent, the human individual (Hauriou, 1896, p. 2). Sociology calls impossible what law absolutely requires, "therefore there is between determinist sociology and the law the same conflict as between this sociology and morality" (Hauriou, 1911a, p. 16) [*"Il y a donc, entre la sociologie déterministe et le droit, le même conflit qu'entre cette sociologie et la morale"*]. The conflict cannot be sidestepped; sociology forcibly introduces a theory on law, for legal phenomena are as much social facts as are economic or political phenomena (Hauriou, 1893c, p. 3). Each speaks of society and is a part of society, so each speaks of the other: law speaks of social science as containing liberty among its data, and social science speaks of law as a natural and law-like phenomenon.

The only solution is by now a familiar one: to admit both. The pragmatic dualism here comes about through each discipline standing on the side unavoidably its own, while trying not to prejudice the presumptions of the other (Hauriou, 1893e, p. 2).

The reconciliation of these two antagonistic conceptions is difficult. Hauriou was trying to effect a reconciliation by working out of the background of a legal method and moving towards sociological methods, whereas social scientists contemporary to him had first been exposed to determinisms of social fact and, from this starting point, found it impossible to gain an adequate appreciation for the legal point of view of freedom and responsibility (Hauriou, 1899f, p. 462). The error of reasoning of the sociologist, as traditional logic knows it, is perfect conversion of a universal affirmative proposition. Sociologists examine the socially useful. For them, whatever is just is useful, for this means that whatever sociologists can observe to be just, to be observable at all, must already be useful. The converse of this, the proposition that whatever is useful is just, is the assimilation of law into social science that Hauriou refuses. Once the limitation inherent to the discipline is accepted by the theorist, each can assist the other; but this is the state of a more self-confident and less threatened sociology. "A little sociology moves away from law, but a lot of sociology rejoins it" (1893c, p. 4) [*"Un peu de sociologie éloigne du droit, beaucoup de sociologie y ramène"*]. A change in sociology is what is needed, and for this reason, Hauriou took up the study of sociology.

As we have seen, the three elements Hauriou finds necessary to make an appeal in law a truly legal matter are all explicitly social: oral conflict between parties; their acceptance of a given solution; a judge available to them who fits the demands of the case (1905, p. 13, and passim). This illustrates that for Hauriou's disciplines, the social and the legal formations are constructed at once from inside by human wills—subjectively—and from outside by social circumstances—objectively (1896, p. 5). Both are meant to protect people from contradictions in the universe; social science, and any science, protects them from contradictions among phenomena, whereas law protects them from contradictions among interests (ibid., p. 109).

Hauriou calls for a social jurisprudence [*jurisprudence sociale*], a jurisprudence penetrated with the public interest, an enlarged justice (1916b, p. 601). The needs of society place whatever demands there are upon law, and direct the evolution of law. "The object to which laws are applied is more than the laws, society is more than the law. A law is not made for itself, it is made for its object" (Hauriou, 1899d, p. 135) [*"L'objet auquel s'applique la loi est plus que la loi, la société est plus que le Droit. La loi n'est pas faite pour elle-même, elle est faite pour son objet"*]. No new social order can be established without a new legal vehicle; once the legislation is passed, it in turn becomes established social fact (Hauriou, 1899a, p. 69).

Legal rules appear as the residue of social relations, which are envisaged as wills; social science views these same social relations as ideas, concepts, and feelings (Hauriou, 1896, p. 309n1). When events and interests materially distinct in society become joined, this does not occur on the grounds of universal concepts. Their conjunction is something artificial and even violent, the result of a decision by will made under the pressure of circumstances. The study of jurisprudence, then, consists of finding the artifact that is employed and the urgent circumstances urging the parties to dispute (Hauriou, 1882b, pp. 6–8). Circumstances even more than the nature of rights determine what kind of action is being effected legally; and legal conflict is acceptable not on account of a claim made but on account of the conflict being externalized into a social fact (Hauriou, 1903b, p. 463; 1905, p. 42).

Law penetrates society, and society is itself related to the universe. So to give a definition of law that is exact and complete, we must have knowledge of all these relations (Hauriou, 1969, p. 131). The context in which the relation of fact to law becomes unavoidable is when we seek to consider the historical origin of law (Hauriou, 1918b, pp. 815–816). But the legal order is almost by definition related to facts of the social order by a relation of opposition; its purpose is to remedy the amoralism found in the brutal forces of politics. So not only by abstraction is law distinguished from politics and economics; they are in opposition and contradiction because legal forces are moral while the others are amoral, being of themselves only brutal forces meant for the exploitation of persons by other persons or the domination of persons by other persons. The war of the legal and the social is, then, the struggle between the just and unjust, a variation of the struggle between good and evil (Hauriou, 1916c, pp. xxv, 10). Legal and social facts are "radically different," and use different categories (Hauriou, 1908b, p. 623).

In an organized society, then, the state of law is more important than the state of fact, because the state of fact makes only rare appearances, with law being the regular organized way for events to occur (Hauriou, 1929c, p. 16). Something is not the way it is outside law first, determining the law in turn; rather, it is the way the social appears to be only because it is first legislated thus (Hauriou, 1879b, pp. 18, 22). The relations of power among people are not purely legal or purely social; the domination by natural necessities is present, but because of human love of liberty, these mechanisms are not admitted as such, being transformed into obedience to themselves, to other human beings, before being acceptable (Hauriou, 1929c, p. 29).

For these reasons, a legal theory can be neither contrary to fact nor simply immersed within fact and indistinguishable from fact (Hauriou, 1912d, p. 5). Law, rather, is a "faithful mirror of society" (Hauriou, 1898, p. 6) [*"le droit, ce fidèle miroir de la société"*]. The representative or legal order is meant neither to kill the real, nor by a deplorable confusion to become the organ of the real. It is meant only to govern the real (Hauriou, 1899d, p. 142). The difference is not in the kind of events which take place, but in the way they take place; the order of law permits persons either to do or not to do what they would do in the order of fact, but to have the same advantage as if they did, in fact, do the deeds (ibid., p. 111).

It is an unreal distinction to distinguish rigidly brute social facts from legal constructions, for the facts that occur in social contexts are already beyond the state of brute facts. Even the merely social is intended by its partisans to escape the way of brute fact, "not to fall . . . into an assault" (Hauriou, 1905, p. 14) [*"ne dégénère . . . en une voie des faits"*], because all social institutions have the same goal, namely, to find peaceful solutions to conflict. The goal is not juridical, but peace loving [*pas juridique mais pacifiste*], and such a goal is no more brutal than it is legal (ibid.). While not legal, social order closely follows it:

> It is a fact that the rule of law is not given as embodying a solidarity indifferent to the idea of justice; it is a fact that the individual today in his relations with his peers cannot make an abstraction from the idea of the just, and that the rule of law appears as an interpretation of this solidarity in a certain direction which is that of justice; this direction imposes sacrifices on people, however, and will not be obeyed without the constraint of an external authority, even though it be recognized. Here is the real truth, banal for being known to all; this is the real datum of the problem, from which no one is allowed to eliminate a single element. (Hauriou, 1902b, p. 354) [*c'est un fait que la règle de droit n'est pas donnée comme incarnant une solidarité indifférente à l'idée de justice; c'est un fait que, aujourd'hui, dans ses rapports avec ses semblables, l'individu ne peut faire abstraction de l'idée du juste et que la règle de droit apparait comme une interprétation de cette solidarité dans une certaine direction qui est celle de la justice; cette direction impose d'ailleurs à l'homme des sacrifices pénibles et partant, quoiqu'il en reconnaise l'existence, elle ne serait pas obeié sans la contrainte d'une autorité extérieure. Voilà la vérité réele, banale à force d'être connue de tous, voilà la véritable donnée du problème dont il n'est pas permis d'éliminer un seul élément.*]

In general, social order conforms to the needs of human nature; it is drawn from the order of things; but everything conformed to the order of things is divine (Hauriou, 1911a, p. 12).

In this way, power, for instance, is not simple force but one able to create law. Power is a free energy endowed with superiority and superiority is something qualitative, a quality of will or intelligence. Brute force is something quantitative, a quantity of willpower backed by physical strength. Separation of powers helps insure that the content of power will be spiritual competence instead of domination, since domination is a strong draw upon power otherwise. Because of this shaping of fact by ideas and morals, as shown in peaceful endurance, the law can be seen to confirm states of fact instead of doing away with them (Hauriou, 1907a, p. 16; 1923d, pp. 143–144; 1933g, p. 103).

To put it differently, neither social solidarity nor legal rules are a purely social product; they are the balance between the action of society and the reaction of the individual self (Hauriou, 1909a, p. 82). Law and rights both come from the social milieu where stabilized situations occur (Hauriou, 1899d, p. 139). The morality of law, which receives its sanction in law, has society as its source. What yields this morality from society is not social solidarity, the simple relationship of individuals in economic private life, but the social structure, the political phenomenon, the primary expression of which is in the institution (Hauriou, 1907a, p. 7). It is a social procedure or social ceremony adapted to the necessities of social life, which is the external form for acts, a form that unites heterogeneous individual acts for a single legal effect.

So much a part of social life is the form for legal acts that it is often not fully voluntary in social life but imposed for the same social needs (Hauriou, 1906a, pp. 150–151). It is by this form that an historical succession resides within the same object, the institution, from a state of force to a state of law. This transformation occupied much of Hauriou's attention and is one of the fundamental problems of law for him (1896, p. 196; 1916c, pp. 10–11).

The legal order does not create institutions proper to itself, for the most part; its activity is simply to regularize and improve the existing factual organizations (Hauriou, 1916c, p. 9). Thus, the legal institutions can be identified by a social rather than a legal approach; the stipulation of an existing law system for some external input to the society is not needed to render social institutions legal.

> These institutions are in a state of perpetual evolution; one would hope that they evolve towards the better, but one does have to recognize that the phases through which they pass have in themselves their own reason for being. (Hauriou, 1905, p. 97) [*Ces institutions sont en perpetuelle évolution; on espère qu'elles évoluent vers le mieux, mais on doit reconnaitre que les phases par ou elles passent ont en soi leur raison d'être.*]

There is no available moment in the history of the state, for example, when there did not exist a law structure already established in the nation prior to that legal system the state would create; in this, as in other social-legal situations, the state is only the reorganization of the nation (Hauriou, 1916c, p. xvi). Social order can generate the necessary preconditions for a legal order, and do it historically, of itself.

If these legal formations are irreducible to preexisting states of law, they are equally irreducible to contractual relationships, even though contractual relationships can also establish states of law. Joseph Albert Broderick (1968, pp. 144–160) has a treatment of Hauriou's appreciation for contract. Hauriou uses the social situation [*situation d'état*] ("state" referring here to stability, not to governance) as the normal social genesis of the legal order. He defines it as "every stable form of social relations which tends to express itself by law or, in a more general way, by legal rules" (1899a, pp. 66–67) [*"Toute forme stable des rapports sociaux qui tend à s'exprimer par la loi ou d'une façon plus générale par la réglementation légale"*]. In turn, the preparation for this fundamental truth [*vérité fondementale*] is balance; the balance of power leads to legal situations (Hauriou, 1909a, p. 85). Hauriou saw his contribution to the growth of law from fact to lie in the social order. Acts and operations in legal categories are each characterized by a determining fact, which becomes the legal cause of the operation or act. The non-legal and legal facts here are not any different, since law intervenes to make the facts a legal basis and cause of law posterior to them. But Hauriou believes that he has introduced the derivation of legal rights from social situations, thereby extending the contact of the factual and the legal (1926c, pp. 384–385; 1925, p. 389).

The crucial question is the point at which the institution passes over from a social to a legal climate. Hauriou answers that this occurs when the social institution progresses from individuality to moral personality. This specification of personality as moral is key; for although at the time Hauriou made this identification, he considered distinguishing moral from legal personality unnecessary, he later did so vigorously. But simply to say the legal personality is legal is tautologous. Instead, Hauriou explains it as follows:

> From the moment that the representative unity gives rise to a new being, the person, it is conformed to our ways of thinking to regard rights, representations, . . . which fundamentally constitute person, as attributes of the person, by an inversion as it were of cause and effect. (1899d, p. 159) [*Du momente que l'unité représentative donne naissance à un être nouveau, la personne, il est conforme à nos habitudes d'esprit, par une sorte d'interversion des effets et des causes, de regarder comme des attributs de la personne les droits, c'est-à-dire, les représentations, . . . qui au fond la constituent.*]

So no institution need be debarred from being a legal reality only because no written text or subjective right exists that makes it so. More important things than the legal aspects of an institution exist in law; most important of all qualifying factors is the social value of resolving a troublesome conflict peaceably (Hauriou, 1905, pp. 11–12).

This "special virtue" comes not from any authority or any general will; it is due, materially, to the adaptation of an institution to the realities of corporate structure. It is due, formally, to its endurance in peace, the fact that manifests the presumed adaptation (Hauriou, 1916c, p. xvii). As groups become less conscious of their originally external and unilaterally imposed form and more conscious of their function, they become legal realities (Hauriou, 1896, pp. 342–343).

The adaptation of social to legal is through characteristics of the social itself, generated from itself. This gives rise to the suspicion, which Hauriou confirms, though not too frequently, that something cannot even be called fully and truly social until it is already legal. To become real, the legal ideals of justice and of peace must become practical, become attached to a determinate organization in the very activity of transforming it. The ideals must characterize the group as its cause. This is, for Hauriou, the joining of both ideals into *une institution qui soit à la fois de fait et de droit*, which becomes at the same time matter for social science and for law (1907a, p. 16).

3. Economic and Legal Order

Society is built upon the force of private property; it balances the political forces and from it, legal relationships of the economic variety grow (Hauriou, 1899a, p. 87). Economic activity is a concrete, living source of law. Its rules are customary, and custom is an abstract source of law. Custom consists of practices found appropriate in a certain society to the necessities of that society. Thus, legal customs, resting on legal postulates, arise to form an economic or commercial relationship that is legal (1916c, p. 185). The economic order's relationships could not have survived without becoming legal relations. Economic relations are not purely social phenomena fitting comfortably within the political order. Instead, economic relations are by nature open, interstitial, and international, at odds with the closed, authoritarian, and disciplinary character of political institution. Economic relations need the protection of law to survive in the political order (ibid., pp. 352–353).

As distinguished from the legal order, the economic order takes no notice of justice in satisfying human desires (Hauriou, 1909a, pp. 35–36). But economics does not cease to be humane for this reason. Economics tries to see money, for example, as eliciting will and action. To do this, it would have to emphasize the power over the fact, the quality of possession over the quantity of wealth; for money elicits will but is immobile without will. Law, on the other hand, recognizes the quality of ownership: wealth has value only because it rouses will and action, but it rouses action only because of the power of possession (Hauriou, 1896, pp. 319–320). Thus, Hauriou distinguishes goods from wealth [*biens et richesses*]. Goods are legal values; they have an unconfused mode of acquisition, and a guarantee of possession. Wealth is an economic value: no set way of acquiring wealth exists, nor any guarantee of keeping it. "Every one of the goods is an enrichment, but not every enrichment is one of the goods" (1907a, p. v) [*"Tout bien est une richesse, mais toute richesse n'est pas un bien"*].

The legal security of goods is not the result of laws, however, but of social institutions, the combinations of active forces. Laws are real, but they are not in the first order of effective forces. Laws set only the external limits and boundaries of things (ibid., pp. vi–vii).

4. Political and Legal Order

Although it is impossible to distinguish the political and the legal strata of society respectively as the real and the ideal plane of public life (Hauriou, 1923d, 444), still no legal order can be separated from the political order, since law's role is to introduce justice into the political. This occurs by the introduction of "states of law," legal situations which, as we just saw, establish themselves (Hauriou, 1916c, p. 7). This condition can occur because the political order contains the initiative for moving itself, while the legal does not put itself in movement; it can only act, or better, react, upon the completed acts of other orders— to govern is to act, not to deliberate [*gouverner c'est agir et non pas délibérer*]. The political power is armed to control the struggle among public powers for control, among the executive, legislative, and elective powers. The legal power is not fitted out for such a struggle towards final supremacy since it can halt no other power, being dependent as it is upon acceptance of decision when public life reaches a certain maturity (Hauriou,1916c, pp. 36–37; 1923d, p. 527).

The explanation for these differences between political and legal phenomena is that political government concerns the "brutal fact" of human beings' rule over human beings, while the legal government is a matter of equilibrium through the establishment of moral personality. If Hauriou early finds this level of personality a fictive one because its only reality is the substratum of individual wills (1892b, pp. 6–7), he soon makes its specific characteristic its attention to rights, at the level of substances. Political life remains a question of services, on the more superficial level of actions (*L'introduction à l'étude du droit administratif français*, n.d., pp. 1, 10).

The concern of legal order is with persons; the political life looks rather to the preservation of functions, a human value, but as a use-value not adequate to the appreciation of persons and their rights (Hauriou, 1897b, pp. 269–270). However, the personal feature and foundation of law extends more to the lived institutional form of law than to the written "legal" law. For the lived institutional form of law concerns a group of people because of their membership in a group, a personal focus; while laws are territorial, applied to people only as present in a particular territory. The determinate character of written legal law and its artificial sanctions make clear that it is less adaptable to personal requirements than the institutional form of law. But institutional law approaches much closer to the lived struggle of political life than does the written law (1907a, pp. 19–20).

Hauriou's essay on decentralization (1892a, pp. 9–10) exemplifies this discrimination of political from legal. Decentralization is a political matter concerned with the way of acting, of giving service; the parallel legal process, concerning the way of existing in a federal manner to alter the ability to legislate, he calls not decentralization but deconcentration. Political decentralization is an analysis of popular wishes and the best way to make citizens participatory in government; legal deconcentration is a structural analysis of the modes of administration. Political analysis is a study of the sources of power at its roots; legal analysis is a study of the limits, interpretations, and direction of power. So the result of political analysis is powers and facts, while the result of legal analysis is notions and ideas (ibid., pp. 17, 30).

As against an increase in power, in the creation of public life, the ways of exercising power, and the number of persons—individual and moral—who exercise this non-political power both increase (ibid., pp. 37–38). As applied to the decentralization and deconcentration of the state, the political aspect views the way to apportion power possessed by the state for the most advantageous results, while the legal point of view concerns the way of existing the state has insofar as it fosters law and legal persons (ibid., pp. 1, 3).

Hauriou does not rigidly separate law and politics, however. He holds that all social institutions need explanation from two viewpoints, one from the point of view of political science and another from the point of view of legal science. While these do not exhaust social reality because of the inherent impossibility that intellectual methods reach living reality, the duality of standpoints approximates the truth of living institutions as closely as it is possible to do so (1905, p. 12n1). A series of examples can illustrate this duality. Voluntary obedience to the law is as much a political matter as it is a legal one. Again, public power cannot enter the realm of free economic forces without making a law (Hauriou, 1899a, p. 12; 1895b, p. 430). As well, the responsiveness of officials to their constituencies is political and legal at the same time (Hauriou, 1923d, p. 244). So also the accusation that legal bodies are obeying political considerations is not always condemnatory, even if true; for the preoccupation with good administration is as much legal as it is political (Hauriou, 1894a, p. 714). Further examples of the closeness come from studies of constitutional law near the end of Hauriou's career.

The sanctions necessary to law are not stated in the constitution regarding the constitution itself; surely natural sanctions do exist, however, such as the suffering and decline of the constituted body. But Hauriou finds this quite difficult to see how this differs from the fate of a political body as it degenerates (1884, p. 15). The ambiguity of constitutional law stems from its threefold structure of order, power, and liberty, with an irresoluble struggle between order and liberty. Power establishes a shifting balance between order and liberty by shifting sides depending on changing needs and dominances (Hauriou, 1923, p. 2). Constitutional law is formal—legally codified and objective; it is politically responsive to real social needs and is not arbitrary. It is systematic and total, these two sides represent the legal and the political demands upon it respectively (ibid., p. 4). The legal forms of its institutions are less important than the political beliefs of individuals; to be legitimate, it is enough that the institutions do not violate these individual actions. Constitutional law is, then, deeply transactional, creating a balance of spiritual forces, namely legal justice and political peace (ibid., p. vi).

With this transactional nature, Hauriou "leaves to the jurists who live in the ideal world the definition of executive power by the execution of the law" (ibid., pp. 445–446) [*"abandonnons donc aux juristes qui vivent dans l'idéal la définition du pouvoir exécutif par exécution de la loi"*]. He defines the executive as being the executrix of things [*la exécutrice des choses*], especially of the public thing. Political reality is not determined by the compartments of legal science. Thus, although legally the government's ministers and the president cannot act independently of each other, politically, and in fact, the president is dominated by the ministers and must follow their lead (Hauriou, 1916c, pp. 383–384; 1923d, p. 450). Similarly, the judiciary is a branch of the executive power, separated from it artificially by constitutional principles but rejoining it naturally and historically (Hauriou, 1923d, p. 481). The relation between constitutional powers politically and legally is shown to be close in Hauriou's overall statement to this effect:

> In a state where the separation of powers exists, the only political power is that of keeping a measure from becoming executive. . . . Once a measure becomes executive, it no longer interests the political power; if it falls into the trap of a conflict after or even before it is executed, this is only a legal accident, and the judiciary which will, because of the conflict, consider the consequences of the execution or annul it before its execution with legal forms, is nothing more than a legal power. The distinction of political and legal takes place between the executive and the judicial powers. But the property of executive power is to make measures executed, and the property of the legal or judicial power is to carry on the conflicts roused by measures already executive, from the point of view of law. (1912c, p. 179) [*Il n'y a de pouvoir politique, dans un État où existe la séparation des pouvoirs, que celui qui a la puissance d'empêcher une mesure de devenir exécutoire. . . . Quand une mesure est devenue exécutoire, elle n'intéresse plus le pouvoir politique; si elle tombe dans la chaussetrappe d'un conflit, après ou même avant son exécution, cela n'est plus qu'un accident juridique, et le pouvoir juridictionnel, qui, à raison de ce conflit, appréciera les conséquences de son exécution, ou qui l'annulera avant son exécution avec des formes juridictionnelles, n'est plus qu'un pouvoir juridique. La distinction du politique et du juridique se place entre le pouvoir exécutif et le pouvoir juridictionnel. Or, le propre du pouvoir exécutif est de rendre les mesures exécutoires, le propre du pouvoir juridique et juridictionnel est de trainer, au point de vue du droit, les conflits provoqués par les mesures devenues executoires*.]

No one decided upon the separation of powers; the pressure of events forced it; countries copied the form from each other. All powers need do is to collaborate, to work together [*aller au concert*]. With this status, they cannot be taken as separated in any but a very supple sense, not rigidly. The distinction of executive and judiciary, and thus of law and politics, is slim (Hauriou, 1923d, pp. 402–403). In Anglo-American constitutions, says Hauriou, the distinction has even less rigidity, since it is not taken as essential structure due to a weak Anglo-American sense of corporate realities (1916c, p. 611).

Seven

APPLICATION OF METHODOLOGY TO LARGE GROUPS

1. Introduction

The problems that arise in distinguishing the methodology of social science from that of law in Hauriou originate in his discussion of existing human groups. Before continuing, a brief review of the analyses examined thus far will be instructive.

History is the way to locate these human groups; procedure is the general classification for them. The institution is the key existent grouping for Hauriou, the grouping in which moral and legal personalities are the culminating phase but which they do not exhaust. The nation has come to be the most concrete and important institution, being mediated toward personality by progressive centralization of government.

For Hauriou, the state is admittedly the peak of this personification, representing both the social and the legal grouping, which has come to provide the fullness of historical realization at this modern age. Hauriou never excludes the surpassing of the modern state, but much earlier in his theory of representative law even provides for that (1899d, Appendix 1).

2. History and Procedure

Hauriou believes anyone not blinded by philosophical prejudice must see that history reveals essential postulates of law as they have been known in the Western world. He concludes that study of the history of civilization reveals that one civilization is superior to all others, namely the Western Mediterranean one. The criterion by which he judges is his bourgeois identification of peace and stability with progress, when accompanied by justice. He derives this postulate from the premise that truth is unique. Finally, penetrating the genesis and survival of this civilization, he finds that it depends upon a constant current of social and moral ideas, namely those of fallible or relative individualism: individualism because liberty predominates, relative because it requires rules and sanctions. Law successively approximates this idea. Individualism places the legal person at the base of legal order, and places individual enterprise at the base of social order (1929c, p. vii). Because this is what law and society depend upon, Hauriou recognized from the beginning of his career that jurisprudential and sociological history must be given the first place in law (1884, p. 13).

History sees only two objects, events that are the subjective work of people, and institutions that are the objective residue of this work (Hauriou, 1923d, p. 75). Those events that do not relate to this residue are not objectively available, so history is not to be occupied with sterile facts or events but only with those that have been imitated to form institutions (Hauriou, 1894c, p. 304). Throughout history, revolutions have been the way liberty has been established. But popular rights come from something at the founding of the historical institution, revolution or no revolution, from a balance established between government-person and community-individual. Historical events are not necessary but accidental; the results could as well have come from normal evolution as from revolution (Hauriou, 1929c, p. 136).

This is not, however, how Hauriou believes history did unfold; in elucidating the concept, he does not mean to imply an evolutionary possibility that events are the fortuitous results of determined universal causes, fortuitous with regard to the institution and determined with regard to nature. On the contrary, he rejects historical evolutionism. Rather, whether revolution or evolution, history is always a revelation, the revelation of virtualities implicit in the spontaneous events of human ideas or insights, virtualities explicated as time unrolls (ibid., p. 65). This also explains the irreversibility of historical process toward institutional types, from aristocracy, to democracy, to administrative empire. It can be hastened or slowed; but until the starting idea is lost or rejected, the virtualities of the same source are appearing (ibid., p. 139).

The events and institutions history reveals are procedures, constant modes of acting. The whole of public life for Hauriou is made up only of ceremonies and procedures; constitutional and administrative law are nothing but vast collections of procedures (1916c, p. 160). It is the constancy of the rhythmic movement of procedure, which people instinctively trust, believing that respect for forms is the fundamental guarantee for everyone who participates in the same action (ibid., p. xix; 1923d, p. 270).

In Hauriou's theory, institution depends upon this, that actions performed procedurally will endure and become facts. The procedure allows certainty and therefore social permanence to the act. It does not remain an act, therefore, but becomes a fact, a past act, which continues by its adaptation to the totality of facts (1912d, p. 106). With such a status, this fact can be the basis for future acts, acts that either accept or change the fact. To demand that the very same act be constantly performed to ensure social solidarity, that the action never be completed but drawn out indefinitely, is inconsistent with the discontinuity so evident in social life as much as in individual life. It is only the presence of a fact, to which a person can adhere or reject that makes the formation of social group reality possible; and this fact depends on prior act and procedure.

The permanence and the type of social institution depends on procedure; to discover what kind of legal entity is present, we must only to look at the procedure of its existence (1879b, p. 26). Hauriou recites the maxim, "form gives being to a thing" [*"forma dat esse rei"*] as more true of social existences than of any others; the legal value of an institution comes from the form of the action, the procedure. "Just as religious ceremonies produce sacramental effects, so the official ceremonies of the cult of the state produce legal effects" (1923d, p. 202) [*"De même que les cérémonies religieux produisent des effets sacramentels, de même les cérémonies officielles du culte d'État produisent des effets juridiques"*].

3. Institution and Personality

For Hauriou, the truly scientific question with regard to society does not revert to absolute origins, whether before society existed, the ideas preceded the facts, or vice versa. The truly scientific question asks whether the organic stratum of society is at every moment in its existence gradually penetrated by the representative stratum, in an historical succession (1899d, p. 101). Guidance by ideas leads a social group not only to be established as social but also to become legal.

"It is, therefore, in the spirit of historical observation, combined with a dialectic of forms, that we must appreciate institutions" (Hauriou, 1923d, p. vii) [*"C'est donc dans un esprit d'observation historique, combiné avec une dialectique des formes, que nous devrons apprécier des institutions"*]. The history and the procedure of the institution are both under a formal logic of ideas [*une logique formelle des idées*], an intersection of forms corresponding to different and even antagonistic ideas. Hauriou gives the example of the intersection of the rights to legitimacy due to the state and the right of revolution due to primitive liberty (ibid). He applies this formal logic of ideas to his conceptualization of the institution. Ideas standing in opposition foster the balance of powers in politics. The endurance of ideas permits the permanence of institutions once willing individuals accept them. Because ideas are limited, they do not allow evolution to progress indefinitely. As with nonhuman animal species, the extent to which social organizations can evolve is limited, because they have fundamental characteristics due to their directive ideas, which cannot disappear until the species itself is destroyed (1916c, p. 347). As a social fact, institution relies on procedure; it does not need the permanence of an act as an act in the same way as a contract does (1907a, p. 24).

Institution need not be debarred from legal order, leaving it as the interest of sociologists only. The lack of a written text to justify its legality is unimportant. Law has factors more important than textual value, chief among them being social value, what meets a social need. The need institutions meet is to resolve troublesome conflicts peaceably (1905, pp. 11–12). It is this that makes institution a legal dimension [*un champ juridique*], a legal identity [*une figure juridique*], and a virtual legal location [*un lieu de virtualité juridique*].

Institutions "secrete" law the way a body secretes fluids (1906a, p. 136; 1907a, p. 17). Institutions do not cease to exist when legal order begins, nor do they simply run parallel with legal order. Instead, the birth, life, and death of institutions of social order is profoundly legal (1933g, p. 126). Law does not create institutions, except exceptionally; in the usual case, law can only regularize and confirm spontaneously existing institutions, which already have a legal character since they are means for harmonizing the individual and the social (1898, p. 139).

The proof that institutions are not only social but already legal is that they are sources of law. It is true that they are organized by law, that legal effects ensue from decisions taken within institutions, and that their personnel are legally responsible for their acts. But these factors only manifest the legal character. The source of it is that institutions create a statutory law, which establishes them before other groupings, externally, and a disciplinary law, which governs them internally. Both are independent of the state and its written law (1907a, p. viii). The basis of law, then, is not contract, statutes, or even the state, but the institution (1918b, p. 313). "It is institutions which make the legal rules, it is not the legal rules which make the institution" (1933g, p. 128) [*"Ce sont les institutions qui font les règles de droit, ce ne sont pas les règles de droit qui font les institutions"*].

For these reasons, even the inner state of a band of robbers or a war party is superior to that of a simple herd of individuals whose chief offers them no goal for collective action (1916c, p. 53). The robbers or the war party is already a legal condition, for it is internally stratified with a view of an end. This places the institution as fully of interest to law as it is to social science. For what is of interest to social science is the power and the peace of society, and the sacrifice, which makes them possible. Egoistic individual motivations are of no interest to social science because power shifts independently of such motivations (1896, p. 328). The institution is defined as a "state of law," "a state of fact prolonged within society in peace." This state may indeed not have the custom, the voluntary obedience and loyalty, necessary to a complete state of law, but it is sufficient to be described in a way that is as legal as it is social 1907a, pp. 15–16).

The legal state, Hauriou's doctrine of the state as public power [*l'état puissance publique*], is only a vaster social state, what Hauriou calls a state of stability [*situation d'état*] and defines as:

> a social situation which keeps itself in an enduring equilibrium; it is characterized, then, by stasis, for stasis is not only immobility itself but every equilibrium which tends toward immobility; the state of stability is opposed to whatever is changing, ephemeral and purely dynamic in the relations of persons. (1899d, p. 107) [*Une situation d'état est une situation sociale qui se maintient dans un équilibre durable; elle se caractérise donc par le statique, car le statique n'est pas uniquement l'immobilité mais tout équilibre qui tend vers l'immobilité; la situation*

> *d'état s'oppose à ce qu'il y a de changeant, d'éphemère, de purement dynamique dans les rapports des hommes.*]

This strictly social concept appears fundamental in each of the definitions of institutions Hauriou offered throughout his career. Several secondary sources have traced the development of Hauriou's theory of the institution through the various stages of development it had. One of the better is Joseph Albert Broderick, who details the progress from the phenomenal through the objective to the more subjective and personalist stages (1965, pp. 281–308).

The first appearance of institution was as the phenomenon of the most important social process, in a functional or verbal sense. "This is no longer an organization, it is an institution, for to institute is to give an inner principle, a soul, and what we are going to describe is the phenomenon of the institution" (1896, pp. 193–194) [*"Ce n'est plus une organisation, c'est une institution, car s'instututer c'est se donner un principe interne, une âme, et ce que nous venons de décrire est le phénomène de l'institution"*]. It is:

> the fact of the redemption of social organizations, which we shall call the *phenonemon of the "institution"*. . . . founded on force, it is necessary that organizations be maintained by it. . . . [But] the holders of power have understood the duties correlative to this power, have understood that their power has become a function. (Ibid., pp. 188, 192, 194) [*le fait de la rédemption des organisations sociales, que nous appellerons* phénomène de *"*institution*"* . . . . *fondées sur la force, il faut que les organisations soient maintenues par elle. . . . les dépositaires du pouvoir ont compris les devoirs corrélatifs à ce pouvoir, que leur pouvoir est devenu une fonction.*]

Ten years later, Hauriou says:

> we must now define the institution. It is a social organization, established in relation with the general order of things, whose permanence is assured by an equilibrium of forces or by a separation of powers, and which of itself constitutes a state of law (*stat per se*). (1907a, p. 8) [*Il nous faut maintenant définir l'institution. C'est une organisation sociale, établie en relation avec l'ordre général des choses, dont la permanence est assurée par un équilibre de forces ou par une séparation des pouvoirs, et qui constitute par elle-même un état de droit* (*stat per se*).]

Another decade later, Hauriou strengthens the emphasis on the legal aspect of social institution:

> But observation proves that there is something other than legal relation [contract] as the source of particular legal existences; there is the *legal institution* which is nothing other than the situation or organization of

> fact, bound to the whole complex of political and legal factors existing in the State, and acquiring just as much as do all general rules a legal value by the phenomenon of confirmation or legitimation which results from the adherence by free minds and also from the buffering of things under the force of inertia, for only the good is stable and coherent. (1916c, p. xx) [*Mais l'observation prouve qu'il y a autre chose que le rapport juridique comme source des existences juridiques particulières; il y a l'institution juridique qui n'est autre que la situation ou l'organisation de fait, reliée à l'ensemble des choses politiques et juridiques existant dans l'État, et acquérant, tout comme les règles générales, une valeur juridique par le phénomène de confirmation ou de légitimation qui résulte de l'adhésion des esprits et aussi de l'accommodation des choses sous l'action de la force d'inertie, parce que le bien seul est stable et cohérent.*]

From the period of constitutional interests onwards, the factor which dominates the institution is the reason *why* it becomes acceptable and is accepted, namely the factor of idea which it embodies. "An institution is a social organization endowed with permanence because it rests on an idea or on a set of ideas in whose service people's wills place themselves" (Hauriou, 1923d, p. 15) [*"Une institution est une organisation sociale douée de permanence parce qu'elle repose sur une idée ou sur un ensemble d'idées au service desquelles se mettent les volontés des hommes"*]. The high point of this stress is his often quoted definition from 1925:

> The major lines of this new theory are the following: an institution is an idea of a task or project which is realized and lasts in a legal manner within a social milieu; for the realization of this idea, a power is organized which gives it organs; on the other hand, among the members of the social group which is interested in the realization of this idea there are produced manifestations of communion which are directed by the organs of power and are regulated by procedures. (1933g, p. 96) [*Les grandes lignes de cette nouvelle théorie sont les suivantes: une institution est une idée d'œuvre ou d'entreprise qui se réalise et dure juridiquement dans un milieu social; pour la réalisation de cette idée, un pouvoir s'organise qui lui procure des organes; d'autre part, entre les membres du groupe social intéressé à la réalisation de l'idée, il se produit des manifestations de communion dirigées par les organes du pouvoir et reglées par des procédures.*]

The final formulation on the same side is from the end of his life:

> In gathering these characteristics of the *instituted social organization*, which is at the same time the *incorporated institution*, we are led to the

following definition: a social organization becomes durable, that is to say, it keeps its specific form despite the continual renewal of the human matter which it contains, when it is *instituted,* i.e., when on one hand the directive idea, which is in it from the moment of its foundation, has been able to subordinate the power of government, thanks to the balances of organs and power, and when on the other hand this system of ideas and power balances has been consecrated in its form by the consent of the institution's members as well as that of the social milieu. . . . In summary, *the form of the institution, which is its enduring element, consists in a system of balances of powers and consents, which is built around an idea.* (1929c, p. 73) [*En rassemblant ces caractères de l'organisation sociale* instituée, *qui est en même temps* l'institution incorporée, *on est conduit à la définition suivante: une organisation sociale devient durable, c'est-à-dire conserve sa forme spécifique, malgré le renouvellement continuel de la matière humaine qu'elle contient, lorsqu'elle est instituée, c'est-à-dire lorsque, d'une part, l'idée directrice, qui est en elle dès le moment de sa fondation, des équilibres d'organes et de pouvoir, et lorsque, d'autre part, ce système d'idées et d'équilibres de pouvoirs a été consacré, dans sa forme, par le consentement des membres de l'institution aussi bien que du milieu social. . . En somme, la forme de l'institution, qui est son élément durable, consiste en un système d'équilibres de pouvoirs et de consentements construit autour d'une idée.*]

If institution is the high point of social reality, the high point of institution is personality. Law is concerned with the activity of persons, so social reality must somehow be seen as personal before law can touch it (Hauriou, 1897b, p. iii). Personality is the "intimate logic" Hauriou uses to tie up all the loose ends he finds in law (1893d, p. 31). Personality succeeds upon the more primitive phase of institution, objective individuality. While in institutional individuality, the group simply functions systematically; in moral personality, the group recognizes itself to have some type, some nature, and is recognized by others to be something peculiar.

Georges Gurvitch is one of the few who distinguish objective individuality from autonomous individuality in Hauriou's grouping, the first corresponding to pre-institutional mass. This has some basis in Hauriou, but Hauriou often uses "objective" also as a qualifier for institutionalized individuality of groups (1899d, pp. 152, 154). The shift between objective and institutional individuality is gradual, and it is less the resulting person available for observation than the process. "It is less the moral person, which is seen, than the fact of the personification of a pre-existing objective institution" (1916c, p. xx) [*"C'est moins la personne morale qui est visée que le fait de la personnification d'une institution objective préexistante"*].

The relation of moral and legal personality is a variant piece of Hauriou's theory. He identifies the two without question in early writing and gives legal personality reality. Later, he distinguishes them and deprives the legal personality of reality. Yet even early, legal personality appears "as a mask applied to a face which does not follow it exactly" (1899d, p. 148) [*"comme un masque appliqué sur un visage mais qui ne le moulerait pas exactement"*]. The face to which he applies it is moral personality, not individuality, and the molding it does is to stabilize the personal life from contingencies, which appear to disperse it. Much later, the same idea is expressed more strongly, that legal personality is a simple legal technique to adapt the moral person to the exigencies of a system of law. It is a stylization of moral personality into which slips, as into every work of art, something artificial. At the extreme, when a legal person is recognized without any moral personality existing, a pure creation of law is created, a pure fiction (Hauriou, 1923c, pp. 335–336).

This is not a practical question for Hauriou, however, and so he does not deal with it willingly. He sees the pertinent question for his day as not the character of moral personality, real or fictive, but the construction of moral personality of subjective and objective forms. "We must change tactics" (1916c, pp. 45, 61, 64–65, 86–87, 87n57) [*"On doit changer de tactique"*]. Subjective and objective personality is a distinction parallel to the two forms of law we encountered in Chapter Four; subjective as related to a manifestation of will, and objective as related to some kind of organization. Subjective personality is for the purpose of life with others; but not all legal situations are analyzed into such a relation among persons. Where they are not so analyzed, legal personality fulfils no useful role (ibid.).

Since moral personality in the subjective sense is only one side of the legal situation, law can be constructed without it. But since it remains at least one side, it cannot be exorcised. It and the objective organization are the warp and woof of one and the same reality (*l'envers et l'endroit d'une même réalité*). Moral personality is the epiphenomenon, while in constitutional law, parliamentarianism is the phenomenon. Constitutional law is the way to establish moral personality, while personality is the transposition of the search for liberty, which makes up the parliamentary pole of such law (Hauriou, 1923c, pp. 331–335).

This attention to the subjective side of law and personality is present throughout Hauriou's work—in his reaction to mechanist sociology, in his criticism of Léon Duguit's Germanic objectivist sources, in his attraction to Jean-Jacques Rousseau's solution while pinpointing the error therein, in his later return to stressing history's individualist direction. But the ultimate perspective on society as, in Hugo Grotius' phrase, which Hauriou adopts, social personality [*un tout social de personalité*], reinforces definitively this direction. By building this social whole, law realizes the synthesis of universalism and individualism, or in his usual terms, of collectivism and individualism. The "whole" is attained by the compact of subjection [*pactum subjectionis*], the conditional agreement in liberty to subject oneself to authority, made on the part of each by adherence to social facts, the residue of social acts. The composition of "personalities" includes individual and social persons alike. These, rather than simply institutions of the objective sort, are the consummate achievement. The degree of subordination of each depends upon the degree of liberty necessary to the superior moral persons, giving no more subordination than is necessary (Hauriou, 1923c, p. 342; 1969, pp. 138–139).

The significance of this orientation is that law will take its root from human moral liberty. Each person is a center of liberty and all rights are meant to allow each to achieve and preserve liberty. Rights are liberties to be claimed, obligations are liberties to be sacrificed; and these particularized transfers constantly have a more or less direct repercussion on the global moral personality of the state (1969, p. 139).

4. Nation and Government

Nation is social moral personality insofar as it is seen to be organized. That is, although it is worked out in a rational manner, it can also be seen as apart from personification (1910, p. x). Even apart, it is a matter for law because it is already legally organized by a series of statutes; it is not just a matter of fact (1907a, p. 6). So the nation, even not personified, can be looked at from the point of view of law, without having to appeal to sociology in general or to philosophical concepts (1912d, p. 129n1). As an institution, the nation has constituted its organization itself. By definition, this is a matter of "fundamental equations; constitution involves an institution, and an institution involves the submission of sovereignty to law by objective means" (1918b, p. 814).

As organized, the nation is a composite unity, the result of composition, the composition of various governmental powers with the general will of the nation (1912d, p. 10). This is the living reality; the state, on the other hand, is more of the nature of an idea (1916c, p. 638). This is the chief distinction of nation from state, that as an organized unity, nation is a composition and therefore decomposable, while as unified personality, although partly abstract, the state is not composed and also therefore not decomposable. Nation comes to be, more or less, whereas state either is or is not (1912d, pp. 7–8).

The nation and the state government need not be in opposition, but ordinarily some degree of opposition exists because nation is a body under this government while being capable of bodily formation itself, with concomitant government. National community is the sum of state plus government; but as an exception, governments can artificially create a nation that had not existed before. As a rule, however, nation aspires to a complete social life by itself, with government being solely the giving of organs to itself (1916c, pp. 321–322; 1929c, p. 79n1).

Because of the difficulty in keeping the point of view of the organized nation without implying in it the personification found in state, Hauriou offers several rules toward this end:

(1) Principle of organized order: admit the superiority in practice of organized order over unorganized. Political organs are instruments through which the ordered community can act effectively.
(2) Principle of composite unity, or of composition of forces: every organized institution tends to constitute a corporative unity, not simple and the result of realizing a unique principle, but composite and the result of recognizing powers that exist. It is the practical result of combining several forces, some of which dominate others and thereby achieve an equilibrium; the equilibrium constitutes the composite unity.
(3) Principle of the necessary bond between political power and organization: admit that power is tied up with organization, that the function of power is to organize and that it must therefore organize itself. (1916c, p. 641)

As the result of this last rule, every power that is unorganized is unfit for government, and every power that is organized tends toward government. The net result is increased liberty, for the self-limitation [*autolimitation*] of power preserves its own liberty and ensures that of individuals by objective procedures established. In the light of this, these members can then subject themselves to the extent necessary.

Social phenomena, with three fabrics, are one reality: political government, which harmonizes these fabrics, is an additional reality, subordinate to and a reaction to social fabric. It is the organ of political unity: for although society is possible without political government, the political unity must cut across the social and professional disintegration. So government is needed to ensure whatever likenesses there are against threats, and to provide itself as an ersatz likeness where no natural ones already exist (1896, pp. 365, 371, 365).

Government is something positive and not merely a neutral servant: it uses force for its purposes and it acts in favor of interests, which are only a part of total social order, since in cases of conflict within society, within the nation under law, only one side can be chosen and acted upon (1897b, p. 9). Government interprets common ideas of the national community, but it must do this by representation, by particular ideas. Consequently, force is indispensible to its favor for parties and interest groups. Yet the government identifies itself with the rational ideal. Its employment of force for this end is itself a rational ideal—ideal unrealized, however, since it is not an immediately evident attribute of government that it is identified with the general interest (ibid., p. 16; 1916c, p. 117).

Because of the specialization toward interest groups, the government must be complemented by the administration, dealing with citizens directly through public services. Administration is not identified with government due to these different orientations (1896, p. 369n1). But in practice, the constitutional government cannot exercise its role effectively without centralizing administration in its hands (Hauriou, 1923d, pp. 518, 521n1).

To centralize government means to put in its hands all the power of the political and temporal order, making the state a political, diplomatic, legislative, judicial, and military unity (1929c, p. 116). This is the precondition for any power to exist at all; for, apart from an accumulation of experience, ideas, procedures, and formulas for governing, the only reality power can have is as a possibility for action. The actual reality of power comes from the phenomenon of "capitalization," the accumulation described; and this is, itself, a consequence of centralization (ibid., p. 118).

Hauriou holds to the political axiom that minority power centralizes, majority power decentralizes (ibid., p. 189). The intersection of these two powers in a balance is the assurance of political liberty. The hierarchy of powers in the government, where the majority is subordinate to the minority, intersects and balances the inverse hierarchy in the nation, where the minority is subordinate to the majority (ibid., p. 27n14). The government has the sovereignty of governing over the nation, the power of centralizing and commanding. The nation has the sovereignty of subjection over government, of accepting centralization and command to the extent necessary. Both are equally real, dominating the other completely in a certain sphere, a domination, totally dependent upon the other's domination of it, in turn, in its complementary sphere (ibid., p. 89). Even the electoral body, which is closer to the nation than the other powers of government, is, as a power of government, a minority power; and when nation appears opposed to government, the electoral body then lies on the side of government (1912d, p. 33).

5. State

Hauriou defines the state, over and against nation and government, as the rational organization of political government. He explains that this means the political unity realized by the metaphysical social fabric, the political unity insofar as it is rationally organized (1897b, pp. ii, 12).

That state is rational means that it is above limitation by fact. It is not only the ensemble of whatever rational likenesses there are; nation itself demands these. It also covers them with a perpetual form and depends upon tools such as credit and communication for success, which are abstract. While in the positive economic and political order opinion rules and a practical morality is sufficient, the state has rule by ideas and a morality of justice. For this reason, the state and its rationality are the normal location for law (1896, pp. 355, 375).

The natural, positive, and primarily social context of the nation takes individuals in their dissipated concreteness, while the metaphysical order of the state can take individuals as unities in terms of the human ideal (1897b, p. 2).

The state is essentially an effort of reflection intended to restore the primitive materiality of social life and to ennoble it, to take up the instinctive forces of family and property and couch them in terms of the intelligent idea of humankind. Family and property remain the fundamental categories of rational private law (1916c, p. 313). Ultimately, although the state redefined as rational is now in conflict with religious and economic powers and intellectual modalities corresponding to them, these latter are not of themselves rational and cannot preserve a unity that is truly human; so the state remains a logical and a practical necessity (1896, p. 401).

There are, however, limits upon the rationality of the state in fitting into its social role, for it does not control the will, for example, the will to be together in political unity, nor sentiments, the sentiments that are the fundamental basis of nationhood. What is not rational in society controls externally the rational state, although state is free internally because it is rational (1897b, p. 23). Hauriou demands of a rational state that it be adapted to deliberation and discussion, but also that it be adapted to present needs. However, the needs are not created by the state's system makers. For this reason, Hauriou disclaims the state's constructs as irrelevant to social science, since social organizations fulfill a function and the functions fulfill needs, which are not due to the state (1896, p. 349). His intention is to elucidate that the state is not necessarily the origin and end of all public activity, that citizens act spontaneously to create other institutions and laws even within the state, and that they did create those upon which the state essentially depends (1907a, p. 6).

Social science and the state are not totally disjoined, however, despite the attraction of the state to the side of law. Hauriou asserts that his later studies on the state were the continuation of his earlier social studies (1916c, p. 15n1). Social order gave birth to the state; state is the most eminent institution to which the social order has given birth (1929c, p. 78). Social order appears as the limit of the state; but it is the state that posits and makes effective those limits upon itself by law (1897b, p. iii).

The state appears as a phenomenon only with the separation of private and public life, which are confused in the organization of the nation prior to the state. The transition comes at the point of contact between a materially advanced civilization and the creation of a new and superior morality, at which time state becomes legally constituted (1916c, p. vii). But nothing can be constituted legally until it has been instituted, and it cannot be instituted until it has a division of powers, For the consciousness of an end is sharpened into rationality by self-limitation of a social group, and such self-limitation is not possible unless there are powers available with which to form the balance to oneself which self-limitation uses (1907a, p. 12). The power that government needs, then, is attained by organizing economic order. From its organization the rationality can be attained, while the economic order itself is the most forceful of social fabrics (1896, p. 390).

The state is achieved by an equilibrium of elements: the power of government culled from the organization of economy, which is the element of coercion; the spiritual unity of the nation, which is the element of consensus; and enterprise, which is the wrestling with a public valued for itself, because it is public, and this is the ideal element (Hauriou, 1929c, p. 86). It is of these partly social and partly ideal elements that state is built; thus integrated, it stands in the same relation to political unity as a structure stands to that of which it is the structure (Hauriou, 1897b, pp. 1–2).

Hauriou believes that the originality of his theory of state comes from keeping the individualist nature in state, despite balancing political forces with economic ones, which many would have taken to be the same as introducing socialist directions into the state (1909a, p. xi). The first job of the state is to protect individual action; any sovereignty it has dissolves logically into individual sovereignty (1896, p. 41). Hauriou's position is that a natural equilibrium exists between individualism and social necessities in the state. This state of affairs always provides sufficient cohesion for individuals to feel persuaded to stay in this form of society and assume its taxing demands (1916c, p. 379).

The new fact that appears in the state is personification. The organization of the nation is a preparation for state; they are different aspects of the same force, with parallel development. But they are not continuous, for the criterion of the state is the indivisibility of personality instead of the decomposability of organization. The personality of state is a total characteristic that cannot be reduced to the forces which make up its parts—the parts of the national organization. Individuals may exercise the state's authority through different representative organs of the national government, but the sovereignty is indivisible (1912d, pp. 7, 11n1, 147–179).

As a person, state is a legal and political superstructure [*superstructure politique et juridique*]; it is placed over the more primitive powers rather than succeeding them. State has profited from their political expression, but it now governs them toward different ends (1929c, p. 79). There is no logical relation of state to nation, only a purely historical relation. The only logic involved is the logic in the power of the state to attempt to absorb completely and to destroy the national infrastructure of more primitive powers and justice (Hauriou, 1923d, pp. 182–183; 1916c, p. 311). The state illustrates the proposition that a given social form cannot evolve beyond certain limits, unless its adaptation to higher functions and a new equilibrium causes it to be absorbed into a more comprehensive, overarching formation (Hauriou, 1916c, p. 320).

The progression toward state personality is, to Hauriou, the most vigorous thrust of all Western civilization. Although state may not be suited to every time, people, and place because it is a special historical product, its directions are those through which a progression from primitive institutions into nations would lead. It is last in intention of the founders of social bodies. First the nation must be centralized in political, economic, and legal contexts; then the state supersedes as the legal personification of the nation, in view of a civil order (ibid., p. 304).

The exposition of the state from a legal point of view rests on the two postulates of a concert of freewills and an organic determinate reality. Both of these are organized around the notion of state personality, one subjective and one objective (1893e, pp. i, v). This state personality is requisite for the law of the state to be seen not as attacks on the rights of private persons but as decisions in accord with the rights of a public person. As possessed of rights due to personality, the state has a natural affinity with law. Every political unity and every social fabric has its law, but only the state, the "state fabric" [*"étatique"*], can at times be constituted solely by law (1896, p. 356). The substance of the state, then, is the centralization of law, with political government providing the sanctions.

This makes of the state a power of domination separable from private property, with these characteristics: written law and formal procedure are substituted instead of custom. Consequently, a greater mobility of the social body ensues due to being freed from inertia of social custom. This in turn is the source of greater liberty and the source of greater danger of revolutions. The swiftness of legal change in the state can outstrip the power of adaptability, assured in advance by a customary regime.

This tendency toward revolution is partly obviated by putting constitutional law in the state into a position of primary respect. The honor accorded it is similar to that accorded a custom. The result is that institutions within the state independent of written law return to vogue, an effect which sustains social life and protection but which the state of the French Revolution had excluded temporarily (1916c, pp. x–xii).

So it is an aberration for the organic and political state to determine the representative and legal state, or for the legal state to be seen as the necessary condition for the organization of political community (1899d, p. 162). First, ideal law stands over and above the state, but positive law is internal to the state and, as a living force, is simply an aspect of its sovereignty.

Second, with regard to the legal state being seen as the necessary condition for the organization of political community, state is not a pre-existing person that organizes political centralization. Instead, state tends toward the legal personification of existing and centralized national community or institution (1916c, pp. xiii, 33). Instead of a pre-existing necessary datum for the social personification of institutions, "for myself, I take it that we can be present to assist at its birth" (1907a, p. xv) [*"Je prétends, quant à moi, que l'on peut assister à sa naissance"*].

The classical opinion concerning the relation of law and the state, an opinion Hauriou supports, is that they are separate systems of ideas, although having a tight relationship. The distinction is very clear only late in Hauriou's career, with his distinction of *Diké* and *Themis*, which I introduced in Chapter Four. *Diké* is a law common to different groups or persons; its source is human sociability, and it derives from the notion of persons. *Themis* is a disciplinary law internal to and organic to an institution, one with the bodily organization; its source is the organization of social materials. *Diké* existed before the state, and although state gradually overtakes it, it is never fused with state. *Diké* is essentially international, it knows no frontiers; while the state is essentially national in a political sense (1929c, pp. 97–101).

Diké among individual and moral persons existed prior to any particular state, among the persons who would come to be its members. *Themis* occurs within these persons as national institution is founded, and can continue to suffice for this institution as it achieves the objective personality of organization. *Diké* subsequently is the form of law that is necessary as the objective personality of the national institution must face out upon other national persons, thereby achieving subjective personality through willing and asserting its existence. This expression of will is made possible through the adherence of the members of the nation to the objective procedure on which was founded the institution.

The submission of the state to law is a useful policy [*politique habile*] for the sake of gaining popular assent, instead of a mysterious penetration of the state by law in accord with some intimate definitional logic. This politics of self-limitation sets poorly with those who dislike an appeal to history and prefer a proof. The only "proof" is that this has always happened in any situation of *Diké* in the formation of states and in the formation of international law today. "This quarrel concerning self-limitation is the proof that law and history cannot be separated. Logically the self-limitation of the state appears to be an absurdity. Historically it is the truth of constitutions" (ibid., p. 101) [*"Cette querelle de l'autolimitation est la preuve que l'on ne peut pas séparer le droit et l'histoire. Logiquement, l'autolimitation de l'État apparaît comme une absurdité. Historiquement, c'est la vérité constitutionnelle"*].

The state is a practical legal synthesis of a theory of subjective law (*Diké*) envisaging the state as a personality, and a theory of objective law (*Themis*) seeing state as an institution, including relations but not personality. In this practical synthesis, objective law dominates because, if subjective law did, it would disallow the objective side. "The individual nation is nothing but the state seen as an objective legal institution" (1907a, pp. xi–xii) [*"Cette individualité objective n'est autre que l'État envisagé comme institution, avec ses ressorts du droit disciplinaire et de phénomène statutaire"*], for social functions are already legal institutions, and the totality of these social functions is itself a legal institution, the nation; the state adds the subjective personality to this objective legal personality, which is identical with the social moral personality of the nation.

In summary, "the theory of the sovereignty of the state . . ., together with the theory of the institution, is one of the cornerstones of the public legal system" (1912d, p. 5) [*"la théorie de la souveraineté de l'État . . . est, avec la théorie de l'institution, l'une des pièces maîtresses du système du droit public"*].

Eight

PHILOSOPHICAL METHODOLOGY

1. Introduction

Throughout his career, Maurice Hauriou intentionally avoided philosophical and metaphysical development of his positive research. At the end, he contributed more towards such a development, for example, in the second edition of *Précis de droit constitutionnel* (1929c), the articles in the first half of *Aux sources du droit* (1933f) and *Introduction à l'étude du droit* (1966a). The legal and sociological theories that he combatted erred, in his estimation, chiefly because of their unacknowledged philosophical premises.

Hauriou wanted to avoid this danger by developing his doctrines in a rigorously observational way. However, his demurrers convinced neither his contemporaries nor later commentators that the philosophical sound of his ideas was not, in fact, philosophy. In combating the philosophy of positivism, he was forced to assert a philosophy of neo-positivism. In evading the anti-realist metaphysics of subjectivism, he had to find what he called a classical spiritualism for an alternative metaphysics. These, in turn, were applicable to non-philosophical disciplines such as law and the empirical sciences; more correctly, they were applicable there only because they had grown from these other disciplines.

What philosophical and metaphysical materials there are, however, are more doctrinal than methodological. We will examine the methodology of the philosophical materials in this chapter.

2. Attitude about Philosophy

The typical attitude about philosophy [*attitude philosophique*] toward Hauriou is that of gratuitous skepticism; critics claim that it is insufficient to solve any seriously posed problems, and must be bypassed for positive investigation (Hauriou, 1899d, p. 58). Critics put philosophical taking sides as much in the camp of the imagination as alchemy or fantasizing about creation myths. Each of these primitive stages must give way to the results of empirical observations: philosophizing to the social sciences, alchemy to chemistry; and archeology displacing creation fantasies. Imagination must be thoroughly exercised before observation can succeed; but eventually observation must supplant it (Hauriou, 1927d, p. 66).

The place metaphysics takes for itself is to speak of absolute principles, principles that go beyond positive observation (Hauriou, 1909a, p. 78). Metaphysics uses the absolute to find in it the reconciliation of contradictory terms, for instance, of science and art, or of sociology and law (Hauriou, 1893e, p. 3). Elementary observation establishes the oppositions; one can then "philosophize" at length upon them, establishing the opposition in its roots and bringing the abstruse notions to the surface light. But the instinctive behavior of the practical and positive jurists in applying their methods, for example, to detail the observed contradiction of subjective economic human needs to objective political human powers, is explained by irreducible contradiction between things; it is this which is fundamental and preferable as a guide to behavior (Hauriou, *Introduction à l'étude du droit administratif français*, p. xviii).

The function of metaphysics is to construct explicative systems of the universe. The net effect of this is to make the unity of beings prevail over their diversity, the principle of identity over the principle of contradiction, and likeness over differences. For no system can be constructed in which there is a predominance of differences over likenesses (Hauriou, 1896, p. 200). The dominant principle of identity in metaphysics excludes even the contradiction of identity and diversity, of simplicity and complexity. But such a coexistent contradiction is needed in adequate concepts, such as that of the state. From the metaphysical point of view, every conceivable division of state will stand in logical contradiction with the substantial unity of the state; both concepts are needed, but the metaphysics of substantial unity as applied to the moral person, state, excludes the division.

As an alternative to metaphysics, Hauriou suggests an experimental and phenomenal point of view, in which no contradiction of logic stands between unity and multiplicity, one in which notions of unitary substance are replaced by those of composite unities (1923d, p. 400). Thus, state's would be a composite of many operations, each the work of a different power, as long as each operation is one that observation and the analysis of observation reveals to be combined in the will of the government; they become one by adherence to a single procedure.

Philosophical theories understand something for the sake of something else, for example, a philosophical theory may understand a phenomenon in terms of a totalized mechanism. Science, on the contrary, takes a given phenomenon without explaining it away and without occupying itself with how the existence in question is explained and fitted into the universe. Positive observation simply observes the modifications, the mode of existence of a certain matter (Hauriou, 1896, p. 3). The gratuitousness of philosophical systems seen in this way explains how Hauriou can say that any one is "not at all demonstrated, and [is] indemonstrable as are all systems" (1893c, p. 6) [*"pas démontré du tout et indémontrable comme tous les systèmes"*].

It is no wonder, then, that Hauriou distances himself from philosophy and metaphysics when they are seen first described as above. He restricts his scope to the direct observation of facts at the point where, otherwise, he parallels his ideas with those of Henri Bergson:

> I have no need to say that this was without any philosophical pretention. . . . I will definitely keep myself from posing the problem in its philosophical terms; this is not my business, I must take the task of representing it in factual situations. (1909a, p. 19n; 1916c, pp. 15–16, 15n1) [*Je n'ai pas besoin de dire que c'était sans aucune prétention philosophique. . . . Je me garderai bien de poser le problème en ses termes philosophiques, ce qui n'est pas mon affaire, je me borne à le signaler dans les faits.*]

Philosophical beliefs are not to be discussed in his work, or at best discussed only obliquely insofar as needed to clear the ground for an issue (Hauriou, 1916c, p. 281). Instead of discussing [*discuter*] the meaning of a philosophical framework, for example, dualism, Hauriou takes his role as simply stating [*constater*] the issue. Thus, to formulate the data of the problem in philosophical terms may sometimes be necessary. For example, he needs some individual freewill and some social determinism in his formulations. Once formulated, it suffices for Hauriou that both are observed to be needed, that they are related by a practical combination, that both transform into rights (ibid., p. 492).

Hauriou appears to yield this same slight nod toward philosophy elsewhere in the demand that the philosophy of some topic be disengaged from all metaphysics; he allows only facts. In his example, this means that what individuals perceive themselves to be, "persons considered as having a power over their conduct and as a subject of duties" (1899f, p. 463) *"l'homme considéré comme ayant un pouvoir de conduite et comme sujet de devoirs"*] is admissible in philosophy, but not the metaphysical entities of the subjective ego [*moi subjectif*] or metaphysical freedom [*liberté métaphysique*], terms which he does not explicitly define. Philosophy of the positivist variety appears to be rehabilitated to some extent, but metaphysical philosophy is constantly excluded, excluded primarily because of its supposed intolerance for manifest contradictions.

3. Neo-Positivism

The impression of Hauriou as positivist is impossible to take seriously, however. Due to what he viewed as positivist philosophy's corrupting influence, during his earlier career, he refused to allow positivist sociology to assist law. Although devoted to positive observation, Hauriou saw clearly the severe problems and dire consequences of positivism, its regression from nominalism to determinism, and into total phenomenalism at last.

Hauriou gives a standard description of nominalism: one admits the ideas of genus, species, and collectivity to be no more than useful vocables, even calling them an empty sound [*flatus vocis*], which correspond to no factual reality. The outcome of this is that the legal personality of social groups can only be a fiction, and that social organization has no real value, ceding to the dream of an inorganic and anarchical social world (1916c, p. 55).

Having given up the determinacy and reality of appearances, the grammar of the universe will be that of connected names only. This is the unilinear determinism that follows from nominalism, "the belief in the entailment of all natural phenomena in a single unique series" (Hauriou, 1911a, pp. 15–16) [*"la croyance dans l'enchaînement de tous les phénomènes naturels en une seule et même série"*]. This restricts the possibility of there being multiple causes, of many antecedent facts combining to cause another, and requires instead a single unique cause for any fact. It makes finality an impossible category; for if acts are rigorously connected in a chain, there is only efficacy, but no direction toward its achievement. It makes order in things impossible; there is no distinction of order and disorder, for if only one series exists, then everything is equally necessary (ibid.).

The only way to get at any differentiation within the primitive homogeneity of the series is to invoke chance (Hauriou, 1894c, p. 303). To Hauriou's way of thinking, the determinism of causality and the futility of premeditated efficiency explain "the impotence of scientific philosophies to engender a morality which is even slightly involved in action" (1919b, p. 692) [*"l'impuissance des philosophies scientifiques à engendrer une morale tant soit peu douée d'action"*] instead of passive acceptance and adjustment. The philosophical hypothesis of universal determinism allows prediction of the future for humanity and discourages the attempt to influence this beyond the laws of its evolution (Hauriou, 1893c, p. 6).

The next movement, out of nominalism to determinism, is into phenomenalism. The denial of spontaneity cannot help but lead to denial of real existences by making all internal phenomena to be explained by the external action of the milieu (Hauriou, 1911a, p. 16). Everything reduces to phenomena ruled by laws, and this law, like the totality of phenomena, is the milieu.

The totality or milieu is a sort of vague entity by which the different forms of existence are explained. In themselves, these differing forms have no real principle of autonomy proper to them; they remain purely verbal phenomena (Hauriou, 1916c, pp. 57–58). This means "any categories . . . are artificial conceptions of our minds" (Hauriou, 1902b, p. 358) [*"les catégories . . . sont des conceptions artificielles de notre esprit"*].

There can be, then, no way to avoid denaturing the political fact: authority, personality, and liberty are lost, with nothing real remaining but solidarity, the milieu existing in a social context.

Hauriou's point of attack upon this unacceptable philosophy is through a reinterpretation of determinism. No less necessary to science, determinism is sufficiently comprehensive if it is a determinism of multiple series. Worked out by Jules Lachelier, Émile Boutroux, and Henri Poincaré, as mentioned in our first chapter, it means to deny that everything is linked by determining causes. The laws of nature leave a certain contingency, a lacuna needing to be filled with spontaneity. There is a place for finality, as a result; for the order in nature is such that in part, at least, it must be willed. Every agent has some liberty; and the result of action is a choice between a good order and an evil one. Not only people, but also atoms—every element in the world—possess this modicum of liberty. As far as scientific discovery is concerned with human individuals, their liberty is conditioned by the presence of liberty in the non-human world, the lacunae left unfilled even after a complete statement of scientific laws (Hauriou, 1916c, pp. 8–9).

This alternative conception of the world is the reversal of roles from those assigned by positivism as it moves into its phenomenalist phase. Instead of the determinism of things being imposed on our thinking, from the external upon the internal, the neo-positivism Hauriou is describing is the imposition of internal thought upon the world outside. Again a reversal: existences are real and determinism is the mere category of our thinking, a category created and employed only for practical ends.

All sciences are founded on practical ends; determinism will be one of the tools to these ends. But if liberty is found to contribute to human individuals' ends in the social order, then this category is on an equal or superior footing with determinism, without the social sciences being any less scientific. The phenomenalist view in old positivism is outmoded, for the reality of categories, genera, and species is necessary to the life of the human spirit and the organization of the social world. Also outmoded is the old monist view, for dualism is the only suitable way of appreciating the conflicts of the social world to cope adequately with them (Hauriou, 1902b, p. 358).

This multi-series determinism [*déterminisme à séries multiples*] admits both continuity and discontinuity in nature: some events are caused by others, but some acts cannot be tied to antecedents, being due instead to the intervention of spontaneity of agents. Spontaneity, in turn, gives rise to a new series of phenomena, which may then be subject to determinism but in a different line than if the intervention had not occurred. Determinism is more a procedure of mind than a reality of things; it cannot be a logical preoccupation to simplify the observation of facts by reducing them to determinism (Hauriou, 1911a, pp. 16–17). Even multiple determinism is incomplete without an "order of things" being added, an order that does not coincide with a universal flux, but which is an arrangement good for things and chosen by them (ibid., pp. 18–19).

In the physical universe, this re-appreciation of the contingency in the laws of nature entails the theory of atomism, for this is a realism insofar as it explains natural phenomena by the existence of beings. Hauriou traces it in modern times to René Descartes, and finds representatives of it in ancient philosophy as well. It is preferable to the phenomenalist view of physical laws and to the third possible direction in physicalist theory Hauriou acknowledges, that of "energism." This is the Newtonian view of the universe, and works itself, too, into pure phenomenalism (1916c, p. 59, 59n1). Because of the carry-over of physical principles, it is not a question for theoretical physics but for philosophy: Is atomic space filled with matter, or is it filled with the forms, which are relationships of particles, relationships equivalent to the energy ascribed to the particles considered as centers of force? (Hauriou, 1899d, p. 91).

From Hauriou's approval of Gottfried Leibniz in several brief mentions, it would probably be true that he would approve of the view of particles as centers of force. In either case, the interaction of atomic particles or centers of energy must be seen in terms of final causality, of a practical science. From a mechanist point of view, we cannot talk of finality; but from the philosophical point of view, we must see the antecedent cause as a final cause (ibid., p. 122).

In the social order, this neo-positivist philosophy has even more important results. Society is complex and pluralized in makeup, for not only are the mechanisms of social inertia at work, but so also are the spontaneous actions of human agents active in liberty. Society admits of the practical combination of diverse elements, elements in contradiction. Human individuals are not only in conformity with each other, but also in opposition to each other. The individuality of any person is opposed to its social nature, and to the social nature of others; their individualities are opposed as well. By observation, social life is made up of oppositions followed by successive reconciliations or by compromises. In society, this occurs not by the external force of natural law, but by reflexive action upon itself by itself, mirrored in the very syntax of its description:

> Society is a form of life where the differences and the contradictions of people reconcile themselves practically; it is a peace, which realizes itself progressively in the midst of perpetual conflicts; it is a synthesis; it founds itself on the combination of feelings and ideas, just as does the organic life on the combinations of chemical elements. Surely it is a whole whose parts are in solidarity with each other, but at the same time it must not be forgotten that the whole creates itself continually and creates itself only by the reconciliation of the conflicts between its parts; there is a twofold constant current: the reaction of the whole on the parts, but also the creation of the whole by the parts. Thus it is not sufficient to set forth the solidarity as existing; it must also be shown as constituting itself laboriously; and the rule of law can no longer intervene just as the application of a pre-existing solidarity but also as an element in the formation of the solidarity. (Hauriou, 1902b, pp. 358–359) [*La société est une forme de vie où se concilient pratiquement les différences et les contradictions des hommes; elle est une paix qui se réalise progressivement au milieu de perpetuels conflits; elle est une synthèse; elle s'établit sur des combinaisons de sentiments et d'idées, comme la vie organique sur des combinaisons d'éléments chimiques. Sans doute, en même temps elle est un tout dont les parties sont solidaires, mais il ne faut pas oublier que le tout se crée continuellement et qu'il ne se crée*

> *que par la conciliation des conflits des parties; il y a un double courant constant: la réaction du tout sur les parties, mais aussi la création du tout par les parties. Des lors il ne suffit pas de montrer la solidarité comme existante; il faut aussi la montrer comme se constituant péniblement et la règle de droit peut intervenir non plus seulement comme l'application d'une solidarité préexistante mais aussi comme un élément de la formation de la solidarité.*]

The idea that disengages itself from this excitement is that the unity realizes itself; it is not the unrolling of a unique principle, but the synthesis of different and contrary principles. In an unending action and reaction of elements, such unity can only be purely practical, impossible to define with one formula because it is only one form of life. Other lives are synthesized with other formulas. The form of life can be judged good or bad, but only according to life itself, not according to abstract principles. The judgment according to life is performed by comparing the history of societies to develop a theory of progress, what living well [*bien vivre*] is in terms of which a judgment can be made (ibid.).

This is the "new positivism" Hauriou finds and accepts—"broader, more tolerant, hence more relative" [*"plus large, plus tolérant par là même qu'il est plus relative"*]. It is dualist, begins from the fact of practical life, which is the conciliation of contraries. Its best proof is that it accords with good sense, a good sense that is fully informed by observation. Its truth is that of virtue, for virtue is found at the mid-point [*stat in medio*], but not noncommittally, for as we have seen, the practical equilibrium has always the dominance of one element chosen to dominate but not exorcise the other. The dualism described under general methodology Hauriou names "neo-positivism," and places it in a philosophical context, as an alternative to the unacceptable philosophy of positivism (ibid.).

In law, the ideal discipline of the rational organization, neo-positivism discovers its true home. For the profound tendency of law is toward philosophical realism [*réalisme philosophique*], realism not in a naturalistic sense but in terms of the problem of universals. This is the reason nominalism, despite its longstanding popularity, has not succeeded in penetrating and dominating the law (Hauriou, 1916c, p. 55). Law requires not just that human beings be organized, but even more that they be organized by ideas. Hauriou calls this kind of organization the condition of status [*statut*] (ibid., p. 59).

Of its nature, law requires one philosophy and excludes another; it requires realism and excludes nominalism. Law takes sides in the problem of universals. A realist, recognizing that the ideas of genus, species, and collectivity correspond to realities, can accept that social organizations have a real existence separable in part from that of individuals. So too can a realist accept that these social beings can evolve toward moral personality seen not as a fiction but as a reality. Legal personality becomes not a pure creation of law but the legal face [*la figure juridique*] of a reality—of moral personality (ibid., p. 51). The question of personality, the key question of social and legal reality and of individual reality, is answerable only in terms of this position on universals. "It is necessary to be realist or nominalist, and it is necessary to be the one or the other in a logical fashion, from end to end" (ibid., p. 54) [*"Il faut être réaliste ou nominaliste et il faut être l'un ou l'autre avec logique, de bout au bout"*].

So also only one philosophy of liberty, for example, is compatible with the law, the philosophy of relative liberty. The maxim of this philosophy is that "everything not forbidden is permitted up to the limit" (Hauriou, 1933d, p. 84) [*"Tout ce qui n'est pas défendu est permis jusqu'à la limite"*]. It contradicts the maxims of the philosophy based on order and authority, that "everything not conformed to the constitution (whatever that might include) is without legal value" (ibid.) [*"Tout ce qui n'est pas conforme à la constitution hypothétique est sans valeur juridique"*], which means in practice that the individual rights of subjects in opposition to the state do not necessarily exist, that there is not necessarily any liberty.

4. Classical Spiritualism

To his strong realism, Hauriou finds opposed an anti-realism, whose legal origins occurred in the nineteenth-century theories of social fictions. The subsequent development of this anti-realism came in the twentieth century with Léon Duguit's denial of social personality (Hauriou, 1916c, pp. 55–57). The personality denied Hauriou equates with the objective focus, while the alternative pursued is what he calls, perhaps surprisingly, the direction of subjectivism (Hauriou, 1896, p. 359).

The most influential expression of this trend was in Jean-Jacques Rousseau's identification of the law with the expression of the general will. As a matter of political philosophy, it was imprudent for jurists to import this into law; but they did so nevertheless (Hauriou, 1933g, p. 91). The error was to think that the general will, in formulating laws, would progressively define the ideas upon which the state rests. Reduced to philosophical terms, to put the idea of the state in dependence upon the common will was to put the intelligence subject to the will. This was, for Hauriou, to prepare the way for Hegelian subjectivism and the new philosophy [*philosophie nouvelle*] of Bergson and Maurice Blondel (1916c, p. 273). The practical impact was that once these philosophical ideas were diffused and enough people clearly saw the complicated incoherences of the state, the Revolution was bound to occur. The anachronism between the authors cited and the social result implies Hauriou would have pushed the origins of these subjectivist ideas back beyond Rousseau, although he does not do so explicitly (1903c, p. 459).

To Hauriou, this philosophical trend that he traces to Rousseau and Georg Wilhelm Friedrich Hegel, found subjective thought to constitute the essential form of being, whether at once or progressively. It found the science of being to be more than being, that being is constituted only by the knowledge it has of itself; Hauriou argues that this is impossible, for organic existence, the body, is always more than its representation. The unthinking precedes the thinking: many organisms never acquire thought. Unthinking body engenders thinking: thought appears only within the history of the organism, and from the virtualities of the organism; yet it never fully controls the organism. Thought gains whatever authority it has from the organic; for example, law is made not for itself but for society (1899d, pp. 134–135).

By contrasting this philosophical subjectivism with the objectivist theories of Descartes, in saying, "There is in me thought, the representative; therefore there is *a form* of being" (ibid.) [*"Il y a en moi de la pensée, du représentatif, donc il y a* une forme *de l'être"*], Hauriou appears to accept Descartes' view. But his stand relative to Descartes becomes clearer later when, in place of his apparent approval, he says, "if in place of 'I think therefore I am,' he had said, "I think, and I think God, and God is, so I am,' then his intentions would have been better understood" (1966c, p. 8) [*"Si au lieu du: je pense, donc je suis, it avait dit: je pense et je pense Dieu, donc Dieu est, done je suis, son intention eut être mieux compris"*].

The intellectualism that led to subjectivism brought on the final stage of *philosophie nouvelle*, a philosophy of action and intuition. From an excess of discursive reason and criticism, it has become clear to Hauriou that metaphysics based on these are not adapted to life, and so intuition is adopted instead. In the order of life, intuition precedes reasoning; intuition directs living bodies, and political science shows that the same is true of social bodies. The fault of the theories of Bergson, Edouard Le Roy, and Blondel is, however, that they neglect to realize that intuition is not sufficient to foster life; it must be controlled by reason, just as the legislative discussion controls the executive intuition (Hauriou, 1927g, p. vi).

Intuition partly coincides with reality, but only partly; for it knows nothing of movement except its action, ignoring that the stability of its existence is equally essential (Hauriou, 1916c, p. xxxi). The same error continues, then, in thinking totally novel creation [*création de nouveau*] or duration [*durée*] suffice; whereas the material aspect of what form is created must condition and influence this purely formal aspect of creation (ibid., p. 15n1; 1929c, p. 69). The philosophy called "new" turns out for Hauriou to have no superiority over the "old," still not having the firmness of a philosophy of concepts and ideas (Hauriou, 1916c, p. xxiv; 1923c, p. 343).

This confusion of philosophical ideas is unacceptable to law. In making social matter to be itself a phenomenon, it has destroyed everything, since the notion of phenomenon vanishes without the notion of matter. It is again confusion of the procedures of knowing with the social forces to be known, to claim law as no longer theological or metaphysical, being no longer related to any subjective and individual input (Hauriou, 1916c, p. 60n1; 1896, pp. 2–3; 1912b, pp. 7–8).

The intellectualist, subjectivist, and intuitionist schools do not offer an adequate philosophy to law and social science. What does, Hauriou says, is the classical spiritualism [*le spiritualisme classique*], which is in the service of the human spirit, eternal object of all philosophy [*l'esprit humain objet éternel de toute philosophie*], refusing to subject it either to its material conditions or its own activity (1916c, p. xxx). Accordingly, the philosophical basis of things is the conformity of conduct to successively hierarchized ideals, but summed up in maximum liberty. This spirit provides the discontinuity sufficient to liberate persons from social necessities by keeping them from resting, in any event, by keeping them from subjection to the factual continuum of natural necessities (Hauriou, 1899d, pp. 112–113). From the philosophical point of view, life and liberty are inseparable (Hauriou, 1892a, p. 26). The viewpoint is not the mere empty and ineffectual belief in a free faculty; for the essence of classical spiritualism is that the reality of will and the belief attributable to will have effects on external data (Hauriou, 1896, p. 39n1).

Hauriou ties the key belief in free individuals and their impact on civilization to "grand transcendent principles," which, perceived by human reason, have descended and made civilization: they are principles of civilization rather than legal norms (1929c, p. 227n2). This is a philosophical belief in the life proper to ideas and in the deeply ideal nature of beings, a sort of Platonic idealism but not strictly that of Plato. The true doctrine of Plato [*La véritable doctrine de Platon*] admits the presence of the idea in beings only by participation; particular beings exist only by their participation in general ideas of type and species.

For Hauriou, however, ideas are themselves beings, the beings par excellence. He appears to understand that such was not Plato's doctrine. Where there is a definitive difference, though, is Hauriou's belief that every being is an idea that realizes itself and becomes more or less conscious (1916c, p. 281, 281n1). Consequently, Hauriou can affirm the objective existence of each human spirit conceived as a particular and different being. He can place this particular existence above the general laws of intelligence, by which it thinks itself, and above the will, without at the same time losing hold of idealist values. It is not a one-sided empiricism to look to the individual, for that is where ideas are found at some stage of development. In employing the adage that there is science only of the general and truth only of the particular, no inconsistency is created between science and truth; for the essence of the individual spirit, and in reduced fashion of all material existence proportionately, is the embodiment of universal ideas (ibid., p. xxxi).

The idealist perspective of Hauriou's classical spiritualism is sufficient to convince him that his is also a doctrine of substance because in philosophy, qualitative differences are understood to be what touch most closely to the subjective substance of things. For example, commerce rests on exchange,

exchange rests on the value of products, and this value of products rests on their qualities, and their ability to satisfy needs and wants (ibid., p. 258). Philosophy is established in the substantial order from the time it lets go of motor reactions to concentrate on ideas; for ideas are the virtualities of sensations and movements. Even in the physical world, what is most substantial are virtualities, those of atoms, underneath the varied surface appearance of things (ibid., p. 264).

Hauriou arrives at this line of reasoning by starting with the common sense fact that we name substances. The name is a capacity for action, and any capacity is a virtuality. A virtuality, since it is not yet realized, sustains itself as homogeneous and indivisible, the characteristics of a substance. Virtuality is more substantial, in fact, than that which is actually realized. What is present and realized is only a passing phenomenon, destroyed as soon as it is built and disappearing as soon as it appears, because it is in the present that it is realized and the present has no endurance. Endurance, and consequently substantiality, exists only in idea: in the past by memory, or in the future by virtuality (ibid., p. 263).

Assimilating substance to a virtuality by idea creates the danger of exaggerating the role of "order in potency." Virtuality can become a specter haunting each act in freedom a person makes, because it might stifle liberty; virtuality as pre-existence allows no spontaneity. Hauriou stresses, on the contrary, that virtuality is not an already fully present but hidden existence; its virtuality is that it is not actual, there is nothing but an idea to develop itself, an idea that appears and exists only as it is exercised (1933d, pp. 76–77). This is why he finds it necessary to check the excessive development of institutions; as a goal becomes more conscious, it begins to pre-exist in a more literal sense and to limit free spontaneous growth.

The sense of substance Hauriou uses is an explicitly positive one and not metaphysical. The positive sense means "a homogeneous reality hidden under the accidents" (1916c, p. 260) [*"réalité homogène cachée sous les accidents"*]. For example, to ask on what something is painted, and to find that it is painted on a roll of cotton, a homogeneous tissue without appreciable accidents when painted, is a question of substance. For Hauriou's purposes, even when the question of substance is posed absolutely instead of relatively, it still has recognizably a positive meaning; for states of matter are more substantial, one more than another, when one sustains another.

In the sphere of personality, where physical uncovering of the positive substance is not possible, the positive meaning can be still maintained and the metaphysical avoided, for the name or title of an individual is something positive. It constitutes the legal reality, expressing a substantial quality of the individual, a quality, which is, in law, that of legal personality. This title is conserved indefinitely without having to be exercised; it is separated from its actual exercise and thus also from the accidents of the present. It is, consequently, the substance of the individual in law; and it is this value, quality, or virtuality, which constitutes "the eminent dignity of the human person" (ibid., pp. 260–261, 492nn2,64) [*"l'eminente dignité de la personne humaine"*]. This is the ultimate justification for the rights of the individual; for philosophers it is identified with the human power of will, and for jurists, it is the fact that the human person is the sole free and responsible being.

In this way, we end up with the substance of legal personality, but we did not begin with it. It is sheer metaphysics to explain the body by the soul, and to explain objective rational nature by subjective personality. For positive science, the body appears before the soul, and so all we can do is posit body first, then introduce person into it as something real. To consider the body to be created by an act of subjective will is metaphysics; the only physical explanation, the only way that falls under the senses and so can be observed, is to have the body created by an objective procedure and then make subjective will appear in it. The definition of person in Boetius, an individual substance of a rational nature [*rationalis naturae individua substantia*], shows the precedence of homogeneous or undivided substance over the rationality, and it is perhaps the prime characteristic of legal personality to jurists that it is indivisible. In philosophical terms, this means that legal personality is continuous and identical to itself (ibid., pp. 85–87, 158, 260).

This is Hauriou's last word on the metaphysics of classical spiritualism. He refuses to go beyond the determination of the phenomenon of objective ideas, a phenomenon evinced throughout the movement of history and fulfilled in the development of each substantial person. Each is identified in substance with its virtuality, the idea being worked out in its life, whether it be social or individual. The presence of the idea is manifested by the continuity of development, for which neither contingent events nor physical law could sufficiently account, since Hauriou has re-appreciated this physical law in his neo-positivism.

Hauriou, however, refuses to inquire whether any substantial spiritual reality corresponds with the objectivity of ideas. He admits that idea appears as a substance, but stops short of asking whether it corresponds to a substance. This is critical to know, however, because if ideas did correspond to a substantial spiritual reality, some ideas could have more reality than others. Some could come closer to truth. But this is the job for philosophers to consider. "We await from them the construction of the metaphysics for this physics which is the vitalism of social institutions" (1933g, p. 128) [*"Nous attendons d'eux la construction métaphysique de cette physique qu'est le vitalisme des institutions sociales"*].

The two people Hauriou found to be carrying out this mission were Georges Dumesnil and Jacques Chevalier, both religious philosophers who identified the reality of ideas with God, in answer to Hauriou's expectation. Hauriou still claimed to be waiting, however, despite the completed work of these two. Their religious affiliation raises the question of how religion fitted into his own scheme.

For Hauriou, scholastic philosophy was only an extension of theology; yet, although medieval thought was not free of dogma, it was more so than the pagan "middle ages," the period just before the golden age of Greek thought (1895a, pp. 530, 539). Hauriou claims the metaphysics he follows is Thomistic, particularly the Thomistic doctrine of soul and body (1916c, pp. xxiii–xxiv). His own doctrine of soul and body differed greatly from this, however. Idea is substance for Hauriou, the "body" not being something divorced from idea but much more likely being an idea in its objective, not yet subjective form, "soul." His religious influences remained, however, that of the medieval Church and its institutional continuation. He never did go on explicitly to work out the importance of his early doctrine, which espoused that putting the idea of God into society is putting into society an infinite sociability, which gives the will new resources (1896, pp. 357–358).

In essence, Hauriou did not indicate how his legal and social theories were to be conjoined with a more fundamental metaphysical stratum. He left the lines of a philosophy, however, as described; for philosophy cannot be cut from beneath any portion of life. It lies hidden but it is there, everywhere. "Beneath all positive theory there is metaphysics" (1916c, p. xxx) [*"Derrière toute théorie positive il y a une métaphysique"*]. "Behind all physical theory there must be laid a metaphysics" (1916c, p. 59n1) [*"Derrière toute théorie physique, il convient de situer une métaphysique"*]. "In the smallest borderline dispute there is metaphysics" (1900a, p. 413) [*"Il y a de métaphysique dans le moindre procès du mur mitoyen"*]. There are philosophical postulates hiding under all judicial systems (1911a, p. 15). This is no open warrant for speculation, however, for besides philosophical truth, philosophical tactics also exist. To Chevalier, Hauriou writes his tactics:

> But I want to explain my frame of mind to you. *I realized long ago that in social science metaphysical argument is no longer any good and must be left aside*. For say to a *listener* that power comes from God and you will turn him to ice; tell him that it belongs to a social elite and you will interest him. But fundamentally it is the same thing; in a social elite, as long as it is not just an aristocratic class, power is an individual possession the infant has at birth, and so it is a gift of God. But we must not say that; we must follow the way of positive knowledge to its last possible reach—in the example of power, the limits of the positive fact of the elite. And there stop. (1923d, p. 168; 1966b, pp. 8–9) [*Mais je tiens à vous expliquer mon état d'esprit.* J'ai constaté depuis longtemps que dans les sciences sociales l'argument métaphysique ne porte plus et qu'on est obligé de le reléguer. Ainsi dites à un auditoire *que le pourvoir vient de Dieu et vous le trouverez de glace; dite-lui qu'il appartient à une élite sociale et vous l'intéressez. Au fond, c'est la même chose; dans l'élite sociale, à supposer que ce ne soit pas une aristocratie de classe, le pouvoir est un don individuel que l'enfant apporte en naissant, donc*

> *c'est un don de Dieu. Mais il ne faut pas le dire, il faut reculer les bornes de la connaissance positive jusqu'à la limite du fait positif de l'élite. Et puis s'arrêter.*]

5. Philosophy of Other Disciplines

The ideas that define persons are revealed in their full impact at their inception; as time passes, the force of these moral and religious ideas weakens. Then comes the time for other disciplines—philosophy, law and social science—which are secondary social phenomena to the human species and its directive ideas. From inauspicious beginnings, these disciplines grow marvelously by the articulation of discursive reason to restore enthusiasm and energize the failing ideals (Hauriou, 1933a, p. 31; 1969, p. 130). The philosophy drawn from the revelations, social and legal, can be applied back to them.

Hauriou admits his *Leçons sur le mouvement social* of 1899 was a philosophy of science (1899g, p. 348). His philosophical attempt therein is to seek out some means to put the ideal elements and liberty back into physical things, to limit mechanism by some element that conditions it (ibid., p. 351). He claims for his endeavor the right to be judged not by the particular techniques of the sciences, but in the name of the synthesis itself, which he creates, and that is worth whatever it is, itself, worth (ibid.).

Hauriou refuses to bow to the scandal lodged by scientists at his nonmathematical use of their theorems; he counters that they are of the same ilk as jurists who express concern over the nontechnical use of legal principles to help construct a moral philosophy or a sociology. He sees them all as refusing to blunt the edges of their terms regardless how much they are needed. "The human race is lost; will it be replaced by scientists?" (ibid., p. 349) [*"La race s'en perdait; va-t-elle donc être remplacée par celle des scientifiques?"*] He claims that they cannot disavow his work, because things have many aspects, all legitimate, if we place them in order. To do this, Hauriou sets up several principles for work in the philosophy of science.

> Only look to physicists when they begin to leave physics; strip physical principles of their quantitative aspects; I retain only the qualitative aspects; I interpret them; finally, work a philosophical rapprochement with social principles. (Ibid., p. 348) [*Ne regarde les physiciens qu'à la condition qu'ils commencent par sortir de leur physique; depouillerai les principes physiques de leurs éléments quantitatifs; je ne retiendrai que leurs éléments qualitatifs; je les interprète; afin d'opérer avec les pincipes sociaux des rapprochements philosophiques.*]

Hauriou found it no less necessary to justify what he was doing in his legal works, for again, some critics lodged vigorous technical accusations against the philosophy of law therein (1899f, p. 471). Hauriou himself was something less than favorable toward the so-called philosophy of law. Its starting point is inviolable human persons and the threats to them. This is non-metaphysical, although philosophical, which is good; but it can lead only to a system that reduces everything to the individual, the error from medieval natural law through eighteenth-century philosophical enlightenment and French Revolutionary thought to the nineteenth-century Hegelian subjectivism in legal philosophy (ibid., p. 464). Philosophy of law ends with seeing political life as the guard for individual relations; so it must be supplemented with social science, which, from a perspective of science rather than individual life, sees social order as the objective of political life. Social science, then, shows the basis from which individualism grows, namely, personality, whether individual or social; while philosophy of law shows the limits beyond which the collective stress of social science cannot pass (ibid., p. 476).

Hauriou found philosophy of law to be a legitimate concern, but not, as it existed, of much concern to him. He felt compelled to try to keep law free from philosophical matters lest it be prejudiced (1893c, p. 4). There is enough overlap between the two disciplines, however, that he felt the need to distinguish them for key terms. As stated, he is going to distinguish the meaning of will, liberty, power, and state, in terms of two disciplines: law and philosophy.

In law, *will* is a phenomenon available in acts, a series of autonomous and changing decisions by practical reason manifested in external attitudes; in philosophy, it is a manifestation of substance, and so is a continuously existing reality (Hauriou, 1898, p. 20). In law, *liberty* means the power to do all that is not forbidden by law, and not to do anything except what is ordered by law; in philosophy, it means the faculty to conform to order while maintaining some choice of means (Hauriou, 1929c, p. 650). The justification of *power* is a philosophical question of its origins; its legitimacy is a legal question of its devolution (Hauriou, 1923d, p. 167). Philosophically, *state* is the guidance of legal order according to ideal right and not natural necessity; legally, it is an ensemble of bonds additional to nation that people freely choose. In terms of social science, state involves an unconscious evolution according to fatalistic laws of nature (Hauriou, 1892b, pp. 2–3).

So it appears that Hauriou does not offer much that he would call a philosophy of law. However, we can reflect upon his work in the following way: First, law ordinarily covers up its metaphysical foundations with legal technicality; but when we remove this covering, as when factual power comes to be legitimatized, and then we discover the metaphysical roots of law (Hauriou, 1929c, p. 29). Next, Hauriou acknowledges that he is dealing with a natural history of law rather than with a philosophy of natural law; yet he promises a later series of essays on natural law (1918b, p. 815). Finally, in beginning that promised series in the same year, he ascribed the positivist method to the study of natural law, insofar as its bases are pre-social and therefore can rest upon nothing but species (1933a, p. 42). The identification of species with idea existing as virtuality provides for its philosophical character and its "social revelation" to positive observation.

Since this method is, however, the way Hauriou proceeded throughout his whole career, we could conceivably, on his authorization, reinterpret his entire career as addressing a philosophy of law. However, we should keep in mind that he never reinterpreted himself in this way.

Nine

THE PHILOSOPHICAL STATUS OF HAURIOU'S METHODOLOGY

1. Introduction

The constellation of many groups of doctrines in Hauriou's work would be considered philosophical materials by many, especially in view of their coherence to his theory of ideas. But because of distinctive characteristics of the idea, it is questionable whether Hauriou would see his doctrines in this way. The specification of his philosophy is problematic. In attempting to relate the problem of specifying his philosophical method to a theory of substance hoped derivable from his work, we can evaluate the lines of thought most characteristic to and explicit in his methodology.

2. System of Doctrines

The universe is composed of matter, which exists in atomic diversity with likenesses but even more with a tendency toward dispersion and expansion because of radical differences. The dispersion is not its ultimate condition, however; matter achieves balances over and above the partially or mutually destructive syntheses it can also achieve. Such balancing of contradictions occurs by convergence around mediating elements of matter, elements, or processes, which have the capacity of representing both contradictions and allowing their mutual penetration and preservation. This spontaneous action of matter is carried out while it remains material. Since the universe is coherent despite its contradictoriness, this function may be extended well beyond Hauriou's use of it in thermodynamics to be considered a capacity of all matter, immense love [*un immense amour*].

Atomic diversity is thus the existence of matter in the form of centers of force not reducible to their measurability, not reducible to their function in theory. The coherence of the universe of matter is not, then, a preliminary given factor but is rather a revelation in the duration of matter in movement, a duration effected through the retarding influence of material species upon the movement of matter.

The species that occur in this durable movement of evolution are fixed species, since species are the successive termini of evolution. Species do not evolve; evolution is a function of individuals, which vary from specific type and eventually consolidate a new identifiable complex of characteristics, a new species equally fixed. Living beings live their species: live up to the species and live beyond it. The species is not the sole existential determinant, then; rather the individual life is. Species is the retardation and stabilization of life in movement. The direction by fixed species is the movement of evolution; into this movement, however, is introduced a counter movement against evolution [*Contr'évolution*] when persons evolve. *Contr'évolution* is the movement wherein individuals seize control of the future of their own species by seeking themselves rather than their species as their identity; this is the beginning of human history. Because of it, human beings are the terminus of evolution beyond which it cannot go.

History becomes an individualistic pessimism [*pessimisme individualiste*] of fall from the human type in the achievement of human individuality. Historical progress becomes the return to type in the achievement of rationality. The formation of the several social fabrics, due to the appropriately adjusted convergent expansiveness inherent even in primitive matter, carries the progressive return through positive, metaphysical, and religious modes of rationality. Another dimension of the same return to rationality is the alternation of ages of belief and of criticism, of medieval and renaissance epochs. The contradiction between them, due to the incompleteness of each, is inexpugnable, but can be mediated or retarded by establishment of a half-medieval age [*demi-moyen âge*], best carried out in the representative administrative regime that succeeds to the rule by aristocracy and by democracy.

Individuals find some of the routes of rationality—the human type—consciously available. Observation extends not just to their organic nature but also to their representational abilities; they can discover their desires, their freedom of will, their intellect and its conceptualization, their organizations, and correlations of matter and of concepts. But these are not fully available nor fully certified by their self-consciousness. Beyond these, some aspects of their selves are not at all available to self-consciousness. Even their lone attempts to alleviate the contradictions among individuals resulting from individual attention yield only an individualistic solution, contract. The conscious deficiencies of consciousness force individuals beyond self-consciousness.

Only objective observation of social order through its history reveals the fullness of the human type, ideal, or species. There, individuals find the need for belief in the constant revelation of humanity, through the intuition of seers of all kinds followed by popular imitation of them, and now still available as a result of the practicality of their insights. The involuntary and the unconscious stratum of the human being found there must be interiorized to achieve human individuality, and subsequently human personality with and before others recognized as human persons. The achievement of soul from body follows this route. These ideas are present throughout Hauriou's second appendix to *La science sociale traditionnelle* (1896), his "*Fragment sur l'évolution et le contrévolution au sens théologique*" (1887a), his "Prologo" to Ruiz del Castillo's *Principios de derecho público y constitucional* (1927f), and "*L'ordre social, la justice, et le droit*" (1927d).

Knowledge of right conduct occurs by this sacrifice of individuality in the face of tradition, and the conduct to which it leads is the sacrifice of restricted individuality in the face of the moral absolute found there. This absolute is the human individual, the human person; but it is discovered in full only through non-individual means. Personality is the good, its value as justice; but because of the indirection toward justice it needs proper external conditions for its realization, and this condition is order.

Person and justice may be the goal, but the end is something less lofty; it is a combination of order with justice, such that the just is realized only insofar as it does not destroy order. Natural law, then, is not equivalent to justice, the principle of which is always the same; natural law is a set of principles dependent upon order, and so it is changing and it is only partly real at any time. It appears highly valued in history during ages of democratic government; but democracy is not necessarily the best means of achieving it, since the moral absolute is never fully dominant over individualistic pessimism.

Value for the person can be, perhaps, even more stifled in democracy. The realization of order cannot be fully insured because it depends upon many discretionary acts. This structure gives the "architecture of the legal system": directives are given, but only on the basis of standards (1933c, pp. 190–191). Both of these are given on the basis of principles, principles that are used in interpreting law and thus are more discretionary than laws, though dependent upon law.

Finally, law, the whole matter of legality, is itself a matter of discretion in view of the ideal of justice and so law exists in function of this ideal without being identified with it. Order always intrudes. The progress toward the foundations of conduct from legality toward super-legality (including the principles of good administration) is embodied in the life of institutions, in their legitimization and then personification, a life spread out over time. Institution is the mediator of organic life toward personal life in society. Because of the dependence of individual knowledge of humanity upon its social revelation, institution also conditions the personalization of individual human beings.

3. Reliance upon Ideas

Throughout the sweep of these doctrines, which we have only sketched here and not attempted to justify, one after another comes back to Hauriou's reliance upon ideas. The likeness of matter and the species that control its movement are identified with ideas; individual sacrifice and intuition occur for the sake of historically revealed ideas, otherwise unconscious. The moral absolute is an idea, and personification takes place as a function of the idea. The presence of God in the world is manifested by the revelation of ideas. Hauriou's more lengthy discussions on the nature of "idea" are found throughout "*La théorie de l'Institution et de la fondation*" (1925c) and the first book of *Précis de droit constitutionnel* (1923c).

Hauriou's structures conditioning dualism, and so also his pragmatism, apply to world, knowledge, morals, and society. These structures—contradiction, mediation, and transaction—appear to be irreducible to idea, yet closer examination reveals that this is not so. The ultimate contradiction, which can be read back and differentiated into lower level contradictions, is between subjectivity and objectivity, between personal will or freedom as over and against the factual and materially observable phenomena. Yet on one side, the person is an idea reaching full explication, and on the other, the objective or material element in many relationships is identified with idea, sometimes with a bizarre appearance. Thus, sociologically, Hauriou calls the form of groups their material element. Yet this form is surely an idea being realized and the material factor in legal phenomena, for example, interpretation, is identified with the spirit of laws. Even in the cosmological order, matter is realized by its own inherent powers, giving rise to the feeling that matter is not exclusively material. We have seen Hauriou occasionally identify contradiction with the traditional disparity of matter and form; but as this works out, the matter is itself something that might be more readily recognized as form. Contradiction, then, does not appear to be contradiction of idea with non-idea, but contradiction between ideas or of idea with incomplete idea (concept), leaving idea as the fundamental stratum of reality.

4. Philosophical Interpretation

We might be tempted to identify idea as the absolute in which Hauriou claims metaphysics synthesizes contradictions, and thus to find it as the home of philosophy for Hauriou. However, several internal facets of Hauriou's writings work against this interpretation. First, we have seen Hauriou, in elucidating his strategy to Jacques Chevalier, espouse that this is not the right era to argue philosophically in law or science. So, if he does in fact follow his own strategy, the arguments he uses cannot be considered philosophical ones, nor can their elements be so considered. Yet Hauriou manifests no reluctance to employ ideas in the ways described. Therefore, we cannot conclude that he views ideas to be the formal objects of philosophy.

Second, we have also seen that philosophy and metaphysics constitute the realm of the supra-sensible for Hauriou. But we have also found that for him, the idea is sensible, or at least objectively available; it is manifested in every order of existence. So, as a result of the extended scope of science and law for Hauriou, idea falls essentially into the purview of science and law, instead of marking off philosophy from them.

Finally, the way Hauriou describes the presence of philosophical and metaphysical issues is as "hidden under" questions in positive science and law. His work allegedly within these areas requires that we seek below its surface categories if we are interested in deriving what is meaningful from the philosophical viewpoint.

Through the extended telescope of science and law, philosophy appears to have a quite restricted realm. Philosophy is supra-sensible, but so much is sensible! What reality philosophy can retain, whether theoretical doctrine or practiced method, is a serious question for consideration. It is not obvious what is the doctrinal residue from other disciplines' materials; disciplines only raise what they can handle, and because of their extension, they appear to raise whatever can be legitimately raised. Philosophy must comprise some set of doctrines for Hauriou, however, because he names several theories he considers wrong as "philosophies."

Yet philosophy is no single set of doctrines, for the same reason. This state of affairs would tend toward the opinion that philosophy is defined by a method, since no realm of existence exists that is set aside as philosophical property; but we do have the description of some doctrines as philosophical. The way of going about an effort, and thereby giving a peculiar quality to doctrines characterized by that method, will not be introspective. Hauriou allows introspective method in every pursuit, but in none is it sufficient for reaching successful conclusions. The external observational method he requires everywhere fails also to characterize philosophy; it may be a part of a philosophical enterprise, but it cannot specify philosophy precisely because we find it everywhere in order.

Overall, Hauriou is not inclined toward specifying anything by method, which he rightly sees to be formal and empty. The importance, for example, of procedure in his social theory is that procedure is not a set of rules but a living existence through time. As a second example, the importance of dualism is that it abides by the contradictory structure of existence.

We fail to locate philosophy for Hauriou in terms either of doctrine or method, but still realize that, while not just a question of idea, philosophy is tied to idea as the summary positive category. In this perplexity, it seems no *tour de force* to look to his demand at the end of the 1925 classic, "*La théorie de l'institution et de la fondation*," that philosophers must supply the substance corresponding to the phenomenally available idea, if such exists (1933g, p. 128). Substance appears as the category taking us into the philosophical order of investigation. How it is derived in its philosophical sense and how it is fulfilled in its philosophical content are tasks that await completion.

The origin of this philosophical category is not in the search for a substrate to appearances; we have seen Hauriou elsewhere explicitly call the object of this search a positive concept and exclude it from the philosophical order, although the tone at that point was to do so at the expense of philosophy. Neither is its genesis found in the search for unity; Hauriou has often been found to decline those metaphysical systems because their logical search for unity has done an injustice to the contradictoriness apparent in positive reality. Nor is substance sought as the correlate of concepts; for the substance in question is the correlate of ideas, and ideas are not concepts. Ideas provide the continuity of social bodies, whereas the conceptualized ends of societies cannot provide these. Hauriou holds that the chief use of concepts is to show the discontinuity introduced by the human order into the continuum of the laws of nature.

Instead, we can find the origin of the philosophical concept of substance in Hauriou's characteristic drive toward practicality. We have seen that he also objects to metaphysics in its unacceptable form because it tends to understand reality for the sake of something else, to explain obtrusive facts away to reach logical unity. To Hauriou, substance appears in the attempt to understand something for itself, without reducing it to something else.

Substance, from this intellectual genesis, comes to approximate the traditional definition of that which exists of itself. The neutrality in the "of" is retained due to the mode in which the concept is acquired; it does not supply the meaning "by" or "from," since the attempt to appreciate substance is the attempt to reach a stable irreducibility (not a finality), not to carry it into self-productivity. The being that this substance is, is a spiritual presence in a milieu for Hauriou; but he identifies this spiritual presence with activity understood as spontaneity instead of self-generation. This substance does perform reflexive action, but it is the action of self-limitation [*autolimitation*] that is also the most characteristic form of activity in human social life.

Spiritual presence in a milieu is evidence for substance, but the evidence is not equivalent to the presence of substance. Self-limitation is the condition for appearance, for unlimited spiritual energy exists not spread out through a process of existence, but exists all at once. Hauriou talks of unlimited energy burning out the world of appearance, of igniting like fireworks. He states this from the point of view of the evidencing of substance, which indeed would not be possible were it to be present without the mediation of its self-limitation. But from the point of view of substance, the spiritual manner of the activity of spontaneous existence, self-limitation is not negative. This inability to appear without limitation implies no negativity in substance, no lack of existence; it implies only that no milieu for it to appear in would exist if it were not for "resistances" or limits that it places upon itself. So the placing of self-limits is, succinctly, the very fact of its coming into evidence.

The correspondence of this substance with the phenomenal idea is not accomplished once and for all then. Ideas are objective and existent because they are substance-appearing; they are not pre-existent to the accomplishment of this appearance. They establish no mirror-image order in the world. Substance, limiting itself as, in turn, each of the appearances in idea do, cannot come to reality all at once. Time and history are not the life of substance but are the only way substance can appear. They can exist in a milieu, because appearance of it occurs through limitations.

Idea, non-contingent and absolute as it is, surely cannot coalesce with substance, because it is mediated through limitations. But if the limitations are themselves the activity of spiritual substance, we must explain how the coalescence is avoided. The self-limitation of substance is not the existence of substance; it is the manifestation of substance, and hence temporal. Limitation is not dissociable from the material existence from which the concept of it is derived. Material limit is a concept derived from material existences, however difficult of unambiguous definition that derivative concept may be. The concept of limitation, then, is inseparable from what is not spiritual substance, from what is the partialization and dispersion of spiritual substance.

The concept of substance, on the other hand, is much less derivative from the material stratum, consisting of a demand arising from human explanatory powers acting toward their completeness, rather than from such an instrumental and imaginative notion as of one block juxtaposed with another block. Remaining humanly based as it does, the concept of substance is less derivable from completed activity than from still open activity. It is a question of degree. But insofar as it is much more likely that the concept of limit originates within experience than beyond it, contrary to the concept of substance, the concept of limit is more recognizably not an essential note of the life that is substance.

To this extent, idea can also be seen as materialized insofar as it is involved with the self-limits of substance, just as much as it should be clear by now that so-called material existence is spiritualized in its modeling of substance's spontaneity. However, it is not a doctrine of "great chain of being," which can meet Hauriou's practical demands, for discontinuity is the immediate evidence of experienced reality and the demand issuing from spiritual substance. Because of this, idea is more ready for relation to experienced existences than is customary in idealistic doctrines. Hauriou believes that idea or ideal being relativized is absurd; but he finds it is quite coherent that it be particularized. Individuals of ordinary existence are ideas in process of realization. The idea they realize is not a generality, applied to them by concept; it is the particularized self-limitation of substance, which, limited temporally through the career of the individual, is also limited spatially among individuals. The limit is not the spiritual substance; neither is the idea. The individual is the substance. The limits of the individual are not obliterated into any generality because its limits are the limits of idea, and the limits of idea are the self-limitations of substance.

As Hauriou well recognizes, all this becomes most clear in the structures of social group moving toward the social person. Idea is revealed historically, but it is not an historical generalization. Rather, the idea in the form of the ideal harmonized the group not with an abstract technological model, but with the demands recognized in the progressive manner of creative artistry as the work advances. It is recognized not by any individual person but by the group, not consciously but unconsciously. It is interiorized by the group, most often without the awareness of individuals, making of the group a social individual. As the members begin to recognize what they and their forebears have done, and to approve that accomplishment, in their turn redoing it, they move toward the explicitness that is social personality.

Attention to the ideal and the resultant options for or against it allow it to be characterized as moral personality. The idea never, however, becomes equivalent to the conceptualization of it by either progenitors or present members. For this conceptualization is punctual, territorially and temporally, whereas the idea is approximated in the objective limits that a social system places upon itself from within itself, limits which insure it against identifying the idea with their conceptualization, with an ineffectual generality.

We must appreciate the contradictoriness of reality as Hauriou affirms in this context of substance. He asserts that reality is internally contradictory; what he refuses, in denying any Hegelian overtones to his work, is any identity of contradictories. He admits identity on the phenomenal plane, but for Hauriou, phenomenal unity always reduces to elemental complexity. The problem comes to the fore in his denial of Otto von Gierke's social theory, a theory, which, as we have seen, Hauriou criticizes as a "sponge colony," meaning it personifies a plurality of individuals without having those individuals first achieve group individuality.

The question that remains is how, since Hauriou is unwilling to leave this elemental complexity under group unity, he can affirm group reality. This problem is similar to the classical quarrel over the presence of real substantial parts as opposed to potential parts, the presence of individuals within an individual without loss of reality by either. The solution demands a reinterpretation of the terms of the problem in the light of the metaphysics of substance, which appears to be required to save Hauriou's demands. One of the difficult sayings which creates the problem, and casts it into the terms above, is his early maxim that the parts act upon the whole more than the whole reacts upon its parts;. This he applied to society and its members. The cogent part of the proposition is not the assertion of atomistic reductivity but the notion of material "withinness," which makes the reduction possible. Parts are within the whole as within a surrounding boundary. In the social application Hauriou makes of this, the basic model appears to be that of a territorial state, a form of organized society that, at the same time, he explicitly refuses to use to model the social order. He clears himself from the whole context later, but a wisp of the problem remains haunting.

Elemental complexity remains present even though the social unity is achieved on more than a phenomenal level. The way these can coexist follows from the metaphysics of substance self-limiting into idea. The identity of elements and of the whole (calling the two individuals by names given in terms of the materialism of the "within" model) comes not from each other, but from the idea fitted to each. "Parts" are no less of an idea, for the idea is particular while it is absolute; and "whole" is no less a particular, for the same reason. Society is implied by the idea of human person, person is implied by the idea of society; but person is not the instantiation of the society as its generalization. They imply each other because the realizing of each idea or type will bring it about that the other is realized. One is not the sine qua non of the other as its temporal prerequisite, but rather in the more literal, neutral and dematerialized sense of sine qua non.

The role of idea in whole and in part as applied to the human order is to make each penetrate the other even as incomplete wholes; to penetrate is another material analogy used as liberation from the materiality of "to contain." Hauriou uses "idea" with the traditional connotation of something mentalistic and with the modern connotation of something living and active. The first supplies the justification for each existence due to its rationality, while the other provides for the continuity in history of the human person and of society. The two meanings can coexist, since for Hauriou, the rationality more literally true of the mental concept derives from idea; concepts are of ideas. The concept inserts discontinuity, while the idea provides continuity; relative to the concept, things either are or are not, while relative to the idea, they are more or less, they become.

To characterize existences in terms of idea allows for a different exposition of individuals as to the sense of undivided [*individua*]. Concretely, every existence is in dispersion: material existence is spatial and temporal, human existence is erratic and fickle. The undividedness of the individual comes, if at all, from the idea, whose role is that of individualizing beings, making them cohere. As Hauriou has mentioned, the good is more coherent than evil, it is a source of greater unification. Idea in this role of coherent good functions not as an end willed by the subject, not as a pre-established order it must follow. However, it partakes of both since idea and end must close upon each other for person to exist, and because an order exists, which is made morally available for choice stage by stage, subsequent to each act, but changing contingent upon what the preceding act was.

Thus, it is context that makes difficulties for the refusal of the "sponge colony" individual. The individual is not undivided from the side of the "colony," its elemental complexity; it is undivided from the side of the idea being achieved. Ultimately, the definitional characterization of substance as existence of itself demands its spirituality, its spontaneous action, an action bound to no making but which, in fact, requires self-limitations. With substance thus dematerialized in concept, wholes and parts unmistakably are structures lying on the side of the self-limitations rather than of the substance. The reaching or fulfillment of these limits through full individualization by idea, through the self-limitations of substance insofar as it is spiritual activity, is an event to which the whole and part structure of containment is much less relevant for the colony.

Contradiction comes out of this conceptualization to be a distinction of the manifold self-limitations of substance, manifested by the exclusivity between the concepts formed about ideas and the incompletenesses in fulfilling ideas. It is not the contradictoriness of propositional logic, for no question regarding deductivity is involved, of deriving from a premise its negative. Neither is it a contradictoriness of coexistence, that demands are placed for existence, which cannot be met without making it impossible to meet demands of the same extremity from the other. It is not simple contrariety or difference, the negation, which is no more than a notational device.

It is a contradiction that permits, in fact requires, the coexistence of both contradictories, for self-limitation is implemented by the mutual limitations within a manifold. It is the contradictoriness, as Hauriou himself says, of matter and form. The only way to explain his use of these categories, which otherwise play little part in his studies, is that all contradictions are not identified one side with matter and the other with form, but that all contradictions exist in the way that the contradiction of matter and form exist. All contradictions as he means them are defined in terms of one another. They must so exist, if at all, since even the ideas toward which they move are the self-limitation of substance by the positing of mutual limitations upon each other. Contradiction is the mode of existence of the world that is not substance.

For this reinterpreted understanding, the notion of the mediation of contradiction toward transaction appears not as essential as Hauriou early made it out to be. A mediation is needed, but perhaps not a mediator. Mediation, as Hauriou first presented it, is a triadic relation, of contradictory, to mediator, to contradictory. Later, however, this relation becomes dyadic; the contradictories limit each other and achieve an equilibrium through the superiority of the one and the conditional submission of the other, a weighting whose quantities are not always the same nor even always in the same distribution. The superiority is posited and is altered in view of the achievement of ideas, for the phenomenal viewpoint, or in view of the effective limitation between ideas, from the viewpoint of substance.

Although this "in view of" structure appears to reintroduce "three-ness," the contradictories are brought to equilibrium long before any conceptualization of the third element enters a situation. Therefore, the relation is factually a duality. The balance by mutual limitation is a definition of each over and against the objective organs, parts, or rights of the other. Hauriou frequently says that the separation of powers takes place originally not because of any difference between their functions but solely because of the need to limit one by the other, to balance one against the other. The peculiar functions accrue later, by appropriation.

5. Evaluation and Application

To apply this philosophical system, which was constructed in section four preceding, back upon Hauriou's methodology is a check upon the degree of accordance between his aims and the metaphysics here reconstructed, and upon the philosophical adequacy of the methodology he developed in the course of his entire study. Therefore, after presenting the metaphysics of idealistic substantialism to the classical queries about any idealistic metaphysics, this section will test it upon Hauriou's dualism, positivism, pragmatism, and personalism. We will conclude by examining the question of its relation to the peculiarities found in Hauriou's sociological and his legal methodologies.

A. Idealistic Substantialism

The idealism to which Hauriou admits is conditioned by his claim that it is not idea that is substance, that idea is related to substance perhaps in the manner we reconstructed above. Consequently, questions usually destructive of idealism may have different results when raised with regard to Hauriou. What is the number of ideas, one or many? As presumed throughout the above discussion, there are many, being not only the self-limitation of substance but also effective in limiting each other. No reason can be found to limit appearance of substance only to individualizations of some higher value; absurdity would arise in giving ideal individuality to the banal individualities of the *Parmenides* only if some individualities were presumed to have a greater claim upon reality than others.

Does some number of substances exist, then, which fully lives up to the demands upon substance? Hauriou's few theological writings lucidly illustrate that he believes all ideas to be the presence of the unique Christian God. From the internal demands he makes, however, such a unity of substance does not appear to be necessary.

If ideas are admittedly numerous and equally real, is there nonetheless a hierarchy of some kind among them? If this hierarchy means a higher value is placed upon some than upon others, a greater affinity to them, then surely Hauriou always takes human persons as the highest value among non-collective existents (although this way of speaking is inappropriate to his insistence upon the elemental complexity of all beings).

In addition, Hauriou insists upon justice in collective existence (again with the verbal restriction). The moderation of justice by order indicates the difficulty of answering the question unambiguously.

If the question of hierarchy means some ideas are more dispensable than others, then some are dispensable, but not in any set or defined way. Since ideas condition each other, it is requisite that they continue conditioning each other so that they remain limited, which their existence always is. In this way, we could fashionably call idealism an ecology of ideas. But no single mode of conditioning is necessary; species, which are one form of ideas, arise and cease, with a resultant shift in the "ecological" balance, but with no final unification of it.

What contact do ideas have with reality? This question presumes that ideas are natively disconnected, somehow unreal; this in turn is due to envisioning ideas as generalizations—conceptualizations. We have already described this view as a connotative aspect of ideas, not fully matching the use Hauriou has for them. Instead, ideas are particular; individuals are not their instantiation, but their realization. Consciousness of idea is not necessary in the development of the idea. In the development of ideas, trials and errors are made in conceptualizing the appearing idea. In this way, we appear to have no need for introducing a "third man" connective whose own status is either unexplained or indefinitely regressive.

How far does the idea extend? Is there, for instance, an idea of contradiction, which might occur between ideas? This variation of the "third man" position is not difficult; surely a concept of contradiction exists. But contradiction is no individual realizing itself; it is a state of affairs between facts, conceptualized no doubt, but requiring no idea in Hauriou's sense. Simply because Hauriou gives many things often considered as relations a more secured existence—for example, social reality—does not mean that relations, combinations, and qualities in the traditional and common-sense usage are forbidden.

An objection raised to Hauriou's theses occasionally, as by Hermann Dooyeweerd, was that criminal association remained unexplained; for, could "bad" ideas possibly exist for criminal coherence? The basis of criminal association can well be the idea of human solidarity, but pursued exclusively of its context. Narrowed into excluding the context in which it occurs, this association is the limitation by an ideal of human individuality under justice. Put succinctly, idea is rigidly conceptualized, and from this comes the potential for its evilness. The most suggestive issue is one that finds it incredible to use the model of idea if it is dissociated from a subject who has ideas, something the human subject clearly does not have in any conceptual way, which is, of course, what my query meant. Hauriou does not posit more than the phenomenal reality of ideas from the side of the human knower; but, after reaching substance on other grounds, he can in turn give idea something more than a phenomenal reality.

To Hauriou's way of thinking, idea is obviously the work of spiritual activity, of substance explained by activity. But it is not subjectivity, which is needed for this form of activity; idea demands only objectivity of spiritual substance. Subjectivity is not needed for self-limitation; spiritual action is needed, but not that which is self-productive.

B. Dualism

The perennial difficulty in dualism is how to relate the duality: immediately? through a mediate third? in parallel? Hauriou insists upon the simplest, traditional meaning of dualism at every turn in his methodology: there exist events and principles that can be understood only in terms of each other and not by themselves. He makes this dualism indefinitely extendable, but pursues it only insofar as it applies to the questions he has chosen to consider, those in social science and law. He specifies the principles there, but not absolutely, since he often traces the development of a present balance to a previous different one. So, the poles of duality would, by definition, be harder to separate, one from the other, than to make them coalesce.

It is helpful that researchers not to be led off into modes of research logically reductive to uniqueness if dualism is the way they are to appreciate things. Hauriou's ventures into metaphysics progress only far enough to let him know that the structures at which he has arrived can be sought everywhere. The partialness of worldly existence requires the balance of partial elements. When metaphysics goes dualist, so will the methodology.

C. Positivism

The positivism with which Hauriou aligns himself has long since been dissociated from data rigidly defined by an arbitrary scientific instrumentality. His positivism embraces facts and events, theories and opinions—everything apparent, and above all, the appearance of idea in history. It is not, then, a positivism falsifiable by the study of individuals; the study of individuals for Hauriou, as we have seen, is the sure way to lead us into a collectivist doctrine. Starting from such an availability of idea, the present study has attempted to construct a metaphysics of substance wherein the status of idea is justified.

Justified in theory as a possibility from the side of history, it remains to be seen whether this sort of positivism is possible from the side of the observer. For that to be so, history would not have to be available in a neutral manner, equally clear on the same data to any observer. The possibility for error can remain here as it does in individual evidence of every fact, even in the interpretation of self-knowledge because no person is just a neutral observer. Persons are involved in interpreting instead of mirroring; this is all the more true of historical knowledge. There is no neutrality before it; people cannot be neutral before their own lives. No positivism, whether restricted or as broad as Hauriou's, can exclude error and interpretation, and since the passivity of positivism is never dispensable in knowing, no positivism can be taxed for not so excluding error and interpretation. The most that can be demanded of positivism is that its data be available apart from deduction, and that some means of testing it be furnished. The test of Hauriou's historical positivism is more history: see how it works in society.

If no reduction will strip history of subjective input, still no amount of active engagement can get rid of the development of idea in history. Idea does not control history; people do. However, people produce historically either in an ephemeral or a durable fashion, preferring the durable. Hauriou looks to the durable to find its source in idea. Since the most durable historical phenomenon is the continual return of a cry for liberty together with stability, he addresses this phenomenon as most revealing of human nature, as manifesting human individuality.

History as a positive phenomenon cannot be claimed as infallibly oriented toward the progress of this idea; but what Hauriou believes can be claimed is that history, when it matches the desiderata of its heroes and its villains, is in the way of stability toward human individuality. The stable balances that Hauriou alleges to find proliferating are what insure freedom everywhere; yet the most tyrannous regime cannot help investing a token opposition with some respectability for the sake of its internal order and survival beyond the day.

Whether Hauriou's observations are correct has, strangely, seldom been criticized, critics preferring to attack his methodology. Yet his methodology appears to be his strongest point, allowing in not only representative knowing but also creative imagination, not a determined progressivism of ideas developing inexorably but the hypothetical observation that if something is to be achieved, something else is necessary for it. The something to be achieved is what all people have found desirable: continued existence.

Idea and substance do not require conduct; they only terminate it. But what does appear through historical acts is the positive structure of humanity and society set out in a conditional proposition: if this is desired, this other must be done.

D. Pragmatism

Success in action is assurance of truthfulness. The action in question is the assemblage of past trial and error in history; and the positivism and pragmatism can so be seen to condition one another. Every action is evidence for or against the relation of an end to an idea; its success is defined in terms of survival, the securing of permanence. Permanence is secured only in peace, and peace only by justice, for example. This does not appear clearly from individual speculation upon doctrines; but it is evinced only by the results, which have accrued from following out those doctrines, something the social group does collectively.

Hauriou's continually announced pragmatism does not leave aside value, but makes the value one that is inarguable: endurance or survival. The pragmatism does not empty out knowing before doing; consummation of action is achieved, although only a relative one. Because of the need for balances, for mutual limitations, any solution achieved will generate its contradictory to balance it, generate it not of itself but from the social milieu wherein it appears. The spiritual action of substance, spontaneity, is the model for worldly production of likenesses among existents; the self-limitation of substance is the concrete basis for differentiation by self-limitation each of others.

E. Personalism

Now that individual is seen to be an idea realizing itself, individual is not like the glassy impenetrability of a hermetically sealed flask [*vase hermétiquement clos*]; it is only relatively inviolable, being open to redirection and to destruction in events, and to definition by contradictions not identified with it. In this light, the individual that is person is the location of only a relative freedom, a freedom that does not extend to all areas of activity because it does not make all areas. The freedom is a correlative of another's spontaneity. "The human individual is essentially free in this sense, that the individual is conscious of a moral law imposed from without as proceeding from the divine order of things, and that the individual has the ability to obey this law voluntarily" (1933a, p. 23) ["*L'individu humain est essentiellement libre en ce sens qu'il a connaissance d'une loi morale qui s'impose à lui du dehors comme précédant de l'ordre divin des choses et qu'il a faculté d'obéir volontairement à cette loi*"].

The receptivity of the individual to essential input from outside itself is related to the question of person in terms of substance. It has seemed implicit in a metaphysics of this kind, that substance is a spiritual one, spontaneous action. It has appeared that the individuals of experience, in being the realization of ideas that are the self-limitations of substance, are not fully identified as substances. But this would be by a freedom of subject making itself substance, the freedom of constituting reality free of other boundaries than a person's own action.

That Hauriou does not find this freedom interesting is patent from the above quote. More proximate than this outcome is the possibility that spontaneity is an insufficiently human liberty, that it differs not at all from cosmic liberty, which as we saw was no more than a resistance to being exhaustively expressed by statistical law. If spontaneity is also the specification of substantial freedom, human liberty appears devalued.

Perhaps the best way back into Hauriou on this point is to realize that person is not identified with subject for him. The development of the individual idea proceeds through the gathering of materials for a nonhuman but psychic body, which makes of the materials organs of activity for itself, an objective individuality. With initial recognition of direction—surely not of particularized idea as the form of this movement, however—an autonomous individuality is established, autonomous because of its own orientation, global and massive as it may be. As members internalize the idea, personality appears for the first time. It is not sheer individuality, for individuals are not their organs, now; the individual members direct organs and establish tools that operate effectively because they balance the action of one another. This is all-important now that the individual, called a person, seizes the idea in conceptualization. The urgency thus given to idea has as its counterpart the possible narrowing of it to extreme abstraction. This demands balance by complementarity to keep the individual development of idea from abstraction.

This is person, due to the conscious internalization of idea and the establishment of objective balance of self-preservation. But this is only objective person, person observed and existing only as a set of circumstances; it is person still only in terms of its internal constitution. Subjective personality can arise only with the recognition that these objective balances are self-limitations, not only constraints, but also the action of none other than itself, and thus indicators of the presence of liberty. The acceptance that liberty is available only on the condition of restraint is the fact about the individual person that makes it fit to face other persons at last, to partake of a social life in which each affirms the others as limits and thereby as guarantors of one's own liberty, and in which each recognizes the need for dominance and superiority as the only mode of survival in contradiction.

In this there is no lack of subjective reality, anymore than there is subjective sole agency. Hauriou does not deny substance of persons. However, as everywhere, it is available only as revealing itself in the realization of an idea, and this means not all at once. It reveals itself historically, in social context, as the actions performed in objective liberty are so recognized and appropriated. Person is not de-substantialized, then, but neither is it de-temporalized. Subjectivity is the orientation of every objective human organization, but the subjectivity can be both gained and lost.

Knowledge of person, so given, surely is able to advance with the positive sciences' knowledge of human beings, since these sciences are objective structures provoked by the need to balance introspection. They are not themselves depersonalized avenues to human knowledge but are facets of its achievement. They are the achievement of personality, although not of subjectivity, because they are ill-recognized to have this role of personalization over and above objectivity. There is no question of human persons abhorring the human sciences due to being tied to any fixed species ideas; for whatever fixity exists is available only at the end of its realization.

F. Social and Legal Methodology

Did Hauriou's philosophical methodology allow him to do anything others could not do in law and social science? It allowed for social existence to be appreciated as irreducible reality without thereby enforcing an alienation from it of its members. If, in this sense, society is "real," it is not the same reality as its individual members, numerically. But it is the members who form among themselves the oppositions, which are the objective limitations and balances making state personality something real. Hauriou's philosophy as developed suffices to give order to processes while leaving them free of theoretical imposition, which might force some legal and social facts to be dismissed as irreconcilable. The legal and social world of Hauriou moves without worry over how individuals' concepts coincide with them; it is not the outgrowth of any philosophy but of the demands that the life of power and fulfillment imposes.

If Hauriou's philosophical doctrines and the socio-legal existence are so non-causal in relation to each other, are his philosophical doctrines of any use at all to jurists and sociologists? First of all, Hauriou excludes some forms of law and social science on the basis of this philosophy, or rather insofar as this philosophy of substance is manifested in ideas. No objectivism can decline will, no subjectivism can reject spontaneous objective and factual growths.

Neither transcendentally complete ideas suffice, nor do thoroughly constructed ends. As a result, social organizations are spontaneous and free of state imposition, while state is loosed from any single power since objective balance of spontaneous powers is needed for survival. Dominance is needed, but it is conditional and shifting.

Can Hauriou's philosophical methodology aid in distinguishing social and legal methodologies? The difference does not lie in the criterion of person, for social reality, too, contains moral personality. The presence of justice does not distinguish them, for survival is duration in peace, and this demands justice. It is not a difference between fact and construct that makes them different, for both are constructs that become facts in procedure. Nor is the distinction even of facts and rights an adequate one to explain the difference, because rights do not depend upon subjective personality, being founded already in the objectivity of social living.

Law is an instrument for bringing social life where it is meant to go: not to pursue a rigidly sedimented conceptual ideal, as a form of social engineering, but to allow a swifter adjustment to new dimensions of idea as it appears with new demands at each moment. Social custom is more inert and moves too slowly to avoid missing new demands until it is too late. That law to meet them requires a more refined level of conceptualization is true; this is why the legal stratum reflects for human beings the model of their proper rationality in the state. But the conceptualization is not allowed to become extreme, since the peculiarity of law is the advent of subjective personality first among individuals and later to society, a subjectivity that recognizes not only the necessity of objective contradictions, but also their desirability in view of the recognition of how idea comes to achievement. Society puts individuals together in service to an idea, however unconscious; law takes the objective balances set up for its achievement, recognizes them as the condition for liberty, and stabilizes them by rationalizing them into language.

What difficulty remains with Hauriou's social and legal methodology is also comprehensible in the light of his philosophy. For the idea of justice could not be formulated without conceptualizing it into an era, and his era was a period when public and private life were still distinct enough for justice to be complemented with the discretionary order of the administrative courts. Hauriou, however, foresaw and forebode the future day when the public and private would be even more merged in the social consciousness than in the confusion of legal institutions.

6. Conclusion

The best criterion of Hauriou's methodology is whether it can be used for doing law, social science and philosophy. The method I have used in this volume does not claim to be positive, dualist, or pragmatic. It has been dialectical. I have compared categories and theses to develop their response to each other. The categories and theses I selected are representative of those most prominent in Hauriou's work. But while he developed them throughout a long life's work, I have joined them together in such a manner as to highlight their appearance as a solidified doctrine.

Over and above this effort, in this final chapter, I have drawn the categories and theses beyond their location in Hauriou's development of them and even his solidified thought. I have drawn them into an even more dogmatic stratum, in which I left his laboratory procedure aside. This has conceptualized the processes Hauriou was content to recognize insofar as he could draw consequences from them, a mode more in accord with their ideal realization.

I am left to question the effect this metaphysics has on Hauriou's methodology. Just as his treatment, instead of simply using methods in law and sociology, widely expanded them into what would otherwise have been called philosophy, so my present treatment, instead of simply using the methods of philosophy, has brought them into contact with a level of reality, an idealism that goes beyond what Hauriou might have seen as philosophical ground.

My purpose has been to satisfy the demands his work makes but does not complete. This metaphysics is not then according to Hauriou's methodology, because it is not positive and descriptive but constructive, or better dialectical, since it takes Hauriou's given propositions and attempts to make them coherent with seemingly discrepant ones by supplying new materials. This is the study of the implicit methodology mentioned in Chapter Two, with the reservation that it is beyond the scope of the present explicit work.

The internal result is, however, that the metaphysics constructed as coherently as possible to accord with the available materials is, even if it is coherent, only one possibility for doing justice to appearance. The appearances in question make up only one set among many sets of appearances perhaps equally legitimate, though implicit.

This is not a metaphysics that Hauriou asked for from his colleagues. Perhaps it is one he would have repudiated. Since it follows his demands upon philosophy, however, he likely could accept it, as supported by his claims and so giving credence to his philosophical methodology. Since his philosophical methodology supports his legal and sociological methodologies, it fortifies them in turn.

These fortified methodologies then make more reliable his theory of institutions as an instrument for analysis of legal and social realities. If that is so, they also make it plausible to accept institution as truly an existent in the field of these realities. This is a welcome correction to our knowledge and a valuable addition to the inhabitants of our social universe.

WORKS CITED

*A complete bibliography of Maurice Hauriou is presented herein for historical purposes. Works actually cited in the text are marked by asterisks.

Aguilar Sahagún, Luis Armando. (2001) "*Del rechazo de los mexicanos a un 'patriotismo constitucional*'" ("Mexican Pursuit of a Constitutional Patriotism"). *Nueva sintesis*.

Amm, Joachim. (1999) "*Der Senat Kanadas; symbolische Stabilisierungselemente eines institutionellen Fossil*," ("The Senate of Canada. Symbolic Support for an Institutional Fossil"). *Kanada-Studien* (Feb.). pp. 73–90.

Apter, David E. (2001) "Structure, Contingency, and Choice: A Comparison of Trends and Tendencies in Political Science," pp. 252–281. In *Schools of Thought: Twenty Five Years of Interpretive Social Science*. Edited by D. Keates and J. W. Scott. Princeton, N.J.: Princeton University Press.

Arendt, Hannah. (1946) "Review of Joseph T. Delos' *Le problème de la civilisation*." *Review of Politics* (January).

———. (1951) *Origins of Totalitarianism*. New York: Harcourt, Brace.

Aubry, Pierre. (1911) "*Essais de critique philosophique*. I. *La philosophie de M. Hauriou*" ("Essays in Philosophical Critique. I. The Philosophy of M. Hauriou"). *Annales de la faculté de droit d'Aix*, 5, pp. 3–11.

Bagehot, Walter. (1882) *Lois scientifiques du développement des nations dans leurs rapports avec les principes de la sélection naturelle et de l'hérédité* (*Scientific Laws for the Development of Nations in their Relations with the Principles of Natural Selection and Heredity*). Paris: G. Baillière.

Barbera, D. (1949) "*Sistema instituzionale del diritto privato italiano*" ("An Institutional System of Italian Private Law"). *Civiltà Cattolico*, 99.

Barrere, Alain. (1971) "*A travers conflits et contradictions, naissance d'une 'autre' société*" *("Beyond Conflicts and Contradictions: Birth of an 'Other' Society")*. *Contradictions et conflits: Naissance d'une société?* Semaines sociales de France.

Bates, David. (2004) "'*Legitimatät*' and '*Legalität*': Political Theology and Democratic Thought in an Age of World War." In *Religion und Nation, Nation und Religon: Beiträge zu einer unbewältigten Geschichte*. Edited by Michael Geyer and Harmut Lehrmann. Göttingen: Wallstein.

———. (2005) "Political Unity and the Spirit of Law; Political Concepts of State in the Late Third Republic." *French Historical Studies*, 28.1.

———. (2006) "Political Theology and the Nazi State: Carl Schmitt's Concept of the Institution," *Modern Intellectual History*, 3:3, pp. 415–442.

Beaud, Olivier. (1989) "*Hauriou et le droit naturel*" ("Hauriou and Natural Law"). *Revue d'histoire des facultés de droit*, 8, pp. 123–138.

Bento, Messias. (1994) "Acórdão n. 481/94 de 12 de Julho [Extradição/ pena de morte]" (Agreement n. 481/94 (July12) [Extradition/Death Penalty]). *Dicionário da Revisão Constitucional*. Edited by José Magalhaes. Lisbon: Publicacaoes Europa-America.

Bernès, Marcel. (1894) *Sociologie et morale: deux années d'enseignement sociologique* (*Sociology and Morality: Two Years of Teaching Sociology*). Paris: V. Giard & E. Brière.

———. (1895) "*Sur la méthode de la sociologie*" ("On the Method of Sociology"). *Revue philosophique* (March/April), 39, pp. 233–257, 372–399.

Bleich, S. (1998) "*Der Einfluss von Maurice Hauriou auf die französische Rechtstheorie und Jurisprudenz*" ("The Influence of Maurice Hauriou on French Legal Thought and Jurisprudence"). *Verwaltungsarchiv*, p. 1.

Bluntschli, Johann Caspar. (1881) *Le droit public général* (*General Public Law*). Paris: Librairie Guillaumin.

———. (1883) *La politique* (*Politics*). Paris: Librairie Guillaumin.

Bobbio, Norberto. (1936) "*Istituzione e diritto sociale*" ("Institution and Social Law"). *Rivista Internazionale di Filosofia del Diritto*, 16.

Bocaç, Erozan. (2004) "An Interpretive Approach to the History of Political Science: Turkey in Comparative Perspective." *European Political Science*. http://www.essex.ac.uk/ECpR/publications/eps/onlineissues/spring2004/profession/erozan.htm (accessed 09 Aug. 2009).

Bonnecase, Julien. (1931) "*Une nouvelle mystique: la notion de l'institution*" ("A New Mysticism: The Notion of Institution"). *Revue générale du droit*, 55, pp. 161–185, 241–254.

———. (1932) "*Une nouvelle mystique: la notion de l'institution*" ("A New Mysticism: The Notion of Institution"). *Revue générale du droit*, 56, pp. 1–12; 81–108, 160–178, 241–263.

Borges, Luiz Ferreira Zavier. (2000) "*A Teoria da Desconsideração da Personalidade Jurídica e sua Aplicação em Análise de Crédito*" ("The Theory of Oversight of Legal Personality, and its Application for the Analysis of Credit"). *Revista do Bandes* (Rio di Janeiro, Brazil) 7:14 (Dec.), pp. 329–350.

Bosserman, Phillip. (1968) *Dialectical Sociology: An Analysis of the Sociology of Georges Gurvitch*. Boston: Porter Sargent.

Bouasse, Henri. (1899) "*Physique et métaphores*" ("Physics and Metaphors"). *Revue de métaphysique et de morale*, 7, pp. 226–241.

Boutroux, Émile. (1874) *De la contingence des lois de la nature* (The Contingency of Laws of Nature). Paris: G. Baillière.

———. (1895) *De l'idée de loi naturelle dans la science et la philosophie contemporaines* (The Idea of Natural Law in Contemporary Science and Philosophy). Paris: Lechène.

Brimo, Albert. (1969) "*La philosophie du droit naturel du doyen Maurice Hauriou*" ("The Philosophy of Natural Law of Dean Maurice Hauriou"), pp. 63–78. In Marty and Brimo, *Journées Hauriou*.

Broderick, Joseph Albert. (1963a) The Institutional Approach to Legal Problems. Master's Thesis. Harvard University.

———. (1963b) "*Sur une nouvelle édition des institutionnalistes français*" ("On a New Edition of the French Institutionalists"). *Archives de philosophie du droit*, 8, pp. 277–284.

———. (1964) "Evolving Due Proces and the French Institutionalists," *Catholic University of America Law Review*, 13, pp. 95–125.

———. (1965) "Hauriou's Institutional Theory: An Invitation to Common Law Jurisprudence," *Sollicitor's Quarterly*, 4, pp. 281–308.

———. (1967) "Maurice Hauriou: His Relevance to Contemporary Legal and Political Thought." D Phil Dissertation. 2 Volumes. Oxford University.

———. (1968a) "*L'influence de la pensée du doyen Maurice Hauriou aux États-Unis et en Angleterre*" ("The Influence of the Thought of Dean Maurice Hauriou in the United States and in England"). In *La pensée du doyen Maurice Hauriou* (*The Thought of Dean Maurice Hauriou*), pp. 271–280.

———. (1968b) "Institutional Theory and a New Private Club," *Nebraska Law Review*, 47, pp. 459–478.

———. (1968c) "*La notion d''institution' de Maurice Hauriou dans ses rapports avec le contrat en droit positif français*" ("The Idea of 'Institution' in Maurice Hauriou; Its Relation to Contract in French Positive Law"). *Archives de philosophie du droit*, 13, pp. 144–160.

———. (1970) *The French Institutionalists*. Edited by J. A. Broderick. Translated by Mary Welling. Cambridge, Mass.: Harvard University Press.

Bustamente, Lino Rodriguez-Arias.(1972) "La teoria institucional del derecho" ("The Institutional Theory of Law"). *Anales de Catedra Francisco Suarez*, 12, pp. 37–64.

Caffaro, Luiz Carlos. (2000) "A improbidade administrativa e sua sistematização" ("Administrative Improbability and its Systematization"). Conference paper. Concurso FEMPERJ-CEJUR, Brazil.

Canhim, Romildo. (1994) "*Codigo de Ética do Servidor Público*" ("A Code of Ethics for the Public Service"). Senado do Brasil (22 June).

Capizio, Jorge. (2000) "*La reforma constitucional de 1999 a los organos protectores de los derechos humanos*" ("The Constitutional Reform of 1999 to Agencies for the Protection of Human Rights"). *Cuestiones* [UNAM e-journal] 3 (July–Dec.), pp. 27–81.

Carré de Malberg, Raymond. (1920–1922) *Contribution à la théorie générale de l'état, spécialement d'après les données fournies par le droit constitutionnel français* (*Contribution to the General Theory of State Particularly in View of Data from French Constitutional Law*). Paris: Libraire de la Société du Recueil Sirey.

Chavreau, Georges. (1888) *Le travail physiologique* (*Physiological Effort*). n.p (as cited by Hauriou).

———. (1891) *Le travail musculaire* (*Muscular Effort*). n.p (as cited by Hauriou).

Cheno, Remi. (2008) "*La pertinence ecclesiologique de la théorie de l'institution de Maurice Hauriou*" ("The Relevance of Maurice Hauriou's Institutional Theory to Ecclesiology"). *Revue des sciences religieuses*, 82:2, pp. 225–243.

Chevalier, Jacques. (1923) *L'idéalisme français au dix-septième siècle* (*French Idealism in the Seventeenth Century*) (as cited by Hauriou).

———. (1927a) "*Le continu et le discontinu*" ("The Continuous and the Discontinuous"). *Aristotelian Society*, Supplementary Volume 4, pp. 170–196.

———. (1927b) "Newman and the Idea of Development," *Revue les letters* (juillet) (as cited by Hauriou).

———. (1929) "*Le concept et l'idée*" ("Concept and Idea"). In Maurice Hauriou. *Mélanges Maurice Hauriou.*

Clemens, René. (1935) *Personnalité morale et personnalité juridique* (*Moral Personality and Legal Personality*). Paris: Sirey.

Cohen, Morris R. (1933) *Law and the Social Order*. New York: Harcourt, Brace.

Collins, Howard. (1891) *Résumé de la philosophie de Herbert Spencer* (*Central Themes in the Philosophy of Herbert Spencer*). Translated by Henry de Varigny. Paris: Alcon.

Cossalter, V. Philippe. (1999) *Les grands arrêts de la jurisprudence administrative* (Major Cases in Administrative Jurisprudence). DEA Thesis in Droit Public. Université de Paris II Panthéon (17 sept.).

Dastre, Albert. (1903) *La vie et la mort* (*Living and Dying*). Paris: Flammarion.

Daviet, F. (2000) "*Le service public peut-il encore innover*?"(" Can the Public Service Still Act Innovatively?"). Nos Congrès SIP XXVIIIèmes. *Journées de la Société de l'Information Psychiatrique*.

Davy, Georges. (1922) *Le droit, l'idéalisme, et l'expérience* (*Law, Idealism, and Experience*). Paris: Alcan.

Declareuil, J. (1929) "*Quelques remarques sur la théorie de l'institution*" ("Some Remarks on the Theory of Institution"). In *Mélanges Maurice Hauriou*.

de Laubadère, André, André Mathiot, Jean Rivero, and Georges Vedel. (1980) *Pages de doctrine: André de Laubadère, André Mathiot, Jean Rivero, Georges Vedel* (*Doctrinal Selections*). Paris: Librairie générale de droit et de jurisprudence.

Delbos, Victor. (1893) *Le problème morale de la philosophie de Spinoza et dans l'histoire du Spinozisme* (*The Problem of Morality in the Philosophy of Spinoza and in the History of Spinozism*). Hildesheim, Germany: Georg Ohms.

Delos, Joseph Thomas. (1931) "*La théorie de l'institution: la solution réaliste du problème de la personnalité morale et le droit à fondement objectif*" ("The Theory of Institution: The Realist Solution to the Problem of Moral Personality and the Law's Objective Foundation"). *Archives de philosophie du droit et de sociologie juridique*, 1, pp. 97–153.

———. (1929) *La société internationale et les principes du droit publique* (*International Society and the Principles of Public Law*). Paris: Sirey.

———. (1944) *Le problème de la civilisation: La nation* (*The Problem of Civilization. The Nation*). Montréal: Éditions L'Arbre.

———. (1950) *La société internationale et les principes du droit publique* (*International Society and the Principles of Public Law*). 2nd Edition. Paris: Pédone.

Dengerink, J. D. (1965) "Hauriou and Dooyeweerd: A Comparison of Some Elements of Their Social Thought." In *Philosophy and Christianity*. Amsterdam: New Holland Publishing Company.

d'Entreves, Passerin. (1967) *The Notion of the State: An Introduction to Political Theory*. Oxford: Clarendon.

Desqueyrat, André. (1935) *L'institution, le droit objectif, et la technique positive: essai historique et doctrinal* (*Institution, Objective Law, and Positive Procedure: Historical and Doctrinal Essay*). Paris: Sirey.

———. (1939) "*L'institution: sa nature, ses espèces, les problèmes qu'elle pòse*" ("Institution: Its Nature and Types; The Problems It Poses"). *Archives de philosophie*, 12, pp. 65–115.

Dooyeweerd, Hermann. (1940) "*De 'Théorie de l'institution' en de Staatsleer van Maurice Hauriou*" ("The 'Theory of Institution' in the Doctrine of the State by Maurice Hauriou"). *Antirevolutionaire Staatkunde*, 14, pp. 301–347.

———. (1941) "*De 'Théorie de l'institution' en de Staatsleer van Maurice Hauriou*" ("The 'Theory of Institution' in the Doctrine of the State by Maurice Hauriou"). *Antirevolutionaire Staatkunde*, 15, pp. 42–70.

———. (1948) "*Een nieuw Geschrift over Hauriou's Leer der 'Institution'*" ("A Recent Text on Hauriou's Theory of 'Institution'"). *Besturs Wetenschappen*, 2, pp. 1–15.

———. (1957) *A New Critique of Theoretical Thought*. Volume 3. *Structures of Individuality and Temporal Reality*. Philadelphia: Presbyterian and Reformed Publishing Co.

Dorssemont, Filip. (2001) *De rechtspositie van de representatieve werknemersorganisaties: Over de problemstische relatie tussen rechtspositie en collectieve actievrijheid* (The Legal Status of Representative Trade Unions: On the Complicated Relation Between the Legal Status of Trade Unions and the Right to Collective Action). PhD Dissertation. Universitaire Instelling Antwerpen.

Duclos, Laurent. (2001) "*Le 'refondation' sociale': entre émancipation contractuelle et proceduralisation*" ("The 'Refounding' of Society: Between Contractual Emancipation and Proceduralization"). *La lettre du GIPMIS* (8 mars).

———, and Olivier Mériaux. (1997) "*Pour une économie du paritarisme*" ("Toward a Stakeholder Economy"). *La revue de l'IRES*, 24, pp. 43–60.

Dufour, Alfred. (1983) "*La conception de la personnalité morale dans la pensée de Maurice Hauriou et ses fondements philosophiques*" ("The Concept of Moral Personality in the Thought of Maurice Hauriou; Its Philosophical Fundamentals"). *Quaderni fiorentini per la storia del pensiere giuridica*, 684, pp. 11–12.

Duguit, Léon. (1901) *L'état, le droit objectif et la loi positive par Léon Duguit, Prof., Bordeaux* (*The State, Objective Law, and Positive Law by Léon Duguit, Prof., Bordeaux*). Paris: A. Fontemoing.

———. (1903) *L'état, les gouvernants et les agents* (*The State, Its Governors, and its Agents*). Paris: A. Fontemoing.

———. (1907) *Manuel de droit constitutionnel: théorie générale de l'état-organisation politique* (*Manual of Constitutional law; General Theory of the State and Political Organization*). Paris: Fontemoing.

———. (1911) *Le droit social, le droit individuel et la transformation de l'état; conférences faites à l'École des hautes études sociales* (*Social Law, Individual Law, and the Transformation of the State: Lectures given at the School for Advanced Social Studies*). Paris: Alcan.

———. (1912) *Les transformations générales du droit privé depuis le code Napoléon* (*The Transformations throughout Private Law Since the Napoleonic Code*). Continental Legal History Series.Volume 11. Paris: F. Alcan.

Dumesnil, Georges. (1892) *Du role des concepts dans la vie intellectuelle et morale* (*The Role of Concepts in Intellectual and Moral Life*). *Thèse*, Sorbonne.

———. (1904) "*Le spiritualisme.*" Annales de l'Université de Grenoble, 16, pp. 453–563.

Durkheim, Émile. (1893) *De la division du travail social: étude sur l'organisation des sociétés supérieures* (*The Division of Labor in Society: Study on the Organization of Developed Societies*). Paris: Alcan.

———. (1894) "*Règles de la méthode de la science sociale*" ("The Rules of Sociological Method"). *Revue philosophique*.

Dwelschauvers, George. (1908) *La synthèse mentale* (*Mental Synthesis*) Paris: Félix Alcan.

Eisenmann, Charles. (1930) "*Deux théoreticiens de droit: Duguit et Hauriou,*" *Revue philosophique*, 110, pp. 231–279.

Emerson, Rupert. (1928) *State and Sovereignty in Modern Germany* New Haven, Conn.: Yale University Press.

Escarrá, Hermann. (1999) *Asamblea Nacional Constituyente*. Paper before the Legislature. 7 Aug. Venezuela.

Escobar, Marcos Carreño. (1980) "*Los estados de exceptión constitucional bajo la vigencia de las constituciones de 1925 y 1980, y su aplicatión prática*" ("Exceptional Constitutional Circumstances under the Control of the Constitutions of 1925 and 1980; Their Application in Practice"). University Paper. *Facultad de Derecho*. Universidad Central de Chile.

Esmein, A. (1896) *Éléments de droit constitutionnel français et comparé* (*Elements of French and Comparative Constitutional Law*). 1st Edition. Edited by Henry Nézard. Paris: L. Larose.

Espinas, Albert Victor. (1877) *Des sociétés animales; étude de psychologie comparée* (*Animal Societies: Study in Comparitive Psychology*). Paris: Baillière.

Farías, Urbano. (1996) "*Marco Jurídica para contribuir al programa de descentralización ambiental de la Semarnap*" ("Trademarks as Contribution to the Progress of Decentralization at Semarnap"). IBENCO (International Business & Environmental NAFTA Consultation, G.P.) (April).

Flores, Hector Astudillo. Untitled paper before the Senado de la República, Mexico, 8 Nov 2001.

Forti, Ugo. (1939) "*Dottrine 'réaliste' di Hauriou*" ("The 'Realist' Doctrine of Hauriou"). *Atti della Reali Academia Pontaniana*, 58.

Fouillée, Albert. (1880) *La science sociale contemporaine* (Contemporary Social Science). Paris: Hachette.

Fourni, François. (2005) *Recherches sur la décentralisation dans l'œuvre de Maurice Hauriou* (Studies on Decentralization in the Work of Murice Hauriou). Lavoisier, Collection thesis, t. 245.

Friedmann, Wolfgang. (1965) *Théorie générale du droit* (*General Theory of Law*). 4th Edition. Paris: Pichon et Durand.

Friedrich, Hansjürgen. (1963) *Die Institutionenlehre bei Maurice Hauriou* (*The Theory of Institutions in Maurice Hauriou*). Mainz: Johannes-Gutenberg-Universitaet.

Fustel de Coulanges, Numa Denis. (1866) *La cité antique. Étude sur le culte, le droit, les institutions de la Grèce et de Rome* (*The Ancient City: Study of Culture, Law, and Institutions of Greece and Rome*). Paris: L. Hachette.

Gascón y Marin, José. (1945) "*La concepción institucional del derecho y la administración*" ("The Institutional Notion of Law and Administration"). *Revista di Estudios de la Vida Local*, 20, pp. 173–181.

Gehlen, Arnold. (1958) *Der Mensch: Seine Natur und seine Stellung in der Welt* (*Human Being: Its Nature and Its Standing in the World*). 6th Edition. Bonn: Athenaeum-Verlag.

Geny, François. (1915) "*La conception sociologique élargie chez M. Hauriou*" ("The Expansive Conception of Sociology for Maurice Hauriou"). In *Science et technique en droit privé positif*. Paris: Sirey.

Gerber, Carl Friedrich von. (1865) *Grundzüge eines Systems des deutschen Staatrechts* (*Foundations for a System of German Public Law*). Leipzig: Tauchnitz.

Giacomuzzi, José Guilherme. (2001) "Common Law Doctrine of Estoppel and Brazilian Constitutional Principle of Administrative Morality." Presented at 13th Minerva Congress. Washington University, Washington, D.C.

Giminez, Joachin Ruiz. (1945) *La concepción institucional del Derecho* (*The Institutional Conception of Law*). Madrid: Instituto de Estudios Politicos.

Gomes, Joaquim B. Barbosa. (1996) "*O poder de polícia e o princípio da dignidade da pessoa humana na jurisprudência francesa*" ("Police Power and the Principle of the Dignity of the Human Person in French Jurisprudence"). *BuscaLegis*.

Gordon, David. (2000) "The Fallacies of Voegelian Antiliberalism," *The Mises Review* (Fall).

Goretti, Cesare. (1933) *Il liberalismo giuridico di Maurice Hauriou* (*The Juridical Liberalism of Maurice Hauriou*). Milan: Pirola.

Goyard-Fabre, Simone. (1998) "*La sociologisation du droit: l'oeuvre de Maurice Hauriou*" ("The Sociologizing of Law: The Work of Maurice Hauriou"), pp. 178–181. In *Les fondements de l'ordre juridique*. "*Que sais-je*?" Paris: Presses universitaires de France.

Gözler, Kemal. (1998) "Realýst Yorum Teorýsý ve Mekanýst Anayasa AnlayiÞi" ("Realist Legal Theory and Mechanist Analysis"). *Anayasa Yargýsý*, 15, pp. 207–249.

———. (1999) "*Hukuk Açisindan Monarþý ve Cumhurýyet Kavramlarinin Tanimi Sorunu*" ("The Question of Defining the Concepts of Monarchy and Republic from the Legal Point of View"). *Ankara Üniversitesi Siyasal Bilgiler Fakültesi Dergisi*, 54, Sayý 1, pp. 51–62.

Gros, Dominique. (2002) "*Le 'status des juifs' et les manuels en usage dans les facultés de droit* (Partie 2)" ("The Status of Jews and the Manuals Used in Law Faculties"). *Cultures & conflits*, 20 (13-06): 15: p. 26.

Gurvitch, Georges. (1931a) "*Les idées-maîtresses de Maurice Hauriou*" ("The Leading Ideas of Maurice Hauriou"). *Archives de philosophie du droit*, 1, pp. 155–194.

———. (1931b) *Le temps présent et l'idée du droit social* (*Contemporaneity and the Idea of Social Law*). Paris: J. Vrin, 1931.

———. (1932) *L'idée du droit social* (*The Idea of Social Law*). Paris: Sirey.

———. (1947) *Sociology of Law*. London: Routledge & Kegan Paul.

Hallis, Frederick. (1930) "The Doctrine of Corporate Personality: M. Hauriou, L. Michoud, R. Saleilles." in *Corporate Personality: A Study in Jurisprudence*. London: Oxford University Press.

Hauriou, André. (1966a) *Droit constitutionnel et institutions politiques* (*Constitutional Law and Political Institutions*). Paris: Montchrestien.

———. (1966b) Introduction. In Sfez, *Essai sur la contribution du doyen Hauriou au droit administratif français*.

———. (1969) *Les derniers aspects de la pensée du doyen Maurice Hauriou et son influence* ("*Journées Hauriou*") (*Final Aspects of the Thought of Dean Maurice Hauriou and His Influence*). Paris: Pédone.

Hauriou, Maurice. (1879a) *Du terme, en droit romain et en droit français* (Term in Roman and French Law). *Thèse de licence*. Bordeaux.

*———. (1879b) *Étude sur la condictio: des contrats à titre onéreux entre époux* (Study on the Condictio: Binding Contracts between Spouses). *Thèse de doctorat*, Bordeaux.

———. (1880) *De l'exercise par les créanciers des droits et actions du débiteur* (*Composition d'agrégation, droit français*) (*Exercise by Creditors of the Rights and Actions of Debtors* [*Composition of aggregation, French law*]). Paris: Larose.

———. (1881a) "*Boni viri arbitrium et clausula doli*" ("The Upright Person's Will and the Clause against Deceit"). *Nouvelle revue historique*, pp. 99–114.

———. (1881b) *L'héritier donataire qui renonce à la succession peut-il retenir sur les biens données, non seulement la quotité disponible mais encore sa part dans la réserve?* (*Composition d'agrégation, droit français*) (*Can the Heir by Donation Who Renounces His Succession Retain Over the Goods in the Gift Not Only the Disposable Amount, But Also His Share in the Reserve?* [*Composition of aggregation, French law*]). Paris: Larose et Forcel.

———. (1882a) *De la conservation du privilège du vendeur d'immeubles* (*Composition d'agrégation, droit français*) (Conservation of Privilege by the Vendor of Immovables[*Composition of aggregation, French law*]). Paris: Larose et Forcel.

*———. (1882b) "*Origine de la corréalité*" ("Origin of the Co-Realty"). *Nouvelle revue historique*, pp. 3–24.

———. (1882c) *Quatenus verum sit venditorem non obligari ut rem faciat emptoris, et quod ibi dicitur de venditione, an ad rerum permutationem trahi debeat?* (*Composition d'agrégation, droit romain*) (*How True Is It That the Seller Is Not Obliged to Perform the Task of the Buyer, and Whether What Applies to Sale There Should Be Applied to Changes in the Thing?* [*Composition of Aggregation, Roman Law*]). Paris: Larose et Forcel.

*———. (1884) "*L'histoire externe du droit*" ("The External History of Law"). *Revue critique de législation et de jurisprudence*, pp. 5–15.

———. (1887a) "*Fragment sur l'évolution et le contr'évolution au sens théologique,*" *Le spectateur catholique*, 8, pp. 55–62.

*———. (1887b) "*Nôte sur l'influence exercée par les Institutes en matière de classification du droit*" ("Note on the Influence of the Institutes on the Classification of Law"). *Revue critique de législation et de jurisprudence*, pp. 5–24.

———. (1888) *Plan du cours de droit administratif, en ce qui concerne la théorie des patrimoines administratifs* (*Plan of a Course in Administrative Law, as It Concerns the Theory of Administrative Patrimonies*). Toulouse, n.p.

*———. (1890) "*Veil.*" In *La jurisprudence administrative*: *Nôtes d' arrêts*. Vol. 3, p. 406.

*———. (1891a) "*Medioni.*" In *La jurisprudence administrative*: *Nôtes d' arrêts*. Volume 1, p. 230–232.

———. (1891b) "*Des services d'assistance*" ("Services of Assistance"). *Revue d'économie politique*, 4, pp. 615–623.

*———. (1891c) "*Soeurs hospitalières*" ("Hospital Sisters"). In *La jurisprudence administrative*: *Nôtes d' arrêts*. Volume 1, p. 473.

*———. (1892a) *Étude sur la décentralisation* (*Investigation into Decentralization*). Paris: Paul Dupont.

*———. (1892b) *Précis de droit administratif.* 1st Edition. Paris: Larose et Forcel.

*———. (1893a) "*Barriat.*" In *La jurisprudence administrative*: *Nôtes d' arrêts*. Volume 3, pp. 94–95.

*———. (1893b) "*Élection de Pluguffan*" ("Election of Pluguffan"). In *La jurisprudence administrative*: *Nôtes d' arrêts*. Volume 1, p. 271.

*———. (1893c) "*Les facultés de droit et la sociologie*" ("The Faculties of Law and Sociology"). *Revue générale du droit*, pp. 3–8.

*———. (1893d) *De la formation du droit administratif français depuis l'an VIII* (*On the Formation of French Administrative Law Since the Year VIII*). Paris: Berger-Levrault.

*———. (1893e) *Précis de droit administratif.* 2nd Edition. Paris: Larose et Forcel.

*———. (1894a) "*Abbé Iteney.*" In *La jurisprudence administrative*: *Nôtes d' arrêts*. Volume 2, p. 714.

*———. (1894b) "*Arrêt Mogambury.*" In *La jurisprudence administrative*: *Nôtes d' arrêts*. Volume 1, p. 316.

*———. (1894c) "*La crise de la science sociale*" ("The Crisis in Social Science"). *Revue du droit public*, 1, pp. 294–321.

*———. (1894d) "*Réponse à un docteur en droit sur la sociologie*" ("Reply to a Doctor of Law about Sociology"). *Revue internationale de sociologie*, pp. 390–395.

*———. (1895a) "*L'alternance des moyen-âges et des renaissances et ses conséquences sociales*" ("The Alternation of Middle Ages and Renaissances, and their Social Outcomes"). *Revue de métaphysique et de morale*, 3, pp. 527–549.

*———. (1895b) "*Ville de Paris.*" In *La jurisprudence administrative*: *Nôtes d' arrêts*. Volume 3, p. 430.

*———. (1896) *La science sociale traditionnelle* (*Tradition in Social Science*). Paris: Larose.

*———. (1897a) *Étude sur le droit administratif français* (*Study of French Administrative Law*). Paris: Paul Dupont.

*———. (1897b) *Précis de droit administratif.* 3rd Edition. Paris: Larose et Tenin.

*———. (1898) "*De la personnalité comme élément de la réalité sociale*" ("On Personality as an Element of Social Reality"). *Revue générale du droit*, 22, pp. 5–23; 119–140.

*———. (1899a) *La gestion administrative: étude theorique de droit administratif* (*Administrative Governance: Theoretical Study of Administrative Law*). Paris: Sirey.

*———. (1899b) "*Grenet.*" In *La jurisprudence administrative*: *Nôtes d' arrêts*. Volume 3, pp. 47–48.

*———. (1899c) "*Joly.*" In *La jurisprudence administrative*: *Nôtes d' arrêts*. Volume 1, p. 490.

*———. (1899d) *Leçons sur le mouvement social* (*Studies on Movement in Society*). Paris: Larose.

*———. (1899e) "*Lepreux.*" In *La jurisprudence administrative*: *Nôtes d' arrêts*. Volume 1, p. 517.

*———. (1899f) "*Philosophie du droit et science sociale*" ("Philosophy of Law and Social Science"). *Revue du droit public*, 12, pp. 462–476.

*———. (1899g) "*Réponse à H. Bouasse.*" *Revue de métaphysique et de morale*, 7, pp. 347–351.

*———. (1899h) "*Villes d'Avignon et Adda*" ("Cities of Avignon and Adda"). In *La jurisprudence administrative*: *Nôtes d' arrêts*. Volume 2, pp. 404.

*———. (1900a) "*Canal de Gignac.*" In *La jurisprudence administrative*: *Nôtes d' arrêts*. Volume 1, pp. 413, 416–417.

*———. (1900b) "*Espitalier.*" In *La jurisprudence administrative*: *Nôtes d' arrêts*. Volume 3, p. 373.

*———. (1900c) "*Héritiers Boucher d'Argis*" ("Boucher Heirs of Argis"). In *La jurisprudence administrative*: *Nôtes d' arrêts*. Volume 2, p. 533.

*———. (1900d) "*Maugras.*" In *La jurisprudence administrative*: *Nôtes d' arrêts*. Volume 2, p. 334.

*———. (1900e) "*Merlin.*" In *La jurisprudence administrative*: *Nôtes d' arrêts*. Volume 2, pp. 222–224.

*———. (1900f) "*Syndicat agricole d'Herbly*" ("Agricultural Union of Herbly"). In *La jurisprudence administrative*: *Nôtes d' arrêts*. Volume 2, p. 247.

*———. (1901a) "*Création de salles de travail à la faculté de droit de Toulouse,*" ("Creating Laboratories in the Law Faculty of Toulouse") *Revue internationale de l'enseignement* 1, pp. 547–558.

*———. (1901b) *Précis de droit administratif.* 4th Edition. Paris: Larose et Tenin.

*———. (1902a) "*Avezard.*" In *La jurisprudence administrative*: *Nôtes d' arrêts*. Volume 1, p. 305.

*———. (1902b) "*Duguit, l'état, le droit objectif, et la loi positive: Comte rendu en collaboration avec M. Achille Mestre*" ("Duguit, the State, Objective Law, and Positive Law: Review in Collaboration with Achille Mestre"). *Revue du droit public*, 17, pp. 346–366.

*———. (1902c) "*Maire de Neris-des-bains*" ("Mayor of Neri-des-bains"). In *La jurisprudence administrative: Nôtes d' arrêts*. Volume 2, p. 249.

*———. (1903a) "*Companie des chemins de fer économiques du Nord*" ("Northern Costed Trains"). In *La jurisprudence administrative: Nôtes d' arrêts*. Volume 3, p. 463.

———. (1903b) "*De la conversion de l'instance en excès de pouvoir en instance en contentieux ordinaire*" ("Conversion of the Suit for Exceeding Powers into Ordinary Litigation"). *Année administrative*. Cited in (1914) "Boussuge." In *La jurisprudence administrative: Nôtes d' arrêts*. Volume 2, p. 418).

*———. (1903c) "*La déclaration de volonté dans le droit administratif français*" ("Declaration of Will in French Administrative Law"). *En collaboration avec M. Guillaume de Bezin. Revue trimestrielle de droit civil*, pp. 543–586.

———. (1903d) "*La force motrice des cours d'eau et le droit des riverains*" ("Waterpower and the Rights of Adjacent Owners"). *En collaboration avec M. Ader. Bulletin de la Société d'études législatives*, pp. 507–531.

———. (1903e) *Précis de droit administratif.* 5th Edition. Paris: Larose.

———. (1903f) "*Rapport adressé à M. de Ministre de l'Instruction publique par le Conseil de l'Université de Toulouse et lu dans la séance du Conseil de l'Université*" ("Report to the Minister of Public Education by the Council of the University of Toulouse, read in the University Council meeting"). (22 Dec.) Toulouse: Edouard Privat.

———. (1903g) "*Recherches de jurisprudence sur les dépenses obligatoires*" ("Jurisprudential Investigation of Required Payments"). *Revue de législation financière*, pp. 3–17.

*———. (1903h) "*Terrier.*" In *La jurisprudence administrative: Nôtes d' arrêts*. Volume 1, p. 459.

———. (1904a) "*Chronique législative*" ("Legislative Chronicle"). En collaboration avec MM. Jéze et Rabany. *Année administrative*, pp. 27–71.

———. (1904b) *Facultés de droit et les élections de 1904 au Conseils supérieures* (*Law Faculties and the 1904 Elections to Superior Councils*). Toulouse: Librairie de droit et de jurisprudence.

*———. (1904c) "*Ville de Lure*" ("City of Lure"). In *La jurisprudence administrative: Nôtes d' arrêts*. Volume 2, p. 602.

*———. (1905) "*Les éléments du contentieux*" ("Elements of Litigation"). *Recueil de législation de Toulouse,* 1, pp. 1–98. (1908, Volume 4, pp. 249–292).

*———. (1906a) "*L'institution et le droit statutaire,*" *Recueil de législation de Toulouse*, 2, pp. 134–182.

———. (1906b) *Principes de la loi de 1905 sur la séparation des Eglises et de l'État.* Paris: Larose et Tenin.

*———. (1906c) "*Syndicat de Quartier Croix-de-Sequey-Trivoli*" ("Union of the Croix-de-Sequey-Trivoli District"). In *La jurisprudence administrative: Nôtes d' arrêts*. Volume 1, p. 26.

*———. (1907a) *Précis de droit administratif.* 6th Edition. Paris: Larose et Tenin.

———. (1907b) "*Du role de la préscription acquisitive en matière de propriété industrielle*" ("The Role of Acquisitive Prescription in Regard to Industrial Property"). *Revue "La Défense de la propriété industrielle.*" pp. 1–19.

*———. (1907c) "*Ville de l'Angoulême*" ("City of Angoulême"). In *La jurisprudence administrative: Nôtes d' arrêts*. Volume 2, p. 764.
*———. (1908a) "*Feutry*." In *La jurisprudence administrative: Nôtes d' arrêts*. Volume 1, p, 585.
*———. (1908b) "*Morizot*." In *La jurisprudence administrative: Nôtes d' arrêts*. Volume 1, p, 623.
*———. (1909a) "*Le point de vue de l'ordre et de l'équilibre*" ("The Point of View of Order and Equilibrium"). *Recueil de législation de Toulouse*, 5, pp. 1–86.
*———. (1909b) "*Winkell*." In *La jurisprudence administrative: Nôtes d' arrêts*. Volume 3, p. 172.
*———. (1910) *Principes de droit public*, 1st Edition. Paris: Larose et Tenin.
*———. (1911a) "*Les idées de M. Duguit*" ("The Doctrine of Duguit"). *Recueil de législation de Toulouse*, 7, pp. 1–40.
*———. (1911b) "*Jacquemin*." In *La jurisprudence administrative: Nôtes d' arrêts*. Volume 3, p. 215.
———. (1911c) *Précis de droit administratif*. 7th Edition. Paris: Larose et Tenin.
*———. (1912a) "*Boussuge*." In *La jurisprudence administrative: Nôtes d' arrêts*. Volume 2, 418–419.
*———. (1912b) "*Les deux réalismes*" ("Two Realisms"), *Recueil de législation de Toulouse*, 8, pp. 3–10.
*———. (1912c) "*Tichit*." In *La jurisprudence administrative: Nôtes d' arrêts*. Volume 3, p. 179.
*———. (1912d) *La souveraineté nationale* (*National Sovereignty*). Paris: Sirey.
*———. (1913a) *Les conditions extérieures du développment du recours pour excès de pouvoir* (*The External Conditions for Development of the Recourse for Excess of Power*). Saint-Petersbourg: Tipografija goubernkago Pravlenija.
*———. (1913b) "*Mure*." In *La jurisprudence administrative: Nôtes d' arrêts*. Volume 3, p. 286.
*———. (1913) "*Ville de Blois*" ("City of Blois"). In *La jurisprudence administrative: Nôtes d' arrêts*. Volume 3, pp. 227.
*———. (1914a) "*Gomel*." In *La jurisprudence administrative: Nôtes d' arrêts*. Volume 3, p. 375.
———. (1914b) *Précis de droit administratif*. 8th Edition. Paris: Larose et Tenin.
*———. (1914c) "*A propos des droits réels administratifs*" ("On Administrative Real Rights"), *Revue générale du droit et de la législation*, 38, pp. 334–338.
———. (1915) *Note sur le principe et l'étendu du droit à l'indemnité pour les victimes des dommages de guerre* (*Note on the Principle and Extent of the Right to Indemnity for Victims of War Damages*). Paris: n.p.
*———. (1916a) "*Astruc*." In *La jurisprudence administrative: Nôtes d' arrêts*. Volume 1, p. 334.
———. (1916b) "*Le Conseil d'État et l'affaire Gaz de Bordeaux*" ("The *Conseil d'État* and the Case of Bordeaux Gas"). *Revue politique et parlementaire*, 88, pp. 40–50.
———. (1916c) "*Le fondement de l'autorité publique*" ("The Basis of Public Authority"). Discussion with Henri Berthélemy. *Revue du droit public*, 33, pp. 20–25.
*———. (1916d) "*Gaz de Bordeaux*." In *La jurisprudence administrative: Nôtes d' arrêts*. Volume 3, pp. 601–603.
*———. (1916e) *Principes de droit public*, 2nd Edition. Paris: Larose et Tenin.

*———. (1916f) "*Vion et fils*." In *La jurisprudence administrative*: *Nôtes d' arrêts*. Volume 1, pp. 41, 46.
*———. (1917a) "*Companie des messageries maritimes*" ("Maritime Message Company"). In *La jurisprudence administrative*: *Nôtes d' arrêts*. Volume 3, p. 616–623.
*———. (1917b) *Notice sur les œuvres de Léon Michoud* (*Note on the Works of Léon Michoud*). Grenoble: Allier Freres.
*———. (1918a) "*Le droit naturel et l'Allemagne*," ("Natural Law in Germany"), *Correspondant* (25 sept.). In *Aux sources du droit*, pp. 13–42.
*———. (1918b) "An Interpretation of the Principles of Public Law," *Harvard Law Review*, 31, pp. 813–821.
*———. (1919a) "*Commune de Cons-la-grand-ville*" ("Commune of Cons-la-grand-ville"). In *La jurisprudence administrative*: *Nôtes d' arrêts*. Volume 1, p. 141.
———. (1919b) *Précis de droit administratif*. 9th Edition. Paris: Larose et Tenin.
*———. (1919c) "*Regnault-Desroziers*." In *La jurisprudence administrative*: *Nôtes d' arrêts*. Volume 1, p. 691–692.
*———. (1920) "*Gaz de Nice*." In *La jurisprudence administrative*: *Nôtes d' arrêts*. Volume 3, p. 635.
*———. (1921a) "*Monsegur*." In *La jurisprudence administrative*: *Nôtes d' arrêts*. Volume 1, p. 9.
———. (1921b) *Précis de droit administratif*. 10th Edition. Paris: Larose et Tenin.
*———. (1922a) "*Boisson*." In *La jurisprudence administrative*: *Nôtes d' arrêts*. Volume 1, p. 150.
*———. (1922b) "*Dourdent*." In *La jurisprudence administrative*: *Nôtes d' arrêts*. Volume 1, p. 658.
*———. (1923a) "*Companie générale des automobiles postales*." In *La jurisprudence administrative*: *Nôtes d' arrêts*. Volume 3, p. 659.
*———. (1923b) "*Couiteas*." In *La jurisprudence administrative*: *Nôtes d' arrêts*. Volume 1, p. 722.
*———. (1923c) "*La liberté politique et la personnalité morale de l'état*" ("Political Liberty and the Moral Personality of the State"). *Revue trimestrielle de droit civil*, pp. 341–346.
*———. (1923d) *Précis de droit constitutionnel* (*Treatise of Constitutional Law*). 1st Edition. Paris: Sirey.
*———. (1925a) "*Mariani*." In *La jurisprudence administrative*: *Nôtes d' arrêts*. Volume 2, p. 389.
———. (1925b) *Précis élémentaire de droit administratif* (*Elementary Treatise on Administrative Law*). Paris: Librairie du Recueil Sirey.
———. (1925c) "*La théorie de l'institution et de la fondation; Essai de vitalisme social*" ("The Theory of the Institution and of Foundation; Essay in Social Vitalism"). *Cahiers de la nouvelle journée*, 4. *La cité moderne et les transformations du droit*. Reprinted in *Aux sources du droit*, pp. 89–128.
*———. (1926a) "*Arrêt Sourisse*." In *La jurisprudence administrative*: *Nôtes d' arrêts*. Volume 2, p. 546.
———. (1926b)"*L'imprévision et les contrats dominés par les institutions sociales*" ("Unforeseeability and Contracts Under the Influence of Social Institutions"). *Revista de Derecho Privado*, pp. 1–13.
*———. (1926c) "*Lefranc*." In *La jurisprudence administrative*: *Nôtes d' arrêts*. Volume 2, pp. 384–385.

———. (1926d) "*Police juridique et fond du droit*" ("Overseeing by Judges and the Basis of Law"). *Revue trimestrielle de droit civil*. Reprinted in *Aux sources du droit*, pp. 147–191.

———. (1926e) *Précis élémentaire de droit constitutionnel* (*Elementary Treatise on Constitutional Law*). Paris: Librairie du Recueil Sirey.

*———. (1927a) "*Charbonneaux*." In *La jurisprudence administrative*: *Nôtes d' arrêts*. Volume 3, p. 762–763.

*———. (1927b) "*Chemin de fer de l'est*" ("Eastern Railway"). In *La jurisprudence administrative*: *Nôtes d' arrêts*. Volume 1, p. 247.

*———. (1927c) "*Dol et Laurent*." In *La jurisprudence administrative*: *Nôtes d' arrêts*. Volume 1, p. 66.

*———. (1927d) "*L'ordre social, la justice, et le droit*" ("Social Order, Justice, and Law"). *Revue trimestrielle de droit civil*, pp. 795–825. Reprinted in *Aux sources du droit*, pp. 43–71.

———. (1927e) *Précis de droit administratif*. 11th Edition. Paris: Larose et Tenin.

*———. (1927f) *Principios de derecho público y constitucional, con un prólogo para la ed. española*. (*Principles of Public Law and Constitutional Law with a Foreword to the Spanish Edition*). 2nd Edition. Translated by Carlos Ruiz del Castillo and Carlos Catalán de Ocón. Madrid, Instituto Editorial Reus. Reprinted 2003.

*———. (1927g) *Prólogo de Autor para la edición española*. In *Principios de derecho público y constitucional, con un prólogo para la ed. española*.

———. (1928) *"Le pouvoir, l'ordre, la liberté et les erreurs des systèmes objectivistes* ("Power, Order, Liberty, and the Errors of Objectivist Systems"). *Revue de métaphysique et de morale*, pp. 193–206. Reprinted in *Aux sources du droit*, pp. 72–86.

*———. (1929a) *La jurisprudence administrative*: *Nôtes d' arrêts sur décisions du Conseil d'État de du Tribunal des Conflicts publiées au Receuil Sirey de 1892 à 1929* (*Administrative Jurisprudence: Notes on Cases on Decisions of the Conseil d'État and the Tribunal des Conflits published by Receuil Sirey from 1892 to 1929*). 3 Volumes. Paris: Sirey.

———. (1929b) *Osnony Publichnogo Prava* (*Droit Public*). Moscow. Translated by M. Oriu. Moscow: Komakad E.B.P.

*———. (1929c) *Précis de droit constitutionnel* (*Treatise of Constitutional Law*). 2nd Edition. Paris: Sirey.

———. (1929d) "*De la répétition des précedents judiciaires à la régle de droit coutumière*" ("Repetition of Judicial Precedents in the Customary Rule of Law"). *Cahiers de la nouvelle journée*, 15, pp. 109–115.

*———. (1930b) *Précis élémentaire de droit administratif* (*Elementary Treatise on Administrative Law*). 2nd Edition. Paris: Sirey.

*———. (1932) *Précis élémentaire de droit constitutionnel* (*Elementary Treatise on Constitutional Law*). 2nd Edition. Paris: Sirey.

*———. (1933a) "*Le droit naturel et l'Allemagne*" ("Natural Law in Germany"). In *Aux sources du droit*. (*See also* Hauriou, 1918a)

———. (1933b) *Hsien fa hsueh ching i* (Chinese translation of *Droit Public*). Peking, n.p.

*———. (1933c) "*Police juridique et fond du droit*" ("Overseeing by Judges and the Basis of Law"). In *Aux sources du droit*, pp. 89–128. (*See also* 1926c)

*———. (1933d) "*Le pouvoir, l'ordre, la liberté, et les erreurs des systèmes objectivistes*" ("Power, Order, Liberty, and the Errors of Objectivist Systems"). In *Aux sources du droit*, pp. 72–86. (*See also* 1928)

———. (1933e) *Précis de droit administratif.* 12th Edition Paris: Sirey.

*———. (1933f) *Aux sources du droit: le pouvoir, l'ordre, et la liberté* (*At the Sources of Law: Power, Order, and Liberty*). Paris: Bloud et Gay.

*———. (1933g) "*La théorie de l'institution et de la fondation*" ("Theory of Institution and Foundation"), pp. 89–128. In *Aux sources du droit.*(*See also* Hauriou, 1925c)

———. (1965) *Die Theorie der Institution; und zwei andere Aufsaetze von Maurice Hauriou.* (*The Theory of the Institution; and Two Other Publications by Maurice Hauriou*). Translated by Hans und Jutta Jecht. Berlin: Duncker und Humblot.

———. (1966a) *Introduction à l'étude du droit.* In Sfez, *Essai sur la contribution du doyen Hauriou au droit administratif français.*

*———. (1966b) *Lettre à Jacques Chevalier, 27 avr. 1921* In Lucien Sfez, *Essai sur la contribution du doyen Hauriou au droit administratif français.*

*———. (1966c) *Lettre à Jacques Chevalier, 16 dec. 1924.* In Lucien Sfez, *Essai sur la contribution du doyen Hauriou au droit administratif français.*

*———. (1966d) *Lettre au rédacteur en chef d'un journal inconnu, 26 juin* (Letter to the Editor of an unknown journal). In Lucien Sfez, *Essai sur la contribution du doyen Hauriou au droit administratif français.*

*———. (1967) *Introduction à l'étude du droit.* In Broderick. *Maurice Hauriou.*

———. (1968) *La teoría de la institución y de la fundación* (*Ensayo de vitalismo social*) (*The Theory of the Institution and of Foundation; Essay in Social Vitalism*). Translated by Arturo Enrique Sampay. Buenos Aires: Abeledo-Perrot.

*———. (1969) *Introduction à l'étude du droit.* In A. Hauriou. *Les derniers aspects de la pensée du doyen Maurice Hauriou et son influence.*

*———. (2003) *Principios de derecho público y constitucional, con un prólogo para la ed. española con un prólogo para la ed. española.* (*Principles of Public Law and Constitutional Law with a Foreword to the Spanish Edition*). 2nd Edition. Edited by José Luis Monereo Pérez. Granada, Editorial Comares. (See 1927f)

*———. (n.d.) *Introduction à l'étude du droit administratif français* (Introduction to the Study of French Administrative Law). *MS. inédit.*

Haynes, Thomas Morris. (1949) Institutional Theories of Law: Hauriou and Jordan. PhD Dissertation. University of Illinois.

Hebraud, Pierre. (1968) "*La notion de temps dans l'œuvre du doyen Maurice Hauriou*" ("The Concept of Time in the Work of Dean Maurice Hauriou"). In Marty and Brimo, Eds., *Journées Hauriou: la pensée du doyen Hauriou et son influence.*

Heuschling, Luc. (1999) "*État de droit, Rechtsstaat, Rule of Law; Quelques réflexions sur les mots et les choses*" ("*État de droit, Rechtsstaat, Rule of Law*; *Some Reflections on Words and Things*"). A.T.E.R. à l'Université de Paris XI (Sceaux).

Hübner Gallo, Jorge Ivàn. (1951) *Introdución a la teoría de la norma juridica y la teoría de la institucion. Carta preliminar de G. del Vecchio* (*Introduction to the Theory of the Legal Norm and the Theory of Institution: Preliminary Sketch by G. del Vecchio*). Santiago, Chile: Edit. juridice.

Imaseki, Motonari. (1982) *"La Limitation de l'état par le droit dans les œuvres de Léon Duguit et de Maurice Hauriou" (I)* ("Limitation of the State by Law in the Works of Leon Duguit and Maurice Hauriou"). *Waseda Law Review*, 57:2, pp. 31–64.

Jabbari, Eric. (2006) "Law and Politics in Interwar France: Pierre Laroque's Search for a Democratic Corporativism." *French Politics, Culture, and Society*, 24:1, pp. 93–113.

Jaurès, Jean. (1891) *De primis socialismi germanici lineamentis apud Lutherum: Kant, Fichte, Hegel* (First Outlines of German Socialism in Luther: Kant, Fichte, Hegel). PhD Dissertation, University of Toulouse.

Jeanneau, Benoit. (1954) *Les principes généraux du droit dans la jurisprudence administrative* (*General Principles of Law in Administrative Jurisprudence*). Paris: Sirey.

Jellinek, Georg. (1904) *L'état moderne et son droit* (*The Modern State and its Law*). Paris: A. Fontemoing.

———. (1922) *Allgemeine Staatslehre* (*General Theory of State*). Berlin: Springer.

Jennings, Ivor. (1933) "The Institutionalist Theory." In *Modern Theories of Law*. Edited by I. Jennings. London: Oxford.

Jones, H. Stuart. (1988) Public Service and Private Interests: The Intellectual Debate on the Problem of "Syndicats de fonctionnaires" in France, 1884–1914. PhD Dissertation. University of Oxford.

———. (1992) *The French State in Question: Public Law and Political Argument in the Third Republic*. New York: Cambridge University Press.

Kelsen, Hans. (1911) *Hauptprobleme der staatsrechtlehre entwickelt aus der lehre vom rechtssatze* (*Major Problems of Public Law Doctrine: Derived from the Doctrine in Legal Opinions*). Tübingen: J.C.B. Mohr.

———. (1926) *Allgemeine Staatslehre* (*General Theory of the State*). Berlin: J. Springer.

———. (1926) "*Aperçu d'une théorie générale de l'état*" ("Overview of a General Theory of State"). *Revue du droit public et de la science politique en France et à l'étranger*, 43, pp. 561—646.

Kurdjian-Fath, Melina. (1997) *L'influence de la pensée de Maurice Hauriou sur le droit constitutionnel de la cinquième république*. (The Influence of the Thought of Maurice Hauriou on the Constitutional Law of the Fifth Republic) DEA Thesis. Université de Nancy.

Laband, Paul. (1895) *Der Staatsrecht der deutschen Reiches* (The State Law of the German Empire). Tübingen: Mohr. French translation: (1900) *Le droit public de l'empire allemande*. Paris: V. Giard & E. Brière.

Lacambra, Luiz Legaz. (1968) "*L'influence du doyen Maurice Hauriou dans les pays latins et latino-américains*" ("The Influence of Dean Maurice Hauriou in Latin and Latin-American Countries"). In Marty and Brimo, *La pensée du doyen Hauriou et son influence*.

Landot, Yann. (n.d.) *La théorie de la connaissance acquise en matière de delais contentieux* (The Theory of Judicial Notice in Delays of Litigation). DEA Thesis, Université René Descartes, Faculté de Droit de Paris V.

Lapradelle, Albert Geouffre de. (1895) *Théorie et pratique des fondations perpetuelles: histoire, jurisprudence, vues critiques, droit français et étranger* (*Theory and Practice of Foundations in Perpetuity: History, Jurisprudence, Critical Perspectives, French and Foreign Law*). Paris: Giard et Brière.

La Torre, Massimo. (1999) "Institutionalist Philosophy of Law." In *The Philosophy of Law: An Encyclopedia*. Edited by Christopher B. Gray. New York: Garland.

Leclerc, Stéphane. (2003) *Les facteurs de convergence de la démocratie locale et régionale dans l'Union Européenne* (Converging Elements of Local and Regional Democracy in the European Union). PhD Dissertation. Université Pau.

Le Bon, Gustave. (1895) *Psychologie des foules* (*Crowd Psychology*). Paris: Presses Universitaires de France.

———. (1905) *L'évolution de la matière* (*The Evolution of Matter*). Paris: E. Flammarion.

Lee, Ian B. (1998) "In Search of a Theory of State Liability in the European Union." Jean Monnet Chair Working Papers, Harvard Law School. http://www.jeanmonnetprogram.org/papers/99/990901.html (accessed 10 Aug. 2009).
Lekeal, Fared. (1989) *Syndicalisme juridique, personalisme et fédéralisme intégral* (Legal Syndicalism, Personalism, and Integral Federalism). PhD Dissertation in Law. Université de Lille II.
Leontoweitsch, Viktor. (1936–1937) "*Die Theorie der Institution bei Maurice Hauriou*" ("The Theory of Institution for Maurice Hauriou"). *Archiv fuer Rechts und Sozialphilosophie*, 29/30, p. 234.
Lequesne, Christian, and Andy Smith. (2002) "*Interpréter l'Europe: éléments pour une relance théorique*" ("Interpreting Europe: Elements for a New Theoretical Beginning"). *Cultures & conflits* (14 June), 18:58, p. 16.
Lissarrague, François. (1941) "*El concepto de institución en el Derecho Público de Hauriou: Su alcance Filosóficosocial*" ("The Concept of Institution in the Public Law of Hauriou: Its Philosophical-Social Combination"). *Revista de la Facultad de Derecho de Madrid*, 6–7, pp. 197–219.
Lopes Meirelles, Hely. (1977) *Direito Administrativo*. (Portuguese translation of Maurice Hauriou's *Précis de droit administratif*). São Paulo: Motonari.
Lubac, Henri de. (1948) *The Un-Marxian Socialist: A Study of Proudhon*. Translated by R. E. Scantlebury. New York: Sheed and Ward.
Lustosa, Eduardo. (1938) "*Teoría de la institución y objetivismo juridico*" ("Theory of the Institution and of Juridical Objectivism"). *Estudios*, 27, pp. 5–14.
MacCormick, Neil, and Ota Weinberger. (1986) *An Institutional Theory of Law*. Dordrecht: D. Reidel.
Machado, José Roberto Lino. (2000) "A Culture dos Operadores do Direito" ("The Culture of Officers of the Law"). *I Fórum Mundial de Juízes, Ajuris Todos*, Brazil (2 June).
Manchego, José F. Palomino. (2000) "La autonomía municipal en la constitución Peruana de 1993" ("Municipal Autonomy in the Peruvian Constitution of 1993"). Conference paper presented at Universitá degli Studi di Siena (3 Nov.).
Marty, Gabriel, and Albert Brimo, Eds. (1969) *La pensée de doyen Maurice Hauriou et son influence* (*The Thought of Dean Maurice Hauriou and His Influence*) (*Journées Hauriou*) . Paris: Pédone.
Maspétiol, Roland. (1968) "*L'état selon Hauriou*" ("The State in Hauriou's View"). *Archives de philosophie du droit*, 13, pp. 249–265.
Maus, Didier. (2002) "*Eloge du doyen Georges Vedel (1910–2002)*" ("In memoriam. Georges Vedel [1910–2002]") (March 14). *Revue française de droit constitutionnel*, 2:50, pp. 259–277.
Mazel, Henri. (1896) *Synergie sociale* (*Social Synergy*). Paris: Armand Colin et Cie.
Mazzantini, Carlo. (1946) "*Una pseudo-stroncatura di un individuo-instituzione*" ("A Pseudo-Structure for an Individual-Institution"). *Giornal di Metafisica*, 1.
Medeiros, Saboia de. (1938) "*Ensayo de Filosofia Concreta Social y Juridica*," ("Essay in Concrete Social and Legal Philosophy"). *Stromata*, 1, pp. 103–159.
Mélanges Maurice Hauriou (*Collected Papers on Maurice Hauriou*) (1929). Paris: Sirey.

Melkevik, Bjarne. (1989) "*Pasukanis: une lecture marxiste de Maurice Hauriou*" ("Pasukanis: A Marxist Reading of Maurice Hauriou"). *Revue d'histoire des facultés de droit*, 8, pp. 295–301, derived from his 1987 thesis on Pasukanis; reprinted as "*Marxisme et le droit*" ("Marxism and the Law"). In *Horizons de la philosophie du droit* (*Horizons of the Philosophy of Law*). Part 6. Sainte-Foy, Quebec City: Presses de l'Université Laval, 1998.

Melle Bonadei, Laurence. (1998) *La comédie de saint-Etienne et son public. Action artistique*. DESS Thesis. Université de droit et de science politique de Dijon (Oct.).

Melville, Gert. (2001) "*Institutionalität und Geschichtlichkeit*" ("Institutionality and Historicity"). Projekt K: "Instrumentalle und symbolische Funktionen von Repräsentationsinstitutionen." *Sonderforschungsbereich* 537, Universität Dresden.

Mestre, Achille. (1929) "Maurice Hauriou (1856–1929)." *Annuaire de l'Institut internationale de droit public*, pp. 269–279.

Meyrier, Virginie. (2002) *Le théatre et le service public, ou l'histoire d'un heritage impossible* (Theater as Public Service: History of an Impossible Inheritance). DESS Thesis (Sept.) Université Lumière Lyon 2.

Michoud, Léon. (1895) "*Étude sur la responsibilité de l'état à raison des fautes de ses agents*" ("Study on the Responsibility of the State for Wrongdoing by its Agents"). *Revue du droit public* (As cited by Hauriou).

———. (1906) *La théorie de la personnalité morale et son application au droit français* (*The Theory of Moral Personality; Its Application in French Law*). Paris: Librairie générale de droit et de jurisprudence.

———. (1911) "*La personnalité et les droits subjectifs de l'état dans la doctrine française contemporaine*" ("The Personality and Subjective Rights of the State in Contemporary French Legal Theory"). In Otto Friedrich von Gierke. *Festschrift Otto Gierke zum siebzigsten Geburtstag: dargebracht von Schülern, Freunden, und Verehrern* (*Festschrift for Otto Gierke on his Seventieth Birthday; Presented by his Students, Friends, and Admirers*). Weimar: Böhlaus.

Millar, Moorhouse F. X. (1932) "Hauriou, Suarez, and Chief Justice Marshall," *Thought*, 5 (Mar. 19), pp. 588–608.

Millard, Eric. (1995) "*Hauriou et la théorie de l'institution*" ("Hauriou and Theory of the Institution"). *Droit et société*, 30/31, pp. 381–412.

———. (2005) "*Os discipulos administrativistas de Maurice Hauriou*' ("Administrativistas: Maurice Hauriou's Followers'"). *Revista opinião juridica*, 3:6, pp. 353–372.

Miranda, Alex. (1999) "*Contribuição Previdenciá—Compensação de Valores cobrados Indevidamente—Remuneração paga a Segurados Empresários e Autônomos—Correção Monetária e Inconstitucionalidade*" ("Anticipatory Contribution—Compensation for Market Shares Acquired Incidentally—Remuneration to Secured and to Independent Investors—Monetary Correction and Unconstitutionality"). *Tribunal Regional Federal da 2a Região, Brazil* (1 Feb.).

Mommsen, Theodor. (1894) *Droit romain public* (*Roman Public Law*). Paris: E. Thorin.

Monaco, B. R. (1932) "*Teoria del l'instituzione nella dottrina di diritto internazionale*" ("The Theory of Institution in the Doctrine of International Law"). *Archivio Giuridico Modena*, 108.

Mondiaire, Gérard, and Sylvie Durousseau. (1999) "*Centralisation et contractualisation*" ("Centralization and Contractualization"). Conference paper. *Institut de décentralisation.*

Mueller, Ludger. (2000) *Glaube und Recht: Institutionnelles Rechtsdenken und kanonisches Recht* (Faith and Law: Institutional Doctrine and Canon Law). Institut für kanonisches Recht Katholisch-theologische Fakultät. Universität Wien.

Neumann, Sigmund. (1934) "Seydel, Max von." *Encyclopedia of Social Sciences*. Volume 14. Edited by Herbert J. Seligmann. New York: Macmillan.

Nguini, Mathias Eric Owona. (1998) "*Juristes-savants, droit de l'État et état de droit au Cameroun: L'enonciation professorale et doctorale de droit de la souveraineté et droit de l'homme au crible d'une sociologie politique du champ juridique*" ("Jurisprudents, Public Law, and Rule of Law in Cameroun: Professorial and Doctoral Pronouncements of the Law of Sovereignty and of Human Rights Law, Screened Through a Political Sociology of the Legal Domain"). Polis/ R.C.S.P./C.P.R.S. 6:2, pp. 31–79.

Olivesi, Claude. (1997) "*Les seize 'capitoli' de la constitution d'Alesani du 15 Avril 1736*" ("The Three 'Chapters' of the Alesan Constitution of 15 April 1736"). University Lecture. Université de Corse, A.D.E.C.E.C.-CERVIONI.

Olsen, Johan P. (2000) "Organising European Institutions of Governance; A Prelude to an Institutional Account of Political Integration." ARENA Working Papers WP 00/2, University of Oslo.

Pascal, Blaise. (1651) *Préface sur le traité du vide* (Preface to Study of the Vacuum). In Hauriou, *La science sociale traditionnelle*.

Pavia, Marie-Luce. (2001) "*Le droit, le jugement et l'équité; La notion de service public*" ("Law, Judgment, and Equity; The Idea of Public Service"). *Le Stat; Le droit public*.

Perroux, François. (1980) "*L'université: une institution dans la société*" ("The University: An Institution in Society"). *Revue universitaire des sciences morales*, pp. 31–34.

Pinheiro, Adenildo Tavares, et al. (1999) "*Ação popular contra venda de carteira imobiliária a preço vil*" ("Popular Action Against the Sale of Undervalued Registrations of Realty"). Conference Paper. *Associação Brasileira dos Mutuários*, Campo Grande, Brazil (20 August).

Pini, Joseph. (1997) "*Autorité et contrat dans l'administration modern en France*" ("Authority and Contract in Modern French Administration"). CRA Études.

Platon, Georges. (1910) *Pour le droit naturel: à propos Les principes du droit public* (*Toward Natural Law: Regarding The Principles of Public Law*). Paris: Rivière.

Poulopol, E. A. (1936) "*Un doctrinar al liberalismulu*" ("A Doctrine of Liberalism"). *Revista de philosofie*, 20.

Pound, Roscoe. (1939) "The Recrudescence of Absolutism." *Sewanee Review*, pp. 6–7.

Proudhon, Pierre-Joseph. (1846) *Système des contradictions économiques, ou, philosophie de la misère* (*System of Economic Contradictions; or, Philosophy of Misery*). Paris: Guillaumin et cie.

Quintão, Geraldo Magela da Cruz. (1998) "Defesa do interesse público na constituição federal" ("Defense of Public Interest in the Federal Constitution"). Presented at Congresso Brasiliense de Direito constitucional (22 Oct.).

Rauh, Frédéric. (1892) *Essai sur le fondement métaphysique de la morale* (*Essay on the Metaphysical Foundations of Morality*). Paris: Alcan.

———. (1892) "*La philosophie de Pascal*" ("The Philosophy of Pascal"). *Annales de la Faculté de Bordeaux*. n.p (as cited by Hauriou).

Reale, Miguel. (1994) "Minhas Memórias da USP [Universidade do São Paulo]" ("A Few Memories of USP" [University of São Paulo]). *Revista Estudos Avançados*, 22 (Sept.–Dec.).

Recaséns-Siches, Luis. (1948) "Human Life, Society, and Law: Fundamentals of the Philosophy of Law." Translated by Gordon Ireland. In *Latin-American Legal Philosophy*. 20th Century Legal Philosophy Series. Volume 3. Cambridge, Mass.: Harvard University Press.

Renan, Ernest. (1882) *Qu'est-ce qu'une nation? conférence faite en Sorbonne, le ll mars 1882* (*What is a Nation? Lecture Given at the Sorbonne 1882*). Paris: C. Lévy.

Renard, Georges. (1922) *Sur quelques orientations modernes de la science du droit* (*Modern Directions in the Science of Law*). Paris: Revue des jeunes.

———. (1924–1928) *Introduction philosophique de l'étude du droit* (*Philosophical Introduction to the Study of Law*). Paris: Sirey.

———. (1930) *La théorie de l'institution: essai de l'ontologie juridique* (*The Theory of Institution: Essay in Legal Ontology*). Paris: Sirey.

———. (1931) "*La doctrine institutionnelle du marriage*" ("The Institutional Theory of Marriage"). *Vie intellectuelle*, pp. 96–123.

———. (1933) *L'institution, fondement d'une rénovation de l'ordre social* (*Institution: Foundation of a Renewal of the Social Order*). Paris: Flammarion.

———. (1939) *La philosophie de l'institution* (*Philosophy of the Institution*). Paris: Sirey.

"Review of *La gestion administratif*." (1899) *Revue du droit public*, 12, p. 192 (as cited by Hauriou).

Reyes, Alfredo Manrique. (2000) "*El alcalde municipal*" ("Municipal Ferment"). Conference Paper. (Oct) Columbia.

Rioldán, Abelardo Rojas. (1998) "*La sociofilosofía jurídica y la teoría universal del derecho*" ("Socio-Philosophy and the Universal Theory of Law"). *Logos* (Jan.-Apr.) Facultad de Derecho, UNAM, México.

Richard, Gaston. (1892) "*Essai sur l'origine de l'idée de droit*" ("Essay on the Origin of the Idea of Law"). *Revue philosophique*, 34, pp. 290–296 (as cited by Hauriou).

Roman, Bernard. (2000) Assemblée nationale Rapport no. 3116 (11 June).

Romano, Santi. (1917) *L'ordinamento giuridico* (*Legal Order*). Pisa: Tipografia editrice cav. Mariotti.

Rossi, Clóvis. (2001) "*Os Coitadinhos*" ("Citizenship"). Conference Paper. *Analista Judiciário*, PCI Concursos (25 Feb) Brazil.

Roux, Christophe. (2004) Half a Century of French Political Science: An Interview with Jean Leca, President of the French Political Science Association. *European Political Science*. http://www.afsp.msh-paris.fr/activite/diversafsp/interviewlecaeps2004.html (accessed 09 Aug. 2009).

Ruiz, Jorge Fernando. (1999) "*A poder et sus typos*" ("Power and its Modes"). *Boletin Mexicano de Derecho Comparado*, 81 [*Instituto de Investigaciones Juridicas de la UNAM*], at VI. *Clasificació organizacional. 2 Poder institucional.*

Ruiz del Castillo, Carlos. (1927a) *Integración de la democracia en una doctrina Corporative del Estado* (*estudio inspirado en la concepción politica-sociologica de Hauriou*) (*The Integration of Democracy into a Corporative Doctrine of the State* [*A Study Inspired by the Sociological and Political Thought of Hauriou*]). Santiago de Compostela, Madrid: Editorial Reus.

——. (1929) "*Un schéma de la Doctrine de la Personnalité de l'État selon la Méthode juridico-psychologique d'Hauriou*" ("An Outline of the Doctrine of the Personality of the State According to the Juridico-Psychological Method of Hauriou"). In *Mélanges Maurice Hauriou.*

Sabatier, Armand. (1892) *Essai sur la vie et la mort* (*Essay on Life and Death*). Paris: Babé et Cie.

Saito, Y. (1993) "*L'État, le droit et le consentement; Essai sur la theorié de l'institution de Maurice Hauriou*" ("State, Law, and Consent; An Essay on the Theory of Institution of Maurice Hauriou"). *Kyoto Law Review*, 131:5, pp. 25–55; 135:4, pp. 70–89.

Saleilles, Raymond. (1895) *Étude sur la théorie générale des obligations dans la seconde rédaction du projet du code civil pour l'Empire d'Allemagne* (*A Study on the General Theory of Obligations in the Second Redaction of the Project of the Civil Code of the German Empire*). Paris: F. Pichon.

Salomoni, Jorge Luis. (2001) "*Reforma del Estado y Mercosur; Hacia la constucción de un Derecho Publico Comunitario*" ("State Reform and Mercasur; Welcoming the Constitution of a Communitarian Public Law"). Documentos de Trabajo No. 65. (May). Buenos Aires, Argentina: Universidad de Belgrano.

Schellekens, J. A. (1945) *De Leer Over de Institution Bij M. Hauriou* (*The Doctrine of Institution of M. Hauriou*). Nijmegen: Centrale Drukkerij N.V.

Schild, Wolfgang. (1974) "*Die Institutionstheorie Maurice Haurious*" ("The Theory of Institution of Maurice Hauriou"). *Österreichische Zeitschrift für öffentliches Recht*, 25, pp. 3–21.

Schmitt, Carl. (1934) *Über die drei Arten des rechtwissenschaftlichen Denkens* (*The Three Types of Jurisprudential Thinking*). Hamburg: Hanseatische Verlagsanstalt.

Schnur, Roman. (1965) *Einfuehrung*. In *Die Theorie der Institution und zwei andere Aufsaetze von Maurice Hauriou* (*The Theory of Institution and Two Other Writings by Maurice Hauriou*). Berlin: Duncker und Humblot.

Schwinge, Erich, and Leopold Zimmerl. (1937) *Wesensschau und konkretes Ordnungsdenken im Strafrecht* (*Essential and Concrete Theory of Order in Criminal Law*). Bonn: Röhrscheid.

Sfez, Lucien. (1966) *Essai sur la contribution du doyen Hauriou au droit administratif français* (*A Study of the Contribution of Dean Hauriou to French Administrative Law*). Paris: Librairie générale de droit et du jurisprudence.

Silhol, Bruno. (2002) "*Maurice Hauriou et le droit du travail*" ("Maurice Hauriou and Labor Law"). In "Les juristes de Gauche sous la III République et sous Weimar," (23 March). Université de Sergy-Pontoise.

Siorat, Lucien. (1969) "*La sociologie du doyen Maurice Hauriou*" ("The Sociology of Dean Maurice Hauriou"). In Marty and Brimo, *La Pensée du doyen Maurice Hauriou et son influence*.

Simmel, Georg. (1989) *Aufsätze 1887 bis 1890: Uber soziale Differenzierung: Die Probleme der Geschichtsphilosophie (1892)* (*Essays from 1887 to 1890: On Social Differentiation: The Problem of the Philosophy of History*). Frankfurt am Main: Suhrkamp.

Siné, Alexandre. (2000) "*Nôte critique pour la chronique bibliographique*" ("A Critical Note on Bibliographical Chronology"). *Droit et Société*.

Smend, Rudolf. (1928) *Verfassung und Verfassungsrecht* (*Constitution and Constitutional Law*). München, Leipzig, Duncker & Humblot.

Spencer, Herbert. (1857) "*Loi et cause du progrès*" ("Law and the Cause of Progress"). Translated by A. Burdeau, *Westminster Review*. In Spencer. (1877) *Essais de morale de science d'ésthetique* (*Studies in Morals, Science, and Aethetics*). Paris: Baillière.

———. (1874–1875/1855) *Principes de psychologie* (*Principles of Psychology*). Translated by Alfred Victor Espinas. Paris: G. Baillière.

Stone, Julius. (1946) *The Province and Function of Law: Law as Logic, Justice, and Social Control, A Study in Jurisprudence*. Sydney: Associated General Publications.

———. (1966) *Social Dimensions of Law and Justice*. London: Stevens and Sons.

Taine, Hippolyte. (1876) *Les origines de la France contemporaine* (*The Origins of Contemporary France*). Paris: Hachette.

Tanuay, Yann. (1991) "*L'institution dans l'oeuvre de Maurice Hauriou; actualité d'une doctrine*" ("Institution in the Work of Maurice Hauriou; The Contemporaneity of a Doctrine "). *Revue du droit public*, 107, pp. 61–79.

Tarde, Gabriel de. (1886) *La Criminalité comparée* (*Comparative Criminality*). Paris: Alcan.

———. (1888) "*Les deux sens de la valeur*" ("The Two Meanings of Value"). *Revue d'economie politique* (as cited by Hauriou).

———. (1890) *Les lois de l'imitation: étude sociologique* (*The Laws of Imitation: Sociological Study*). Paris: Alcan.

———. (1891) *Philosophie pénale* (*Penal Philosophy*). Paris: Storck.

———. (1892) *Études pénales et sociales* (*Studies on Penalty and Society*). Lyon: Storck.

———. (1893) *Transformations du droit* (*Transformations in the Law*). Paris: Alcan.

———. (1895) *La logique sociale* (*Social Logic*). Paris: Alcan.

———. (1898) *Les lois sociales: esquisse d'une sociologie* (*The Laws of Society: An Essay in Sociology*). Paris: Alcan.

Timasheff, N. S. (1946) "The Sociological Theories of the French Institutionalists," *Thought*, 21, pp. 493–512.

Teubner, Günther. (1996) "*Globale Bukowina; Zur Emergenz eines transnationalen Rechtspluralismus*" ("A Global Bukowina; On the Emergence of a Transnational Legal Pluralism"). *Baslerschriften zur europäischen Integration*, Nr. 21, Europainstitut de Universität Basel.

———. (2006) "Rights of Non-Humans? Electronic Agents and Animals as New Actors in Politics and Law." *Journal of Law and Society*, 33.

———, and Peter Korth. (2009) "Two Kinds of Legal Pluralism: Collision of Law in the Double Fragmentation of World Society." Translated by Anna Furness. Presented at: Regime Interaction in International Law: Theoretical and Practical Challenges. Lauterpacht Centre for International Law, Cambridge, UK: 26–27 June. http://ssrn.com/abstract=1416041 (accessed 09 Sept. 2009).

Trejo, José Capetillo. (1999) "Hacia una Reforma Constitucional integral." (" For a Full Constitutional Reform"). *La Revista* (Feb.) (Mexico).

van Heemstra, Tjalling Ulbo Sixma. (1954) *De Staatsopvating van Hauriou* (*The Treatise on State by Maurice Hauriou*). Leiden: Rijksuniversiteit te Leiden.

Viehweg, T. (1937) "*Husserl, Hauriou und die deutsche Rechtswissenschaft*" ("Husserl, Hauriou and German Legal Theory"). *Archiv fuer Rechts und Sozialphilosophie*, 32, pp. 84–89.

Vélez, Ignacio M. (2001) "Potestades conferidas por la concesión y sus limites" ("The Powers Conferred by Concession and their Limits"). In *Opiniones de Interés* (*Views of Interest*). Abogados, Argentina: Badeli, Grau & DeGrazia.

Vilmos, Huszáar. (1993) "*Kollektív jogok—kollektív javakat illetô jogok*" ("Collective Obligation—Collective Obligation of Advocates"). *Mayyar Kisebbseg*, 17.

Vitta, Cino. (1920) *Gli atti collegiali : principi sul funzionamento dei concessi pubblici con riferimenti alle assemblee private* (*Collective Acts: Principles of Operation Granted with Public References to Private Assemblies*). Rome: Athenaeum.

———. (1929) "*Les personnes morales de droit public en France et en Italie*" ("Moral Persons in the Public Law of France and of Italy"). In *Mélanges Maurice Hauriou.*

Voegelin, Eric. (2000) "*Authoritarian State*" (Volume 4) and "Economic and Political Phases of the Reality of the State." Volume 11. *Published Essays 1953–1965.* In *Collected Works.* Edited by Ellis Sandoz. Columbia: University of Missouri Press.

von Gierke, Otto Friedrich. (1880) *Johannes Althusius und die Entwicklung der naturrechtlichen Staatstheorien; zugleich ein Beitrag zur Geschichte der Rechtssystematik* (*Johannes Althusius and the Beginnings of the Natural Law Theory of State: Also a Contribution to the History of the Legal Classification*). Breslau : W. Koebner.

———. (1887) *Die Genossenschaftstheorie und die deutsche Rechtsprechung.* (*The Theory of Knowledge and German Determination of Law*) Berlin: Weidmann.

von Jhering, Rudolf. (1877–1883) *Der Zweck im Recht* (*Purpose in Law*). Out of print, but available online at:
http://www.archive.org/details/derzweckimrecht04jhergoog (accessed 18 Aug. 2009).

———. (1883) *Geist des römischen Rechts auf den verschiedenen Stufen seiner Entwicklung* (*Spirit of Roman Law at Various Stages of Its Development*). Leipzig: Breitkopf u. Härtel.

———. (1895) *Les Indo-Européens avant l'histoire* (*Indo-Europeans before History*). Paris: Librairie A. Marescq.

Waline, Marcel. (1929) "*Les idées maîtresses de deux grands publicistes français: Léon Duguit et Maurice Hauriou*" ("The Leading Ideas of Two Prominent French Public Law Jurists: Léon Duguit and Maurice Hauriou"). *L'année politique*, pp. 39–63.

———. (1949) *L'individualisme et le droit* (*Individualism and the Law*). Paris: Domat-Monchrestien.

Worms, René. (1894) "*Observations critiques*" ("Critical Observations"). *Revue internationale de sociologie*, pp. 395–399.

———. (1896) "*Review of La science sociale traditionnelle,*" *Revue du droit public* (as cited by Hauriou).

Zuccerino, Ricardo. (2000) "*Exposition, Apertura V*" ("Presentation at the Opening, Fifth National Conference on Municipal Law"). *Jornadas Nacionales Derecho Municipal*, México (4 Aug).

ABOUT THE AUTHOR

CHRISTOPHER BERRY GRAY was born in 1941 and reared near Paterson, New Jersey. He received his Bachelor of Arts degree in Philosophy from St. Bonaventure University in Olean, New York, in 1963. After leaving the study of theology with the Friars Minor, his interest in ecclesiology led him to research moral and legal personality for his Master of Arts degree in Philosophy in 1965, and his Doctor of Philosophy degree in Philosophy in 1970, both at The Catholic University of America in Washington, D.C. He married his wife Kathleen Gray (née Schroth) in 1967, and in 1967 emigrated to Canada to continue teaching philosophy at Loyola College of Montreal, merged to become Concordia University in 1974. Dr. Gray is currently a professor of philosophy at Concordia. Pursuing his research into legal philosophy, he studied at McGill University Law School to receive his B.C.L. in civil law in 1978, and his LL.B. in common law in 1979. He was a founding member of the Canadian Section of the International Association for Philosophy of Law and Social Philosophy (CS-IVR), and belongs to its American section (Amintaphil). Dr. Gray serves as consulting editor to the online *Encyclopédie de philosophie du droit*, and until recently, was on the editorial board of the *Encyclopedia of the Philosophy of Law* (IVR, online). He has edited *Philosophical Dimensions of the United States Constitution* (Edwin Mellen, 1990), and *The Philosophy of Law: An Encyclopedia* (2 vols., Garland Press, 1999). He has authored *Philosophy of Man at Recreation and Leisure* (Peter Lang, 2007), as well as numerous papers in collections, proceedings, and in journals of law as *Revue générale de droit*, *Eurocriminology*, *Les Cahiers de droit*, *Legal-Medical Quarterly*, *European Journal of Law, Philosophy and Computer Science*, *International Journal for the Semiotics of Law*, *Canadian Journal of Law and Jurisprudence*, *Archiv für Rechts- und Sozialphilosophie*, *Rivista internazionale di filosofia del diritto*; and in journals of philosophy such as *Metaphilosophy*, *Review of Metaphysics*, *Journal of Value Inquiry*, *Patristica et mediaevalia*, *Journal of Social Philosophy*, *Franciscan Studies*, *Canadian Philosophical Reviews*, *Journal of Thought*, and *American Catholic Philosophical Quarterly*.

INDEX

VIBS

The **Value Inquiry Book Series** is co-sponsored by:

Adler School of Professional Psychology
American Indian Philosophy Association
American Maritain Association
American Society for Value Inquiry
Association for Process Philosophy of Education
Canadian Society for Philosophical Practice
Center for Bioethics, University of Turku
Center for Professional and Applied Ethics, University of North Carolina at Charlotte
Central European Pragmatist Forum
Centre for Applied Ethics, Hong Kong Baptist University
Centre for Cultural Research, Aarhus University
Centre for Professional Ethics, University of Central Lancashire
Centre for the Study of Philosophy and Religion, University College of Cape Breton
Centro de Estudos em Filosofia Americana, Brazil
College of Education and Allied Professions, Bowling Green State University
College of Liberal Arts, Rochester Institute of Technology
Concerned Philosophers for Peace
Conference of Philosophical Societies
Department of Moral and Social Philosophy, University of Helsinki
Gannon University
Gilson Society
Haitian Studies Association
Ikeda University
Institute of Philosophy of the High Council of Scientific Research, Spain
International Academy of Philosophy of the Principality of Liechtenstein
International Association of Bioethics
International Center for the Arts, Humanities, and Value Inquiry
International Society for Universal Dialogue
Natural Law Society
Philosophical Society of Finland
Philosophy Born of Struggle Association
Philosophy Seminar, University of Mainz
Pragmatism Archive at The Oklahoma State University
R.S. Hartman Institute for Formal and Applied Axiology
Research Institute, Lakeridge Health Corporation
Russian Philosophical Society
Society for Existential Analysis
Society for Iberian and Latin-American Thought
Society for the Philosophic Study of Genocide and the Holocaust
Unit for Research in Cognitive Neuroscience, Autonomous University of Barcelona
Whitehead Research Project
Yves R. Simon Institute

Titles Published

Volumes 1 - 182 see www.rodopi.nl

183. Daniel P. Thero, *Understanding Moral Weakness*. A volume in **Studies in the History of Western Philosophy**

184. Scott Gelfand and John R. Shook, Editors, *Ectogenesis: Artificial Womb Technology and the Future of Human Reproduction*. A volume in **Values in Bioethics**

185. Piotr Jaroszyński, *Science in Culture*. A volume in **Gilson Studies**

186. Matti Häyry, Tuija Takala, Peter Herissone-Kelly, Editors, *Ethics in Biomedical Research: International Perspectives*. A volume in **Values in Bioethics**

187. Michael Krausz, *Interpretation and Transformation: Explorations in Art and the Self*. A volume in **Interpretation and Translation**

188. Gail M. Presbey, Editor, *Philosophical Perspectives on the "War on Terrorism."* A volume in **Philosophy of Peace**

189. María Luisa Femenías, Amy A. Oliver, Editors, *Feminist Philosophy in Latin America and Spain*. A volume in **Philosophy in Latin America**

190. Oscar Vilarroya and Francesc Forn I Argimon, Editors, *Social Brain Matters: Stances on the Neurobiology of Social Cognition*. A volume in **Cognitive Science**

191. Eugenio Garin, *History of Italian Philosophy*. Translated from Italian and Edited by Giorgio Pinton. A volume in **Values in Italian Philosophy**

192. Michael Taylor, Helmut Schreier, and Paulo Ghiraldelli, Jr., Editors, *Pragmatism, Education, and Children: International Philosophical Perspectives*. A volume in **Pragmatism and Values**

193. Brendan Sweetman, *The Vision of Gabriel Marcel: Epistemology, Human Person, the Transcendent*. A volume in **Philosophy and Religion**

194. Danielle Poe and Eddy Souffrant, Editors, *Parceling the Globe: Philosophical Explorations in Globalization, Global Behavior, and Peace*. A volume in **Philosophy of Peace**

195. Josef Šmajs, *Evolutionary Ontology: Reclaiming the Value of Nature by Transforming Culture*. A volume in **Central-European Value Studies**

196. Giuseppe Vicari, *Beyond Conceptual Dualism: Ontology of Consciousness, Mental Causation, and Holism in John R. Searle's Philosophy of Mind*. A volume in **Cognitive Science**

197. Avi Sagi, *Tradition vs. Traditionalism: Contemporary Perspectives in Jewish Thought*. Translated from Hebrew by Batya Stein. A volume in **Philosophy and Religion**

198. Randall E. Osborne and Paul Kriese, Editors, *Global Community: Global Security*. A volume in **Studies in Jurisprudence**

199. Craig Clifford, *Learned Ignorance in the Medicine Bow Mountains: A Reflection on Intellectual Prejudice*. A volume in **Lived Values: Valued Lives**

200. Mark Letteri, *Heidegger and the Question of Psychology: Zollikon and Beyond*. A volume in **Philosophy and Psychology**

201. Carmen R. Lugo-Lugo and Mary K. Bloodsworth-Lugo, Editors, *A New Kind of Containment: "The War on Terror," Race, and Sexuality*. A volume in **Philosophy of Peace**

202. Amihud Gilead, *Necessity and Truthful Fictions: Panenmentalist Observations*. A volume in **Philosophy and Psychology**

203. Fernand Vial, *The Unconscious in Philosophy, and French and European Literature: Nineteenth and Early Twentieth Century*. A volume in **Philosophy and Psychology**

204. Adam C. Scarfe, Editor, *The Adventure of Education: Process Philosophers on Learning, Teaching, and Research*. A volume in **Philosophy of Education**

205. King-Tak Ip, Editor, *Environmental Ethics: Intercultural Perspectives*. A volume in **Studies in Applied Ethics**

206. Evgenia Cherkasova, *Dostoevsky and Kant: Dialogues on Ethics*. A volume in **Social Philosophy**

207. Alexander Kremer and John Ryder, Editors, *Self and Society: Central European Pragmatist Forum*, Volume Four. A volume in **Central European Value Studies**

208. Terence O'Connell, *Dialogue on Grief and Consolation.* A volume in **Lived Values, Valued Lives**

209. Craig Hanson, *Thinking about Addiction: Hyperbolic Discounting and Responsible Agency.* A volume in **Social Philosophy**

210. Gary G. Gallopin, *Beyond Perestroika: Axiology and the New Russian Entrepreneurs.* A volume in **Hartman Institute Axiology Studies**

211. Tuija Takala, Peter Herissone-Kelly, and Søren Holm, Editors, *Cutting Through the Surface: Philosophical Approaches to Bioethics.* A volume in **Values in Bioethics**

212. Neena Schwartz: *A Lab of My Own.* A volume in **Lived Values, Valued Lives**

213. Krzysztof Piotr Skowroński, *Values and Powers: Re-reading the Philosophical Tradition of American Pragmatism.* A volume in **Central European Value Studies**

214. Matti Häyry, Tuija Takala, Peter Herissone-Kelly and Gardar Árnason, Editors, *Arguments and Analysis in Bioethics.* A volume in **Values in Bioethics**

215. Anders Nordgren, *For Our Children: The Ethics of Animal Experimentation in the Age of Genetic Engineering.* A volume in **Values in Bioethics**

216. James R. Watson, Editor, *Metacide: In the Pursuit of Excellence.* A volume in **Holocaust and Genocide Studies**

217. Andrew Fitz-Gibbon, Editor, *Positive Peace: Reflections on Peace Education, Nonviolence, and Social Change.* A volume in **Philosophy of Peace**

218. Christopher Berry Gray, *The Methodology of Maurice Hauriou: Legal, Sociological, Philosophical.* A volume in **Studies in Jurisprudence**

www.ingramcontent.com/pod-product-compliance
Lightning Source LLC
LaVergne TN
LVHW102227300926
849160LV00005B/50

9789042030077